SWANTS OF WADI

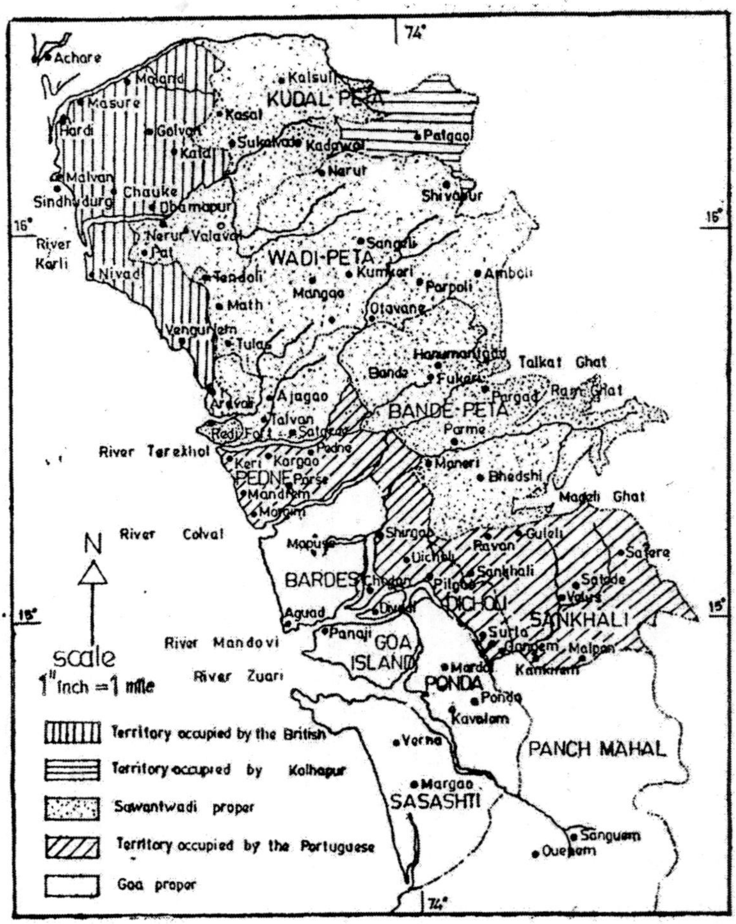

Frontispiece Map

SWANTS OF WADI

Coastal Politics in 18th and 19th Centuries

S.K. Mhamai

CONCEPT PUBLISHING COMPANY PVT. LTD.
NEW DELHI-110059

The Xavier Centre of Historical Research, Goa, gave the financial support towards the publication of this work. However, the responsibility for the content of the book—facts, opinions, material used, etc—is entirely that of the author and not of the XCHR.

ISBN-13: 978-81-7022-131-9

Edition 2018

Published and Printed by

Concept Since 1974 **Concept Publishing Company Pvt. Ltd.**
A/15-16, Commercial Block, Mohan Garden
New Delhi-110059 (India)
T: 25351460, 25351794, *F*: 091-11-25357109
E: publishing@conceptpub.com, W: www.conceptpub.com

Cataloging in Publication Data--Courtesy: D.K. Agencies (P) Ltd. <docinfo@dkagencies.com>

Mhamai, S. K., author.
Sawants of Wadi : coastal politics in 18th and 19th centuries / S.K. Mhamai.
pages cm
Reprint. Originally published: 1984.
Includes bibliographical references and index.
ISBN 9788170221319

1. Savantvadi (Princely State)--Politics and government--18th century. 2. Savantvadi (Princely State)--Politics and government--19th century. I. Title.

LCC DS485.S39M47 2018 | DDC 954.792 23

TO
THE MEMORY OF
HARI GANESH KAMAT MHAMAI

Preface

A comprehensive history of Konkan is a desideratum, and Sawantwadi being an integral part of this region, it deserves special attention of the scholars. Throughout the long course of their history, the Sawant Desais of Wadi had to face many encounters till its ultimate union with India. However, we hardly get a detailed and scientific account of Sawantwadi based on authentic sources scattered in many languages like Marathi, Halkannad, Persian, Portuguese, English, etc. Since the publication of Vithal Sitaram Pingulkar's *History of Sawantwadi* in 1911, no attempt has been made by any scholar either to revise or rewrite it by consulting the new material available on this subject. Dr. S.K. Mhamai deserves congratulations for presenting an authentic account of the activities of the Sawants of Wadi in the context of coastal politics in the 18th and 19th centuries. He has ransacked all possible sources shedding light on coastal politics. The reign of Khem Sawant II (1701-1709) was brief but decisive in laying the foundations of this State on sound footing and Dr. Mhamai has done full justice in narrating his role in the history of this State.

The State went through all the vicissitudes in its long course of history. The animosity between the Chhatrapatis of Satara and Kolhapur, in a way helped the State to preserve its identity, for a fairly long period. But the family disputes and the changing phase of the Konkan history made the Sawants to succumb to the Portuguese, a dominant power in the Konkan, and by 1781, it ceded Dicholi (Bhatgram) and Sakhali (Sattar) to them. These new acquisitions of the Portuguese were called New Conquests or *Navi Kabijad.* Surprisingly the English remained silent spectators while the Portuguese were spreading their sway in the Konkan. Thus by the close of the 18th century the Sawants were reduced to a minor power in the coastal politics.

To support his arguments, Dr. Mhamai has appended a few original Marathi and Portuguese documents from the Historical Archives of Goa and from the National Archives of India. This has certainly enhanced the value of this monograph. The present work is a version of his doctoral dissertation submitted to the University of Bombay, and it has been written with an eye on the general reader. The material incorporated is based entirely on authentic sources, but the normal scholarly paraphernalia of references and footnotes has been dropped for making the text less cumbersome to the ordinary reader. A discer- ning scholar may go through the bibliography and documentary appendices to satisfy his critical requirements.

I hope that this account of Sawantwadi presented by Dr. S.K. Mhamai in precise and accurate form would inspire the research scholars to dig the archives in Goa, Maharashtra, Portugal and other places, and attempt a comprehensive history of the Konkan depicting its political, social and economic aspects.

Vijaya Dashami A.R. Kulkarni
27 October 1982 Poona

Acknowledgements

Much of the research for this book was done while I was employed in Goa Historical Archives, and this was possible only because of the encouragement and support extended to me by its former Director, Dr. V.T. Gune. He and the Archives provided me with much required emotional and academic sustenance and staple.

Next chronologically, not in importance, comes by indebtedness to Dr. B.K. Apte, who never grudged his time and attention in guiding my research to its completion for obtaining my doctoral degree from the University of Bombay.

If the end crowns a work, it is to Dr. T.R. de Souza, S.J., and to the Xavier Centre of Historical Research, that I owe much for enabling me to place the fruits of my labour for the appreciation of the public.

There are many others who in many ways have contributed their mite and have lightened my burden. They include the staff-members of various research institutions where I collected my documentation, namely the National Archives in Delhi, the Bombay Archives, the Post Graduate Centre in Panjim, the Central Library in Panjim, and the Goa Historical Archives. I greatly value their cooperation.

PANJIM, GOA. S.K.MHAMAI

Contents

1

SAWANTWADI AND GOA
A Historical Backdrop

LOCATION

Goa and Sawantwadi lie adjacent to each other on the mid western coast of India. To the East lie the Sahayadri Hill Range. To the North and East of Sawantwadi lie the Ratnagiri and Kolhapur districts of Maharashtra State. South and East of Goa are the Karwar and Belgaum districts of Karnataka State.

Sawantwadi has an area of 925 sq. miles and Goa covers 1429.3503 sq. miles. Both territories have a narrow coastal plain rising sharply into the hills about 3000 ft. high. The climate is tropical, warm in summer, cool in winter and very wet during the monsoon, with over 200″ rainfall in parts. In the plains the chief crops are rice, nachni, kulith, chauli, mug, coconut, mangoes and jackfruit. In the hilly tracks are found cashews and pineapples. Besides papayas, bananas, melons, cucumbers, lady-fingers, onions, chillies, ginger and turmeric also grow in abundance. The thickly wooded forests, due to the heavy rainfall, are rich in jack, mango, tamarind, jambul, żambo, marta, teak, sisso, sivan, pat-panas, cumbyo, vod, bhendi, bamboo, nano, rosewood, ain, amba, kinjal etc. This was very useful for shipbuilding for which teak was the most important. The dense forests also held tigers, leopards, hyenas, bears, wild boars, monkeys and jackals.

Sawantwadi is drained by five rivers namely, Karli (Sarambal), Terekhol (Banda), Gaduadi (Kolawalchi Khadi), Tilari (Kudasi) and Hiranyakeshi. The last flows eastward to join the Krishna. The others flow into the Arabian Sea and are barely 30—40 miles long. They are not navigable to sea-going craft except for a few miles inland and are angry swirling torrents during the monsoon.

Goa is possessed of four rivers namely, the Terekhol, the Chapora (Kolwale), the Mandovi (Gomati), the Zuari (Aghanashini) and smaller ones like Baga, Sinkeri, Sal, Talpona and Galgibaga. The Mandovi and the Zuari are the most important being longer (62-63 km), broadest, and allowing ocean-going vessels to go quite a way inland. The excellent ports of Panaji and Marmagoa lie on these rivers. Marmagoa harbour is open to ships throughout the year and is the best natural harbour on the west coast of India. It was the terminus of the India Portuguese Guaranteed Railway, now a branch of the South Central Railway, and the only railway line linking Goa with the rest of India. A sand bar at the mouth of the Mandovi blocks the entrance to Panaji harbour during the monsoon. The other ports were mainly used by smaller crafts. Forts command the entrances to the rivers and formed an essential first line of defence for the Portuguese whose navy was reputed to be the best in the world in the 16th to 17th centuries and held absolute command over the Eastern Seas from Madagascar to Macau.

Sawantwadi kept its navy in the Karli and Terekhol rivers. Ships were constructed in the former. The fortresses constructed by the rulers, besides those that came into their possession were strongly garrisoned.

At the height of its power the Sawantwadi State included Dicholi, Sakhali (also known as Sattari) and Pedne. At that time Goa comprised only the islands of Goa, Bardesh and Salcete. Around 1763, Portuguese rule extended to Phonda, Canacona and Sanguem. By 1781 Dicholi and Sakhali formed part of Goa. In 1783 a part of Pedne and then in 1788 the whole of Pedne was incorporated into Goa. Contemporary Portuguese documents emphasize the need to capture the coastal taluka of Pedne and the territories of Dicholi and Sakhali in the interior as a safeguard to Bardesh from external attack.

Maland, Masura, Warad, Vengurla and the fort of Reddi were held by the British for 15 years from 1765-80. The Patgaon Karyat on the borders of which stands the strategically important fort of Rangna (Prasiddhagad) often changed hands between the Bhosales of Sawantwadi and the rulers of Kolhapur.

The major trade in Sawantwadi passed through Vengurla and Terekhol along the coast and through the Ram and Amboli which passes in the hills. Phonda and Porpoli were also passes much used for trade.

Goa is rich in minerals and besides ore exported coconuts, betelnuts, mangoes, dry fish and cashew. It was a centre of trade between the East and the West.

Brief histories

Inscriptions indicate that the Konkan was ruled by the Chalukyas in the 6th, 7th and 8th centuries A.D. The Nerur and Kochre grants show that Chandraditya, the eldest son of Pulakesin II, governed the western parts of the Chalukya dominions which included Ratnagiri and Sawantwadi. The Yadavas succeeded the Chalukyas in the 10th century and the Chalukyas again came to power in the 13th century (1261). At the close of the 14th century (1391) Sawantwadi came under an officer of the Vijaynagar dynasty with headquarters at Goa. About the middle of the 15th century (1436) it formed part of the territory of a powerful, local Brahmin dynasty.

In 1485, the independent Adil Shah kingdom was established and the area from Kudal in the north to Chintacora (Chitakul) in the south constituted a province of the Adil Shah Sultans of Bijapur called the Talkonkan.

In 1510, the Portuguese under Albuquerque, first conquered Goa. By the middle of the 16th century, Bardesh and Salset were united into what is known as the Old Conquests. The family name of the Sawants was Bhosale and they were remarkable as commanders of infantry, a service well suited to the country which they occupied. The district of Bijapur was distributed among five divisions (*parganas*), two extra divisions (*karyats*), one sub-division (*vilayat*), twelve petty divisions (*tarafs*) and one Port under a chief styled as a Desai of Kudal.

The five divisions were Phonda, Maneri, Pedne, Dicholi and Sakhali. The two extra divisions that is, the *karyats* were, Nerur and Patgaon. The sub-division, *vilayat*, was Banda. Of the twelve petty divisions, Manohar, Talavda and Mangaon were in Wadi;

Ajgaon and Santarda in Banda; Pat, Haveli, Kalsuli and Bordava in Kudal; and Maland, Varad and Masura in the territory transferred to the British Government in 1812-13. And the one port was Vengurla. In each *pargana*, the Deshmukh was the chief. Kudaldeshasth Prabhus were the Deshmukhs of the Kudal Pargana. In the mid of 16th century Bhauji Prabhu the Deshmukh, with Deo Dalvi as Senapati, sought the help of the Sawants in a revolt against the Bijapur Kingdom. Mang Sawant, the founder of the Bhosale family of Sawantwadi, set himself up as independent chief with headquarters at Hodavda, 9 miles from Wadi. Troops sent from Bijapur could not subdue him and he maintained his independence throughout his lifetime. His successors accepted the sovereignty of the Bijapur Sultans. With the decline of the Bijapur power in the early 17th century Khem Sawant (Fond Sawant's son) who held part of the Wadi country as Jagir, made himself independent.

By the middle of the 17th century, the Dutch were threatening Portuguese interests at sea. The Dutch blockaded Goa from February—April 1637 and again at the end of 1638 burning three Portuguese galleons without opposition. They obtained permission from Adil Shah to establish a fortress and factory at Vengurla. Later the Dutch power at sea waned and the Portuguese tried to rebuild navy.

The Bhosales in the meantime were becoming stronger. The Bijapur Kings who had risen with the fall of Ahmednagar, now began to feel the pressure of Delhi. Lakham Sawant, who had succeeded Som, and his brother Fond, together with his nephew Khem, and an infantry of 12,000 captured the Desai of Kudal, put him to death and took possession of his lands. From this time (till 1670) Wadi was the headquarters of the Sawants, who now called themselves Chiefs of Kudal.

Relations with the Marathas

Shivaji's power being in the ascendent, Lakham Sawant tried to get himself confirmed as Sardesai of the whole South Konkan. However, in the treaty of 1659 between Lakham and Shivaji, it was decided that half of the revenue of the territory of the Sawant should go to Shivaji, collected by his agents and the other half remain with Lakham who also had to keep a body of 3000 infantry ready for service and garrison the forts. In 1660, with the murder of Afzul Khan, Shivaji carried the war into Bijapur possessions plundering Rajapur and burning Dabhol. Bijapur the Siddi and the Sawants united against Shivaji. In the fight that ensued, Shivaji's commander, Baji Phasalkar and the Wadi Commander, Kay Sawant, both perished. The Sawants had to surrender part of the Konkan south of Salshi Mahal (the whole of the present Malwan sub-division and a part of the Wadi district).

Gomaji Prabhu, in charge of the Deshmukhs, sought Bijapur's help to drive out the Sawants. However, Bijapur was in no position to help as Shivaji could not be stopped. In May 1663, Shivaji took Kudal, marched to Vengurla, then further south. The Adil Shah Havaldar of Dicholi and Sakhali, as well as Lakham Sawant, fled. Soon after, Pedne, Sattari, Maneri and Bhatgram were occupied by Shivaji. Shivaji's forces were defeated sometime in May 1664 by the combined forces of Adil Shah and those of the Desais. For his services Lakham was rewarded by an *inam* of Malwan, Masura, Pendur, Ghavnale, Malgao, Math, Hodavde, Araveli, Reddi and Aravande. In December 1664 by a series of surprise attacks Shivaji defeated the combined forces of Bijapur and the Desais and captured the Rangna Fort. Lakham Sawant and the Desais fled to Portuguese territory. A month earlier Shivaji had granted the Deshmukhi to Krishna Sawant. Failing to get the help of Bijapur in ousting Krishna Sawant, Lakham succeeded in arresting him and putting him to death in 1665. In March 1666, Shivaji laid siege to the fort at Phonda. This was viewed with some trepidation by the Portuguese, who secretly helped the keeper of the fort and encouraged the Desais of Kudal, Pedne, and Dicholi to assist the garrison at Phonda. Shivaji thus had to give up the siege.

Shivaji attacks Bardesh

Lakham Sawant and other Desais from their refuge in Portuguese territory, carried out raids on Shivaji's conquests. In September 1667, Naroba, the nephew of Lakham, attacked the Dutch factory at Vengurla, now under Shivaji's patronage. In November 1667, Shivaji, encouraged by the Dutch, attacked and looted Bardesh. The treaty of 5 December 1667, with the Portuguese, provided for the expulsion of the Desais from Goa if they transgressed into Shivaji's lands. Necessary orders were issued to the Desais by the Viceroy on 17 December 1667. However, this did not stop the Desais from violating these orders and in June 1668, Lakham was ordered to leave Goa. He soon offered his allegiance to Shivaji and was reinstated on his ancestral Jagir on the condition that he would live at Kudal and neither build nor repair the forts, nor keep a large body of troops.

Lakham was succeeded by his brother Fond. In 1675, Fond's son, Khem succeeded him and was successful in extending his territory by helping the Mughals against Shivaji and by frequent raids into Portuguese territory.

Khem-Portuguese-Sambhaji

On the death of his father, Sambhaji ascended the throne. He established factories for manufacturing gunpowder at Dicholi and Kudal. A few years later, in 1686, the Bijapur kingdom was conquered by Aurangzeb. Thus ended the hopes of the Prabhus to take charge of their Deshmukhi. Earlier in November 1683, the Portuguese with the help of Khem attacked Phonda but could not take it from Sambhaji's forces. In January 1684 the Mughals attacked Dicholi, burnt Kudal and Banda, and looted Vengurla. For Khem's allegiance to them, the Mughals re-affirmed the Deshmukhi bestowed on him and even bestowed a Mansabdari of 4000 to 1000 cavalry on him and Fond Sawant. Sambhaji had kept a major part of the vatans of the Desais. Fearing an invasion of Sambhaji, the Portuguese made a secret treaty (8 February 1685) with Khem who it seems was acting as representative of all the Desais of the Konkan. A few days later, the families of all the Desais were sent to Goa to be under the protection of the Portuguese. Khem was the most powerful of these Desais. In 1687, a part of the army of the Mughals attacked Sindudurg and looted Kudal which was in the hands of Sambhaji. For his part in helping the Mughals, Khem was bestowed with the Kudal Pranth Sardeshmukhi.

Rajaram, on succeeding Sambhaji in March 1689, proceeded to Karnataka. The Nawab Bahadur Khan requested the Portuguese to arrest him. The Governor of Goa wrote to Bahadur Khan on 12 May 1689 informing him that he had instructed Khem to do the necessary. Khem entrusted this work to his nephew Babu Desai, and Mamba Sawant and others.

Khem Sawant now became more powerful and by 1695 he possessed a number of merchant ships and 8 battleships operating from the Karli creek. He planned an attack on the Maratha ports but without the help from the Portuguese he had to give up the idea.

Thus the Maratha-Mughal conflict enabled Khem Sawant Bhosale as also the other Desais to establish themselves independently to some extent. In August 1696, Khem took the fort of Kudal, killing Narayan Prabhu and causing his kinsman Jogan Prabhu, to flee. Shortly after, he besieged Vengurla. He then set up a mint at Dicholi after capturing that territory and Sakhali and Pedne as well. Thus by 1698, he was master of Dicholi, Sakhali, Kudal, Banda and Pedne.

Khem now turned his attention to Phonda besieging that fort. The Nawab of Phonda appealed to the Portuguese for munitions, offering them the villages from Bardesh. With Portuguese help in the form of gunpowder and cannon-balls, the Mughals attacked Khem's surrounding forces and in spite of heavy losses, including the Killedar of the fort, Sayyad Gulam Ibrahim, forced Khem to retreat. The Portuguese aided the Mughals as they felt Khem was getting too strong and was also troubling their shipping. Finally Khem signed a treaty with the Portuguese on 2 September 1699 becoming their feudatory and accepting their security and help. Thus the Portuguese were able to safeguard their territory by keeping Sawantwadi as a buffer state, yet making the Sawantwadi their feudatory.

Bassalatkhan, the brother of Gulam Ibrahim, after receiving sympathy and promises of help from the Portuguese, gathered a force to attack Dicholi. However, Khem Sawant's army being too strong and the monsoon being too near, the Mughals and Khem concluded a secret treaty resented by the Portuguese.

Khem Sawant, now, with ammunition from the Portuguese attacked Pargad and occupied it, getting rid of Hari Gawas, the chief Desai of Maneri. Thus by 1701, Khem was master of Kudal, Banda, Pedne, Dicholi (Bhatgram), Sakhali (Sattari) and Maneri.

The major interest of the Portuguese was to maintain Sawantwadi as a buffer state between their Goa territory and the powers beyond Sawantwadi like the Chhatrapati of Satara, Chhatrapati of Kolhapur, Tarabai and the Angres. It has to be remembered that it was not the policy of the Portuguese to annex Sawantwadi of the Bhosales to their Goa territory. It is with this consideration that they made Khem Sawant their feudatory. The Portuguese preferred a Hindu ruler as their neighbour than a Muslim power. In this affair, the Portuguese were playing a double game as they could not afford to displease the mighty Mughals nor their powerful neighbour Khem Sawant.

During the reign of Khem Sawant, the Marathas were engaged in a life and death struggle with Aurangzeb from 1689 to his death in 1707. Khem Sawant in his long struggle was never inspired by higher aims to help the Marathas in their war of independence. He had only a limited purpose, namely, of keeping Dicholi, Sakhali, Pedne, Kudal, Maneri and Banda in his own hands. With this in mind, it was his cunning policy not to displease his powerful neighbour the Portuguese who had well settled in Goa since 1510. There was no reason why he should join Rajaram and draw upon himself the wrath of Aurangzeb. His policy clearly was to make the most out of the situation. In annexing the territories mentioned above, Khem's conflicts with the Mughals were inevitable. But the risk involved in this was limited as the Mughals were on the retreat at many places in their war with the Marathas. Khem had chosen the right time in capturing the above territories situated to the south of Sawantwadi.

2

KHEM SAWANT II : (1701-1709)

The history of Sawantwadi at the commencement of the eighteenth century opens with the rule of Khem Sawant II, Bhosale Sardesai. He had been hereditary servant of the Adil Shah Kingdom of Bijapur which had been conquered by Aurangzeb in 1686. With the fall of Bijapur, all the territories once under its Sultanate including Sawantwadi came to be occupied by the Mughals. One of the important tasks, therefore, with which Khem Sawant II had to engage himself was to free Sawantwadi from the Mughal hands. With a strong army and a small navy, he guarded his territories from external foes and expanded it when the situation was favourable. Khem Sawant had at the beginning of the 18th century five Mahals viz., Kudal Pargana and Banda, Maneri, Dicholi, Sakhali and Pedne. It was from these five Mahals that the Sawants came to be addressed in all their official correspondence "Sardesai *Pargane* Kudal and Mahalanihai".

The political condition, when Khem Sawant came to power, was changing very fast. The Mughals were on the retreat on a number of fronts in the Deccan. Tarabai was opposing Aurangzeb tooth and nail after her husband's death. After the death of Aurangzeb in 1707, the attitude of the Mughal officers was one of compromise. The Prabhus of Kudal who were hostile to Khem Sawant II were trying to retain their own power by seeking help from the Mughal officers. Khem Sawant II had to establish his hold over Sawantwadi in this situation.

The Kudal Deshastha Prabhus held Deshmukhi vatans from the Bijapur Adil Shah. Khem Sawant in his attempt to establish his rule over Sawantwadi had to put down the armed resistance of the Prabhus who were always a thorn in the side of Sawantwadi State. In 1704, Narayan Prabhu tried to regain power with the help of the Mughals. The then Mughal officer

provisions for the conquest of Dicholi, held by the Bhosales of Sawantwadi and Phonda and Pancha Mahal which were under the ruler of Sunda. These territories had been given to Shahu by the Mughals by the Sanad of Swaraj. Shahu also demanded from the Portuguese the islands of Kharjuvem and Paneli captured from the Sawants of Wadi.

All the demands of Chhatrapati Shahu were considered by the Goa Council and a reply was sent. The Portuguese agreed to help Shahu against the Sawants of Wadi as they were the enemies of Goa Government. Regarding Phonda and Pancha Mahal, the reply was that the Portuguese had no interest in them as they had been leased by the Mughals to the ruler of Sunda after recovering them from the Sawantwadi ruler, and Shahu may continue the lease. So far as the islands of Kharjuvem and Paneli were concerned the Portuguese communicated to Shahu that they were not prepared to surrender to them as a part of Kharjuvem belonged to Bardesh, and the other part including the island of Paneli was gifted to them by the Mughals.

Thus, in the struggle between Tarabai and Shahu it seems that Khem Sawant's demand of collecting mokasa from the six districts under Kudal was to avoid future conflict with any authority laying claim on the territory of Konkan. Internally, the mokasa rights strengthened his financial and hereditary position.

Having thus secured for himself what was necessary, Khem was virtually independent in his territory. He then made Charata his headquarters, which in due course became his it seems, was not in a position to offer substantial help to Narayan but only granted him 1001 Hons out of the total revenue of Kudal, for the maintenance of his army. By this grant, the Mughal officer could keep the Sawants and the Prabhus of Kudal at war to his own advantage, when he himself was not in a position to do anything as the Mughal power itself was passing through a very critical period just a few years prior to the death of Aurangzeb. With Aurangzeb's death the Mughal power which was extended to the south recently began to crack fast.

KHEM SAWANT IN THE STRUGGLE BETWEEN TARABAI AND SHAHU

Shahu, the eldest son of Sambhaji, was released from Mughal custody soon after the death of Emperor Aurangzeb. His release triggered off a civil war in the Maratha Kingdom. The conflict that arose between Shahu and Tarabai for the gadi was advantageous to Khem Sawant, since his territory was adjacent to that of Tarabai. And since Tarabai was in full control of her territory, the best alternative for Khem was to lend support to her cause.

Tarabai was badly in need of help coming from any quarter to maintain her position at this critical juncture, and was ready to pay any price. It is significant to observe here that the role of the neighbouring powers was always that of opportu-

capital, renamed as Sundarwadi. Here he built a palace and appointed various officials to look after the administration.

ROLE OF KHEM IN THE STRUGGLE BETWEEN THE MARATHAS AND THE MUGHALS FOR PHONDA

Rajaram died on 2 March 1700, and his minor son called Shivaji succeeded him. At this time, the Portuguese supported the weaker Marathas fighting with Aurangzeb for their independence. The memory of the retreat of Chhatrapati Sambhaji from the Goa island which he was about to conquer was still fresh in Maratha minds. Now they had an opportunity of falling on important stations belonging to the Mughals bordering on the Portuguese territory. In October 1702, the Maratha forces attacked Phonda alias Antruj Mahal. The powerful Maratha forces surrounded the Mughal territory and pushed forward in spite of heroic and continuous resistance from the Mughal troops who sent frequent piteous appeals to neighbouring powers. The Sunda ruler who had a stake in the Phonda Mahal rushed his forces to their aid. The Portuguese at Goa afraid of the Marathas so close to their borders secretly supplied the Mughals with ammunition. But the Mughals, not satisfied with this, requested the Portuguese Viceroy for two hundred soldiers. The Portuguese to avoid direct confrontation with the Marathas sent ammunition with Ahmed Sarang, the envoy of Saif Khan, the Subhedar of Belgaum. In fact, the Portuguese at this time do not seem to be in a position to send a large army to help the Subhedar as their troops were then away, and many of their soldiers were sick. The remaining forces were necessary for guarding the frontiers of Goa. Probably, this was an excuse the Viceroy of Goa was placing before the Mughals to maintain neutrality out of fear of the Marathas. Having received help from the ruler of Sunda and ammunition from the Portuguese the Subhedar made an all-out effort to drive the Marathas from the Phonda region, which proved ineffective and the Maratha arms captured Phonda Mahal in January 1703. With the capture of Phonda Mahal the Marathas surrounded the fort of Mardangad, built by Chhatrapati Sambhaji in 1683. This further weakened the position of the Subhedar. It is evident that the Portuguese were restless when the Marathas occupied Phonda Mahal and besieged Mardangad. In the event of the strategic fort of Mardangad falling into Maratha hands, Goa was bound to come under their perpetual threat. The Portuguese to avoid this, without open war with the Marathas, therefore, encouraged the Sawants of Wadi to fight against the Marathas as Khem's help was sought by the Mughals.

Khem Sawant had been informing the Portuguese about the activities of the Marathas in the Phonda affair. The aim of the Portuguese was to drive the Marathas out of Phonda Mahal by encouraging Khem to help the Mughals. This provided an opportunity to Khem to further his interest who sent his forces to help the Mughals. The net result was that the Maratha forces faced by the combined armies of the Mughals and the Sawants were defeated and had to give up the siege of Mardangad fort. The fort was taken possession of by Khem Sawant on 28 September 1703. But he did not return it to the Mughals and retained it for nearly two years to the exasperation of both the Mughals and the then Portuguese Viceroy of Goa, Caetano de Mello de Castro.

Terribly dissatisfied with Khem, the Portuguese Viceroy suddenly changed his attitude and called Khem a "traitor" and "scoundrel", in his correspondence with Krishnaji Pant and Hindurao Ghorpade. He also promised all kind of help to the Desais of Maneri, Haria Gaons and Heroji Rane of Sakhali against Khem Sawant. All this, however, could not dislodge Khem from Mardangad. Such was the nature of changing politics in the Phonda affair.

The Portuguese Viceroy now tried to punish Khem Sawant by inciting his enemies. The relations between the Portuguese and the Bhosales now deteriorated and ultimately resulted in conflicts in the years to come.

On 14 November 1703, the Maratha officers Krishnaji Pant and Hindurao Ghorpade sought the help of the Portuguese whose forces were not accustomed to guerilla warfare and hence could not help Krishnaji Pant and Hindurao Ghorpade very much. However, they incited the Desais of Maneri and Sakhali against the Sawants. But undeterred, Khem Sawant continued to be in possession of Mardangad in spite of the opposition from both the Portuguese and the Marathas.

With mounting pressure from the Marathas, the Portuguese and the Mughals, Khem found it difficult to maintain his hold on Mardangad as there was scarcity of foodgrains and essential goods in the Wadi territory. Taking advantage of this state of affairs, the Mughals suddenly attacked Mardangad. After several skirmishes Khem Sawant was defeated and forced to give up the fort. The Mughals then took possession of Mardangad fort in the beginning of June 1705.

Later in 1706, the Mughals signed an agreement with the King of Sunda who had helped them in the Phonda affair handing the fort over to the King of Sunda, who was to pay rupees eighty thousand annually to the Mughals. The Mughals preferred to keep Phonda Mahal and the fort of Mardangad with the weak King of Sunda than either with the Portuguese or Khem Sawant. The Portuguese on their part preferred this arrangement as it kept the territory free from the hands of their troublesome neighbour Khem Sawant. It was also advantageous for them to have the King of Sunda at Phonda rather than the powerful Mughals. In this regard, it is significant to note the instructions of the Viceroy of Goa Conde de Ericeira in 1720, to prefer Sunda King as a neighbour to any other power at Phonda. He observed that the ruler of Sunda was basically interested in trade than in war. He felt that he would be a useful and friendly neighbour to them. Thus, the fort of Mardangad and Phonda territory went under the King of Sunda to the exclusion of the powerful Mughals and the troublesome Khem Sawant. At this time, Mirza Nizamutidin was the fauzdar of Phonda.

MARDANGAD TAKEN BACK BY KHEM SAWANT

With the death of Emperor Aurangzeb in February 1707, Khem thought the time ripe for action. He succeeded in bribing the Mughal *fauzdar* and the fort was taken into possession by the forces of Khem. The Portuguese Government always preferred a Hindu ruler as their neighbour, yet between the Bhosales and the Sunda ruler they chose the latter. The

Portuguese Government took serious note of the situation and despatched their army to help the Sunda ruler. The combined forces attacked the fort of Mardangad and forced the Bhosales to withdraw. There was no other alternative left to the Bhosales but to retreat. While withdrawing the Bhosales destroyed the fort and devastated the territory. In May 1707, the Portuguese repaired the fort and handed it over to the Saundekars.

WAR WITH THE PORTUGUESE

The Portuguese at this time were in possession of the Velhas Conquistas, (Old Conquests) which included Ilhas, Bardesh and Salset.

The Bhosales having freed themselves from the Mughal supremacy, frequently plundered the Portuguese territory. In March 1702, nearly 102 soldiers selected from different forts of the Bhosales attacked and plundered the village of Asnoda in the Bardesh territory. Many people were captured and a large number of animals were taken away. The Portuguese lodged a strong protest against this action and urged Khem Sawant to maintain peace. But Khem continued burning and plundering Portuguese territory. For these marauding activities, the Portuguese nicknamed Khem Sawant as "Queimar Sant" meaning saint who indulges in burning.

Khem Sawant also possessed a small navy, which fell upon Portuguese ships and looted them when possible. The Viceroy's repeated warnings to Khem Sawant to stop his nefarious activities on sea and numerous reminders of the help rendered to the Sawantwadi state by the Portuguese in times of need going unheeded, the Viceroy of Goa, Caetano de Mello de Castro, attacked the strongholds of Khem Sawant. It may be observed here that the administration of this Viceroy was chiefly noted for his endeavour to extend the Portuguese power in the districts bordering Goa.

In the month of July 1705, the Viceroy turned his attention to the fort of Amona which was occupied by the forces of Khem Sawant Bhosale. Amona is situated to the east of the river Mandavi at a short distance from its bank. Opposite Amona, on the other side of the river, that is, to its west is the famous Island of St. Stephen, also known as Santo Estevam or Juva. Khem Sawant, in order to safeguard his position on the fort of Amona had blockaded the Mandavi river, making it difficult for the Portuguese to attack him. The Portuguese Navy attacked the fleet of Khem Sawant blockading the Mandavi river and cleared the blockade. The Portuguese ships, superior both in tonnage and guns scored an easy victory over the small fleet of Khem Sawant. The Portuguese crew received 300 xerafins each for its victory over the navy of the Sawants.

Having cleared the blockade, the Portuguese army straightaway attacked the Amona fort, and heavy fighting took place in which the Bhosales suffered more loss than the Portuguese. They had no support from any neighbouring power. Moreover, the Viceroy himself was leading the attack in order to encourage his soldiers.

A distinguished Brazilian woman soldier Dona Maria Ursula de Abreu de Alem Castro, daughter of Joan de Abreu de Oliveira, had come to Portuguese India in the monsoon of 1700. She was just 18 years old and with the assumed name of Baltazar do Couto Cardozo, took part in the attack on the fort of Amona. Her brilliant tactics won victory to the Portuguese. After this, she married Captain Afonso Teixeira Arrais de Melo, who had come to Portuguese India in the same year.

A contingent of troops under his command which lay hidden in the impenetrable forests, was suddenly attacked by the forces of the Bhosales. This surprise attack put the Portuguese soldiers in a state of confusion and panic. Hand to hand fighting took place. At this critical moment, the wife of the Captain, the Brazilian woman, fell upon the Bhosales impetuously with her soldiers, and ultimately succeeded in rescuing her husband back. In this operation, she was gravely injured. This was a notable feat of bravery to the credit of this heroic woman. Her action proved to be a turning point in the siege of Amona. In the face of this situation, Khem Sawant realized the futility of continuing the war. Almost all the defenders of the fort were killed in the siege. The loss on the Portuguese side according to both the contemporary Portuguese and Marathi sources was nil, though one finds it difficult to believe. Khem Sawant surrendered the fort to the Portuguese. In recognition of her heroism in the battles of Amona, Dicholi and other places the Portuguese Government granted her two pieces of groves of palm trees situated in the city of Chaul.

Immediately after the capture of the Amona fort, the Viceroy of Goa despatched orders to demolish and level it to the ground, so that the Bhosales might not make use of it again in future.

With the loss of the fort of Amona, one important phase of Bhosale-Portuguese conflict came to an end.

Following their success at Amona, the Portuguese attacked the fort at Valvai. After a few skirmishes, the Portuguese captured the fort and levelled it to the ground.

Khem Sawant now started peace overtures with the Portuguese but they continued their military operations against him. Meanwhile, the forces of Khem Sawant now entered the Portuguese territory of Bardesh and set fire to the Rectory of Revora in a retaliatory move. They particularly wanted to punish the church authorities who guided the policy of the Portuguese Government.

In December 1705, the Portuguese troops were ordered to march on Dicholi fort, another strategically important stronghold of the Bhosales. This fort was situated in the heart of the Province of Dicholi, on the bank of a small tributary of the Mandavi river. In the words of the Viceroy of Goa, the fort of Dicholi was one of the best among those Khem Sawant possessed in the Konkan territory. Khem Sawant often boasted that it was impossible for the Portuguese to capture it. This was a sort of challenge to the Portuguese Viceroy and therefore a matter of prestige.

The Portuguese Viceroy mobilized his army and led an attack on the fort of Dicholi and another fort situated nearby. The aggressive Portuguese played havoc among the armed and unarmed population, plundering Dicholi and other places, but they were suddenly attacked by an overwhelming forces of Khem Sawant. The Portuguese troops fled and the angry Bhosales slaughtered some of the Portuguese soldiers. The Viceroy had planned well by keeping his forces under strict control. Since the Portuguese troops were armed with all the necessary weapons and had a strong contingent of select troops, the sudden attack by the Bhosales was repulsed effectively with heavy loss to the Bhosales. The European artillery was of great advantage to the Portuguese. The artillery bombarded the fort continuously for ten to twelve hours and forced the Bhosales to surrender.

While the Dicholi campaign was in progress, the Maratha Subhedar Daudkhan, who was in the service of the Marathas, tried to attack a few ships of the Bhosales with horses aboard lying in one of their ports. The Portuguese promised to offer all kind of help to the Maratha Subhedar. But the Sawants who got timely information of the intention of the Subhedar successfully foiled his attempts.

It is to be noted that in this expedition led by the Viceroy against the fortifications of the Bhosales, the Franciscans played a dominant role. Three Franciscans, Manoel Graça, Belchior dos Reis, and Francisco de S. Rosa accompanied the expedition. The Franciscans helped the Portuguese with a view to punish the Bhosales who had attacked the Rectories of the Franciscan friars and killed their Provincials.

The expedition of Dicholi was highly successful and the Portuguese Viceroy caused Khem Sawant's troops to flee, and captured the two forts of Dicholi. Immediately after the capture of the Dicholi forts, the Viceroy ordered their demolition, and handed over the territories attached to Dicholi and Sakhali, to the king of Sunda for governance. He then entered into a treaty with the Sunda chief, whereby the latter agreed to be a feudatory of the king of Portugal. It is to be noted that the Sawantwadi rulers rebuilt the fort of Dicholi after some years when they got possession of it.

The Portuguese Viceroy after his success in securing these important forts of Khem Sawant ordered his troops to burn his villages. Accordingly, the Portuguese army burnt down Dicholi, and the territory around it upto a distance of three kms. The Viceroy further boasted that he did not leave a single building in Dicholi standing. His justification for these barbarous acts was that he never wanted Khem Sawant to become another Shivaji.

In 1706, the Portuguese troops concentrated for an attack on the islands of Kharjuvem and Paneli. These had been captured by Khem Sawant from the Portuguese in 1705. The two small islands had earlier been donated to the Portuguese by the Mughal Emperor Aurangzeb when Rev. Father Frey Luis da Piedade went to his court as an ambassador. These islands were very important for the defence of Goa. The island of Kharjuvem lies to the south-east of the village of Aldona in Bardesh and is separated from it by the Mhapsa river, which ultimately joins the river Mandavi. Further to the south of Kharjuvem is the island of Paneli.

The main object of the Portuguese was to secure these strategically important islands. They attacked the islands with their navy and land forces. The Bhosales stoutly resisted but were finally forced to leave the islands, upon which the Portuguese occupied them. It is not known whether on this occasion Khem Sawant had brought his fleet for the defence of the islands as in the case of Amona. The Portuguese artillery was again most effective in forcing the Bhosales to quit the islands. On all occasions, we find that Khem Sawant had neither a matching navy nor an artillery to defend his positions.

While at war with the Bhosales, the Portuguese were also instigating Ramchandra Pandit, a Maratha nobleman to fight against Khem Sawant. In one of the letters addressed to him the Portuguese Viceroy requested him to declare a war on Khem Sawant, because long ago, the great Shivaji had communicated to him (to the Viceroy) his intention to attack Khem Sawant, and had expressed his desire that the Viceroy should join him. However, Ramchandra Pandit does not seem to have responded to the Viceroy favourably.

The campaign against the Bhosales proved a resounding success to the Portuguese. The Bhosales suffered more heavily than the Portuguese both in men and money.

Khem Sawant was smarting under the defeats he had suffered at the hands of the Portuguese. He appealed to Hindurao Ghorpade for help, but help was not forthcoming from this quarter as there was an agreement between the Portuguese and Tarabai under whom Hindurao was serving. In appreciation of this, the Viceroy thanked Hindurao Ghorpade and communicated to him that he had noted Hindurao's friendship towards the Portuguese which would be duly rewarded on an appropriate occasion. At this very time, it was reported to the Viceroy that a small force of Tarabai had come to the aid of Khem Sawant, as far as Jambaulim. He, therefore, wrote to Hindurao Ghorpade expressing his surprise as to how Tarabai could send her force to help Khem Sawant without his knowledge. He could not understand how this decision was taken when Khem Sawant had been an enemy of Tarabai and Tarabai herself had once communicated to the Viceroy that she would fight out Khem Sawant till he was completely destroyed. The Viceroy further wrote that if Khem Sawant had given any promise to Tarabai he should not be relied upon as he was a most untrustworthy man he had ever come across. In conclusion, the Viceroy stated that he had full trust that Hindurao Ghorpade would consider this matter and would not offer any aid to Khem Sawant. Tarabai's small force if it had come as far as Jambaulim does not seem to have had any effect upon the Portuguese.

Khem Sawant Bhosale in his struggle with the Portuguese for strategic places and for the extension of his territory was defeated by the Portuguese. Khem Sawant was unsuccessful everywhere because he did not have an artillery and a navy which could match with the one possessed by the Portuguese. No neighbouring power seems to have come to the aid of Khem Sawant. He was at war more or less continuously from 1703 to 1707, first with the Mughals and then with the Portuguese. This had its adverse effect on the economy of Khem Sawant.

Caetano de Mello de Castro succeeded Dom Rodrigo de Costa as Viceroy on 28 October 1707. This change of Viceroyalty was a welcome opportunity to Khem Sawant to establish peace with the Portuguese. He congratulated the Viceroy when he took office. The Viceroy in his reply brought home to Khem Sawant that he had committed a mistake by his hostility with the Portuguese though he had been under their protection according to the treaty of 2 September 1699. Actually, by this treaty, he was a Portuguese feudatory. Yet he waged wars against them when it was advantageous to him as is commonly done by bordering opportunist state. The Portuguese on their part forgave him his misdeeds and requested Bhosale to send his envoy for establishing good relations.

Friendly relations between Khem Sawant and the Portuguese worried the ruler of the small neighbouring state of Sunda as he feared aggressive action from Khem Sawant. To safeguard his own interest, he requested the Portuguese that he should be consulted in the event of fresh peace settlements between the Portuguese and Khem Sawant. His request was complied with. The King of Portugal too advised the Viceroy of Goa to safeguard the interest of the Sunda kingdom while entering into an agreement with Khem Sawant.

Actually it is not known whether any peace settlement between Khem Sawant and the Portuguese took place in 1707, as we have no original records to support this.

The Sunda's fear of aggressive action from Khem Sawant turned true. In February 1709, Khem Sawant attacked the territory of Sunda with 2000 infantry, 150 cavalry and a small navy. Khem's forces plundered and burnt a number of villages belonging to Sunda and surrounded a church and a house of a priest Sebastinao Lopes of the Society of Jesus, a missionary in the Sunda kingdom. Bhosale forces also wounded a number of Portuguese subjects. In this critical situation, the Sunda ruler sought Portuguese help and succeeded in driving out the forces of Khem Sawant.

Khem Sawant died in 1709, leaving no male successor to the gadi of Sawantwadi. He had three daughters. He ruled for thirty-four years. He was successful in securing Deshmukhi of Kudal from the Adil Shah of Bijapur. Later when the Adil Shah kingdom was conquered by the Mughals, he established himself as an independent ruler. With the establishment of Shahu's rule, he secured from him the *Sanad* of the six districts of Kudal. Thus technically he became a vassal of Chhatrapati Shahu.

The rule of Khem Sawant Bhosale II was crowned with events of outstanding importance. It revealed to the Portuguese the strength and power of the small bordering kingdom even though the Portuguese won wars against it.

3

FOND SAWANT II (ANASAHEB) : (1709-1738)

After the death of Khem Sawant in 1709, his nephew Fond Sawant alias Anasaheb, oldest son of his brother Nar Sawant, succeeded him to the gadi of Sawantwadi.

The 42 year old Fond Sawant immediately began to strengthen the defences of his State. He built the forts of Hanumantgad at Fukeri, Narayangad at Gole, Mahadevgad at Ambolim, Narsinhgad alias Songad at Sonvade, Bharatgad at Masura' Sidhagad at Ovaliyen (*Taraf* Maland), Nivty at Kochren. With the help of British engineers he also renovated the fort of Dicholi which was in a dilapidated condition. The other forts which he renovated were those of Kudal, Banda, Sakhali, and Vengurla. He strengthened the army and naval establishments and introduced changes in the administration of his kingdom.

At this time, the political situation in the neighbouring kingdoms was more or less the same as under his predecessor. While the war of succession was going on in the Mughal Empire, the relentless struggle for supremacy between Tarabai and Shahu continued till the treaty of Varna was concluded in 1731. Till about 1718, Fond Sawant had no trouble from external enemies.

Sawants and the Prabhus

Once again in 1718, Narayan Prabhu besieged the fort of Kudal. Forced to retreat, he sought the help of Sambhaji of Kolhapur. Sambhaji seized the opportunity and ordered his commander at the fort of Sindhudurg to render all assistance to Narayan Prabhu, and himself despatched a strong column against the Sawants. The combined forces of Narayan Prabhu and Sambhaji marched against Kudal. Fond Sawant had to abandon his capital and flee for safety. Meanwhile, Kanhoji

Angre arrived with his forces near the neighbourhood of Fond and requested Sambhaji to hand over the fort of Kudal to him in return for a sum of Rs. 30,000. Furthermore, he informed him that while waiting for his reply he had restrained his troops from attacking Fond's territory. In this dire hour of difficulty, Fond Sawant had no other alternative but to appeal to the Portuguese at Goa for immediate help. The Portuguese who always preferred a weak neighbour, unhesitatingly supplied twenty barrels of gunpowder to Fond Sawant with a request to convey the news of all the movements of the Marathas and the Angres so that they might remain alert in case the Angres and the Marathas join the enemies of Fond Sawant.

Having received fresh succour from the Portuguese, Fond Sawant swung his army into action to drive out the aggressors. Immediately after the defeat of Fond Sawant, Sambhaji had withdrawn the forces from Sawantwadi since he was engaged in warfare at home with his rival Shahu. So the only enemy left in the field for Sawant was Narayan Prabhu. As soon as the forces of Sambhaji withdrew, Fond Sawant attacked the Prabhus at Kudal. Heavy fighting broke out resulting in loss to the Prabhus and the capture of the fort. Ultimately Narayan Prabhu was defeated and his kinsman, Jogan Prabhu was killed. The Prabhus being the vassals of Sambhaji Raje, a grant of village was announced to the widows of Jogan Prabhu. In fact, after this great blow, Prabhus never dared to invade the State of Sawantwadi during Fond's regime.

Conflict with the Angres

The Angres were a constant source of trouble to the Sawantwadi rulers and the Portuguese who being on friendly terms with Fond Sawant in the early part of his career invited him to join them against the Angres. In 1718, Viceroy Dom Luis de Menezes, Conde de Ericeira persuaded Fond Sawant to join in an alliance against the Angres. The Portuguese supplied Fond Sawant with gunpowder and shot which he needed most, and in return Fond Sawant kept the Viceroy well informed about the activities of the Angres.

Fond Sawant invaded the territory of Kanhoji Angre in 1723, in the absence of Kanhoji who had been to the court of

Shahu. The Angre was a power to be reckoned with and there was not much difficulty in resisting and repelling the attack of Fond Sawant who was ultimately defeated. Fearing complete destruction, Fond appealed to the Portuguese for timely help. But the political situation not being very encouraging for the Portuguese, they sent help secretly to Fond Sawant. The Government of Goa knew that a threat to the State of Sawantwadi would pose danger to Goa. So it was natural that they preferred Fond Sawant in the neighbourhood rather than the mighty Angres. With Portuguese succour reaching Wadi State the Angres realized the gravity of the situation and abstained from attacking the territory of Fond Sawant.

Kanhoji Angre died on 4 July 1729 and he was succeeded by Sekoji Angre who continued at war with Fond Sawant for a long time. Meanwhile, Sekoji was at war with the Portuguese too. When the latter asked help from Fond, he was not in a position to give it.

At this very time, the English who had suffered a great loss at the hands of the Angres entered into a treaty with Fond Sawant in 1730, with a view to effectively resisting the attacks of the Angres. In this treaty, the Governor of Bombay Robert Coven was the representative of the English and Bapuji Naik Tendolker, the Naval chief, the emissary of Fond Sawant.

Relations with the Portuguese

In Goa, Dom Rodrigo de Costa who had succeeded Caetano de Mello as a Viceroy on 28 October 1707, was still in power when Fond Sawant came to the gadi of Sawantwadi. The political situation in Kolhapur was still fluid and unfriendly to Fond Sawant owing to his hostile attitude towards the Panhala faction of Tarabai. The Angres too were harassing the Wadi ruler both by sea and land. During the last days of Khem Sawant, the Portuguese were very hostile to him. He endeavoured to gain the friendship of the Portuguese, but in vain. His successor, Fond Sawant, with great difficulty, succeeded in establishing amicable relations with the Portuguese, expressing his repentance for the attacks his predecessor, Khem Sawant, had launched earlier on the territory of Goa. In consequence he accepted the terms of the treaty of 7 April, 1712, which were more favourable to the Portuguese. By this treaty, the Portuguese gained whatever they desired by admitting Fond Sawant as their friend. The Portuguese, by one of the terms of this treaty forbade Fond Sawant from meddling with the territory of Phonda, on the pretext that it was placed under the king of Sunda. Further, the Portuguese also protected the interests of Desais and the merchants who were their vassals. The Portuguese forbade him to trade with the Arabs who were their arch-enemies. It seems that the Revora Church which was demolished sometime in 1706, was to be compensated for by Fond paying Rs. 10,000 xerafins for its reconstruction. Fond also agreed to return to the Portuguese some Negroes who had crossed into his territory.

In 1715, Nar Sawant, one of the sons of Fond rebelled against him causing havoc in the Wadi State. The panic he created, affected the neighbouring powers of Kolhapur and Sunda. The Viceroy Vasco Fernandes Cesar de Menezes who was watching the disturbances in the neighbouring State feared that Nar Sawant would attack the territory of Phonda. With a view to avoiding such an eventuality he remained neutral towards both Nar Sawant and the king of Sunda, who were vassals of the Portuguese. At the same time, he kept his forces ready to avert an armed encounter between Nar Sawant and the kingdom of Sunda.

In Goa, the new Viceroy Dom Luis de Menezes, Conde de Ericeira took charge of the administration of Government on 16 October 1717, and held it up to 1720. In the last year of his Viceroyalty a Mughal Officer in consultation with some Maratha Nobleman attacked the kingdom of Sunda and captured the fort of Samrani in February 1720 as part of their future plan to attack the territory of Phonda. The Viceroy, therefore, alerted Fond Sawant on these developments and asked him to strengthen the defence of the Sawantwadi frontiers and prevent the entry of Gaji Beg's men and the Marathas into his State. Meanwhile, a person by name Balu Bhat Bakre had informed the Portuguese of an understanding reached between the Marathas and Fond Sawant and also of the news that the Marathas had granted some concessions to the Sawants and of the movements of the army of Chhatrapati Shahu. The

Portuguese Viceroy had his own reservations about the Sawantwadi ruler's motives and actions and kept his frontiers well defended.

In March 1720, the fort of Samrani was returned by the Marathas to the Sunda Raja on receipt of rupees one lakh. They also promised not to carry incursions into his territory.

Fear of a fresh Maratha invasion seems to have been current. For, the Viceroy informed Fond Sawant that the Marathas were marching towards Phonda by way of Quel Ghat. He, therefore, cautioned him to strengthen his defences in the said Ghat with a view to obstructing the Maratha march.

There is no doubt that the Portuguese were afraid of the Maratha power coming closer to their border. The Viceroy of Goa therefore informed Fond Sawant about all the activities of the Marathas so that he might take necessary precautionary measures to safeguard his territory, as any threat to Sawantwadi state meant danger to the Portuguese state.

On 12 September 1720, Viceroy Francisco Jose de Sanpaio e Castro arrived in Goa and took charge of office two days later. The first important thing he did was to strengthen the defences of the Portuguese possessions in the North. An equally significant achievement to his credit was the treaty which he concluded with the English on 20 August 1721, against the Angres. It went a long way in establishing friendly relations with the English.

Portuguese fugitives in Sawantwadi Territory

On receipt of the information from the Bardesh General regarding the Portuguese soldiers who had fled to Sawantwadi out of fear, the Viceroy on 26 June 1721, wrote to Fond Sawant requesting him to send them back as per the agreement he had signed with the previous Viceroy. But Fond Sawant turned down the request of Viceroy stating that there were no Portuguese soldiers in the Wadi State. The Portuguese soldiers who had stayed in Sawantwadi were not at all willing to go back to Goa as they were afraid of being punished. Their presence there in fact was of great advantage to Fond Sawant as he could utilize them against the Portuguese in various ways. The Viceroy drew Fond Sawant's attention to the fact that he had turned down the request made by his son Nag Sawant for help against him. He was surprised Fond Sawant was not prepared to return the Portuguese fugitives back to Goa when there was a treaty of friendship between them.

The Viceroy was not in a position to wage a war against Fond Sawant for at this time he was busy with the invasions of Bajirao Peshwa I on the Northern Provinces. This helped the Sawantwadi ruler to consolidate his territorial positions.

FOND SAWANT ATTACKS PHONDA

In July 1725, news reached Goa from one Rudraji Naik that Fond Sawant had collected a force of 2,000 strong on the frontier for the capture of the Phonda fort. The commander of the army of Salsete, Dom Antionio C. de Mello informed the commission which was in charge of Goa administration following the death of Viceroy Castro, and the commission in turn informed the Governor of Phonda, who collected the forces of Jambaulim and Sanguem for the defence of Phonda. The commission asked the commander of Salsete to supply four barrels of gunpowder if asked for by the Subhedar of Phonda.

Meanwhile, the Portuguese Government received information from their intelligence cell that Fond Sawant was giving up the plan of his attack on the Phonda fort. Though the Portuguese believed that the Sawants had abandoned the idea of attacking the fort, they took care to inform the commander-in-chief of Salsete to instruct the Subhedar of Phonda to be alert, as Fond Sawant had still kept his troops on the border. Fond Sawant seems to have withdrawn his forces about September 1725, and later when the situation was favourable he attacked the fort of Phonda.

On 28 October 1725, João de Saldanha de Gama was nominated as the Viceroy of Goa. The seven year tenure of Gama's office turned out to be full of important happenings. The Mughal power near the Portuguese territory had become weak. The Marathas who had grown strong were advancing rapidly towards the borders of the Portuguese possessions in the North. Friends of the Portuguese who had for some time turned their backs on them now showed signs of unity, a factor favourable to the Portuguese.

Fond Sawant Bhosale who knew very well when to act, did not lag behind in making capital of this situation. He seized and robbed many of the Portuguese vessels at sea and also made several incursions into Portuguese territory. In 1726, he collected his troops and attacked the fortress of Phonda which was in the hands of the Sundas who could not match the powerful army of the Bhosales, and the fortress fell to the Sawants. The king of Sunda appealed for immediate assistance to the Viceroy of Goa who despatched Portuguese troops. Having received fresh succour from the Portuguese, the Sunda forces renewed their attacks on the fortress of Phonda, and finally forced the Bhosales to give up the fort. Thus the Phonda fort came back into the hands of the king of Sunda, the Protegee of the Portuguese.

Fond Sawant and the Portuguese-Maratha Conflict at Bassein in 1731, 1736

During the Viceroyalty of Gama, the Marathas were advancing towards the Portuguese possessions in the region of Bassein. The Portuguese were aided by the British against the Marathas who had now appeared before Manora on 27 February 1731, with two thousand infantry and five hundred horses. Prior to this, the island of Salsete (Thana) had been the target of the Maratha attacks, but they could not succeed because the British forces went to the rescue of the Portuguese. Now however the Marathas could capture some of the areas in the neighbourhood of Manor by 1 March 1731. They harassed the Portuguese considerably but the latter on receiving reinforcement forced the former to retreat. Meanwhile, the Portuguese Governor of the North Martinho da Silveira de Menezes was informed that Fond Sawant Bhosale was rushing his troops to his help. But, the Viceroy informed the Governor of the North in his letter that there was no such move and made it clear to him not to be misled by such news. Fond Sawant was not in a position to send his troops outside his territory as he feared a threat from the Angres.

The aforesaid Maratha-Portuguese conflict came to an end with the conclusion of a treaty between them, on 3 July 1731. According to this, it was agreed between the two parties that the losses on both the sides, should not be further referred to; that the territories occupied by the Marathas in the Northern Provinces should be evacuated; that the Portuguese artillery captured by the Marathas should be returned to them; that without any ransom all the prisoners of war should be repatriated; the two merchant ships laden with salt and captured by the Portuguese should be returned to the Marathas. Any other ship that might have been captured during the war should also be returned to the Marathas.

Viceroy João de Saldanha de Gama before returning to Portugal opened the patent of succession in 1732. Having named this commission and handing over the charge to them. Viceroy Gama left Goa on 23 January 1732.

There was no change in the political situation in the neighbouring kingdoms when the commission was in charge of the administration for nine months till Dom Pedro Mascarenhas, Conde de Sandomil took over as Viceroy of Goa on 7 October 1732. The new Viceroy always held the view, "that the Indians in general respected the Portuguese only when they feared them". On these grounds, the Viceroy framed certain charges against Ramchandra Sawant Bhosale, Fond Sawant's grandson and determined to punish him. Accordingly Viceroy immediately issued orders to the troops and three companies attacked the territory of the Bhosales and burnt and pillaged a number of villages. But they were taken by surprise by a small powerful group of eighty of the Bhosales who surprised them in a ferocious attack and forced them to flee. The defeat of the Portuguese troops was a personal defeat for the new Viceroy who was acting upon the conviction that the Portuguese could command respect from the Indians by terror.

On 11 July 1736, Fond Sawant deputed Vishram Anant with a letter to the Viceroy suggesting him that the Bhosale-Portuguese differences should be ended and friendship established. He also expressed repentance for seizing Parangues and light boats belonging to the Portuguese vessels and made a representation to them so that they should remain satisfied with regard to the said crafts. Such expressions of repentance are common in a treaty when a weak party is required to accept it. He requested the Portuguese to observe the treaty of Peace which he had signed with them on 24 August 1726. The details of this treaty are discussed relevantly under "Rebellions of the Sawant brothers Naroba and Nagoba". The Portuguese considered the representation of Fond Sawant and finalized an inventory of crafts and goods captured by Fond Sawant, to be restored to them. The Portuguese on their part acquitted Fond of the annual gift which he had failed to pay to them for nearly ten years. At this time, the Portuguese wanted to curb the nefarious activities of Nagoba, the son of Fond, who had been a thorn in their side for quite sometime.

While these developments were on the Portuguese were at war with the Marathas in Bassein. The Portuguese were badly in need of troops and efforts were made to recruit them from various places. The Portuguese requested Pandurang Vishram, the Minister of Bhosales to see if the people from Dicholi and Kudal would be available on payment to fight against the Marathas at Bassein. The Government of Goa was confident that people from Dicholi and Kudal would join them. In the event of their joining them they were to be transported to Bassein via Reddy or any other suitable port. In this hour of difficulty the Portuguese sought the help of the Bhosales.

Role of the Portuguese in the Sawantwadi-Kolhapur Conflict

The rulers of Kolhapur, never friendly with the Sawants of Wadi, resented the hostile policy of the Fond Sawant with the Panhala faction in the civil war raging between Shahu and Tarabai. A chance to march against the Sawantwadi State was provided to the Kolhapur state in 1718, by Narayan Prabhu's revolt, but since the Portuguese rushed succour to Fond Sawant, this attempt fizzled out.

Yet another opportunity was provided for the Kolhapur Ruler to attack Sawantwadi in 1724, in the disturbed political situation following the death of emperor Aurangzeb. Exploiting the confusion that prevailed, the Marathas also created disturbances in the Northern Provinces of the Portuguese that is, in Bassein.

In July 1724, the Raja of Kolhapur with a heavy force attacked the territory of Sawantwadi. The Portuguese Viceroy wrote to the General of the sea to send intelligence personnel to Sawantwadi to find out the motive behind the attack which he viewed as a serious danger to Goa.

The attack was too strong for Fond Sawant to face and therefore he sought Portuguese help. He sent all crippled persons, animals, prostitutes and dancing girls to Goa. The Portuguese knew in advance that Fond Sawant would send the refugees to Goa if the contingency arose and necessary orders were issued to the General of the sea to allow them in the Portuguese territory. It is worthwhile mentioning that even though the Portuguese had accepted the refugees, separate arrangements were made in regard to prostitutes and dancing girls. They were transported to the island of Kumbarjuva, a small island adjoining the island of Goa. To safeguard the territory of Goa from enemy attack, the Portuguese authorities also wrote to the General of Bardesh, Joao de Mello de Ataide to make all arrangements to defend Bardesh. To safeguard the ports, the Portuguese had moved some companies of troops for their defence. The General was also ordered to recruit people who were capable of handling arms.

On 24 May 1724, the Archbishop Primates de Mello de Andrade issued an order to help Fond Sawant. Acting on the orders of the Archbishop, the Portuguese General extended all help to the Sawantwadi ruler. A strict watch was kept on the prostitutes and dancing girls and they were forbidden to move outside the island of Kumbarjuva, and punishment was also announced for the violation of this order. The General was ordered to house them in a gunpowder storehouse if they violated the law. Such strong measures were adopted to prevent their contact with the Portuguese soldiers.

With such encouragement and help from the Portuguese, Fond Sawant carried out his counter attacks on the Kolhapur forces with fresh vigour. The result was obvious. The Kolhapur Raja had to retreat.

A few months after this on 20 November 1724, Udaji Chavan one of the trusted Sardars of Sambhaji Raje arrived with two thousand cavalrymen and five thousand armymen near Shahapur fort. The General of Bardesh contacted the Government of Goa and apprised it of the fresh activities of the Marathas. The Portuguese remained in touch with the Sawantwadi ruler and also informed him of the activities of Udaji Chavan. Fond Sawant on his part kept his frontiers well protected to meet any eventuality. Udaji Chavan seems to have given up the idea of attacking Sawantwadi. Udaji Chavan of Atheni in this period of political confusion was emboldened to attack even Chhatrapati Shahu.

The Kolhapur ruler again attacked Sawantwadi in 1730, under Udajirao Mohite but this attack too was unsuccessful. Hostilities between Shahu and Sambhaji ended with the conclusion of the Varna treaty, 1731 but it did not bring to an end the conflicts between the other neighbouring powers like Sawantwadi, the Angres, Sambhaji, Amatya etc. In June 1732, Fond Sawant despatched a party to fortify the hills of Bolvan Ghosrani, but his plan was forestalled by Bhagvantrao Amatya who alerted Kolhapur Raja. The timely action of Sambhaji Raje forced Fond Sawant to withdraw. Again in August 1732, Fond Sawant attacked Sadanandgad fort and was defeated. In fact Fond Sawant's actions were nothing but retaliatory measures to punish Sambhaji Raje.

Thus, Fond Sawant consolidated his position in the Sawantwadi state and brought about several changes in the administration till his death. He died on 2 January 1738 and was survived by six wives, eleven sons and six daughters. Out of these Nar, Nag, Jairam and Som Sawant distinguished themselves and played significant roles in the history of Sawantwadi.

REBELLIONS OF THE SAWANT BROTHERS NAROBA AND NAGOBA SAWANT

Fond Sawant was a man of frugal habits and managed the affairs of his State in an economical manner. But his two sons Nar and Nag seriously differed from him and wanted to live an easy and aristocratic life. The result was that the two sons rebelled against him. The available evidence does not indicate any serious reason other than this that led to a rupture between Fond Sawant and these two sons.

Naroba alias Nar Sawant Bhosale, son of Fond Sawant from his first wife Laxmibai, revolted against him in 1715 and began creating disturbances not only in Sawantwadi but also in the neighbouring territories of Kolhapur and Sunda. Sambhaji, the ruler of Kolhapur, taking advantage of the disturbances created by Nar in his territory, appealed to the Portuguese for help, to crush Fond Sawant. Actually the Government of Goa had entered into a treaty with Sambhaji Raje on 21 March 1716. The treaty of alliance had an important clause which stated that Sardesai of Kudal, Naroba Sawant was a friend of the Portuguese, and being a vassal paid an annual tribute to them. It further stated that unless there was some compelling reason, the Portuguese Government would not declare war against Naroba. In the event of a war between Sambhaji Raje and Naroba Sawant, the Portuguese, therefore, could not assist Sambhaji. In view of the friendship between the Portuguese and Sambhaji Raje, the latter immediately sought the help of the Portuguese to fight Naroba Sawant, who was disturbing the peace of Kolhapur. The Governor of Goa asked the ruler of Kolhapur to send their diplomat Hindurao Ghorpade for talks as the previous envoy was incompetent to hold talks with the Government of Goa. The Portuguese were not willing to help the Kolhapur Raja against Sawantwadi and, therefore, they seem to have played delaying tactics.

While negotiations were yet to take place, Sambhaji's Sardar, Ramrao, attacked the Portuguese territory of Salsete. Several villages were looted and a rich church was attacked. The loot in gold and silver worth about ten lakh Pardao, was carried away. The Portuguese resented this act of the Maratha Sardar and wrote to Sambhaji that the question of any help to him against Naroba Sawant would not be considered at all unless the loot was returned.

After the attack of Ramrao on Salsete, Sambhaji Raje gave up the idea of fighting against Naroba Sawant. In fact, the

Raja of Kolhapur had gained much more by way of loot than what he could have by attacking small pockets held by Naroba Sawant. It is also true that since the Portuguese did not help the Kolhapur Raja, the latter gave up the idea of attacking Naroba. There is no doubt that the Maratha attack on the Portuguese territory was in a way profitable to the Sawantwadi ruler. Had the Kolhapur Raja succeeded in getting help from the Portuguese, the Sawantwadi state would have faced a calamitous situation.

Like the ruler of Kolhapur, the Sunda Raja too was worried about an attack on the fort of Phonda from Nar Sawant. He, therefore, requested the Portuguese for help to safeguard his territory against any possible attack. Nar Sawant made several attempts to intrude into the territory of Phonda. With a view to capturing the fort of Phonda, he asked for Lascarins from Essoba Rao, one of the Desais of Phonda. The Portuguese Government, however, never took Naroba's overtures seriously, but as a precautionary measure kept their forces on the alert to meet any eventuality. They were friendly towards Naroba as well as the Sundas, because both of them were their vassals. Goa was trying to safeguard the interests of both by pleasing them. From the complaints Sunda had lodged with the Portuguese it seems that Naroba was unsuccessful in capturing the Phonda fort, though he robbed their territory, yet he was a source of trouble internally to Fond Sawant and externally to Kolhapur and Sunda.

Fond Sawant who tried for a long time to prevent his son from his rebellious acts, at last mustered courage to put an end to this menace and immediately despatched a contingent against him. Nar Sawant had taken shelter in the fort at Wadi. In the fight that ensued he was accidentally shot while looking out from a window in 1716. Thus came to an end the rebellion of Nar Sawant. At the time of his death his son Ramchandra was hardly four years old. His wife Rajasbai requested Fond Sawant to look after her son, before she immolated herself as Sati.

The death of Naroba distressed his mother, Laxmibai very much. She blamed and cursed her husband. In order to pacify her and to regain his own peace of mind, Fond vested the seal of power with his minor grandson, Ramchandra, the son of Nar and he himself looked after the administration.

Had Nar Sawant's revolutionary spirit been directed properly, he would have been a source of great help to his father in his fight against internal and external foes. Naroba had made some land grants to temples at the time when he was acting independently during the period of his rebellion. In 1716, he gave a *sanad* to a temple at Banda which was honoured as late as 1911, the first decade of 20th century. Had Nag survived he would have posed a perpetual danger to his father playing into the hands of the Portuguese, as is seen from the rebellion of his son Nag, who was used by the Portuguese as a tool.

Nagoba's Rebellion

Exactly ten years after the rebellion of Naroba Sawant another rebellion broke out in the State of Sawantwadi. The leader of the rebellion was Nag alias Nagoba Sawant Bhosale Sardesai, son of Savitri, Fond Sawant's second wife.

Fond Sawant made several attempts to bring about an understanding with him. The Portuguese banked upon the strained relations between the father and the son. They helped Nag Sawant and utilized him as a tool against his father. It will be seen in the next chapter how Nag Sawant for his own interests made an alliance with the Portuguese against Ramchandra Sawant and Jairam Sawant, his brother and nephew. The Portuguese would not have helped Nag Sawant against his father, if Fond had maintained good relations with the Estado. When Nag Sawant requested the help of the Portuguese to wage a war with Fond Sawant in 1721, the Government of Goa turned down the request taking into consideration the friendly treaty that was signed with Fond Sawant.

In 1725, the Portuguese Viceroy attacked the fort of Dicholi belonging to Fond Sawant. This was an opportunity to Nag Sawant to revolt against his father and the Portuguese Government helped him in this rebellion. The Viceroy captured the fort of Dicholi and handed it over to Nag Sawant with a view to aggravate the conflict between the father and the son.

After the revolt against his father, Nag Sawant sought

asylum in the Portuguese territory. This was exactly what the Portuguese desired in order to have their own interests served. But Nag Sawant, it may be observed, did not fall an easy prey to the Portuguese designs. He was clever enough not to get entangled into the trap laid by the Portuguese, at least for some time. For instance, when the negotiations for a treaty which were carried through his envoy Bhairu Dalvy, were not favourable to him, he detained for many months the General of Bardesh, Francisco da Guerra de Mesquita in the fort of Dicholi which was handed over to him by the Portuguese Viceroy. He also insulted and maltreated the captives. All this was intended to squeeze out favourable terms from the Portuguese, which unfortunately for him did not succeed. At last the Portuguese entered into a treaty with him on 27 May 1726.

By this treaty, the Portuguese handed over the fort of Dicholi and the districts to Nagoba Sawant on certain conditions. On careful scrutiny of these conditions it is seen that the Portuguese were trying to give him a separate position like his father. In one of the conditions, the Portuguese made him to accept their vassalage his father had agreed upon through the bond signed by him. Further, in the event of Nag Sawant being the Lord of the Sea-Forts, he was to give free shipping to the Portuguese, and was to inform the Portuguese whenever any of his ships left his Port. Nag was also to return the runaway Portuguese soldiers and Negroes in his territory. The prostitutes were to be kept outside Dicholi and those found there could be kidnapped by the Portuguese soldiers. The district to be handed over to him was to remain free from corrupt practices and casteism.

Now seeing the danger from Nag on one side and from the Portuguese, on the other, Fond Sawant deputed his envoy Shambu Shenvi for talks with the Portuguese with a view to reaching an understanding with Nag Sawant who had taken shelter with the Portuguese. Fond Sawant offered to pay eight hundred xerafins per month for the maintenance of Nag on the condition that he would not take asylum in the fort of Dicholi. But, according to Nag the matter was over as he had chosen to stay in the fort of Dicholi.

Meanwhile, Fond Sawant complained to the Portuguese Government about Nag Sawant's orders for the demolition of the fort of Dicholi. The Secretary of State immediately wrote to Nag Sawant not to indulge in the destruction of the fort and the houses surrounding it, and further that if such activities were not stopped, the Portuguese would consider that Nag had violated the promises given to them.

At this juncture, the ruler of Sawantwadi saw the necessity of signing a treaty with the Portuguese, knowing fully well the attitude of the Portuguese, and the danger of Nag Sawant whose sole intention was to capture the territory of Fond Sawant with the help of the Portuguese. The Portuguese were trying to isolate the father from the son by creating conflicts. Fond Sawant thought it wise to enter into a treaty with the Portuguese on 13 August 1726.

The Peace terms between Fond Sawant and the Portuguese in the first part reproduced all the terms of the treaty of 1712. The second part of this treaty adds a few more clauses concerning the non-interference of the Portuguese in the event of a conflict between Fond Sawant and Nag, the troubled question of the prostitutes in the border area, observation of the shipping rights of the Portuguese by Fond Sawant, and the run-aways from the territory of Fond to that of the Portuguese and vice versa.

In the letter to Shambu Shenvi, the envoy of the Fond Sawant, the Secretary of the State made it clear that as soon as the treaty would come into force Nag Sawant would be required to leave the territory. The Portuguese also ordered Nag not to lodge unnecessary complaints against Fond Sawant. But Nag Sawant did not accept his father's offer of eight hundred *ashrafins* for his maintenance, and stuck to his claim of Dicholi region including the fort. To acquire this, he was even ready to wage a war against his father.

While the struggle between the father and son was going on, the Marathas were locked in a conflict with the Portuguese at Bassein. The Portuguese were rather afraid that Nag Sawant might join the Marathas and hence kept a constant vigil over him.

The Viceroy of Goa in his letter to the king of Portugal brought to his notice the political situation of India, in which he stated that so far there was no proper understanding between Nag and Fond Sawant. Both had requested that the fort of Dicholi should remain in the possession of the Portuguese with the garrison. Further they had also asked the mediation of the Viceroy in this conflict. The Viceroy of Goa had no desire to solve the conflict as he wanted to exploit it to the advantage of the Portuguese. The Viceroy also made it clear that once the rift between the father and the son was over, they would ask the Portuguese to vacate the fort and if the Portuguese failed to do so they would wage a war against them. In the event of an attack, the Viceroy further stated that it would be difficult for the Portuguese to defend the fort. Under the circumstances, the Viceroy requested the king's advice in the matter.

The Viceroy of Goa on the advice of the king launched a war against Fond Sawant. The king congratulated the Viceroy for actually waging the war and instructed that the fort of Dicholi should be demolished so that it should not be used in future by Nag or his father. The king feared that Nag like his father would be inimical towards the Portuguese state. The king had specifically ordered that while waging a war with the rebels their navy and strategic places should be destroyed as the Portuguese could not afford to prolong the war. In the end the king advised a treaty if the Sawants were sure to observe the terms thereon. Accordingly the Portuguese entered into a peace treaty with Fond Sawant on 22 August 1726.

The Portuguese suggested that Fond should observe the treaty signed with them in 1712. They also inserted some new conditions to be observed by him. In one of the clauses, Fond Sawant was asked to pay his son Nagoba food allowance of eight hundred xerafins, however if Nagoba refused to accept this amount, he was to be given free passage to the fort of Dicholi. The Portuguese promised neutrality in the event of a war between Fond and his son Nag. The prostitutes were forbidden to reconstruct the houses on the banks of the rivers of the two bordering states. They also imposed cartage on the ships of the Bhosales.

Nag Sawant comes prominently in this treaty, while subjects like prostitutes and navy which were very common are repeated.

On 20 April 1727, the Viceroy wrote in detail to the Secretary of the State of Portugal showing how Fond Sawant had grown impudent. The Sawantwadi ruler had challenged the Portuguese taking advantage of the following facts : the death of the Viceroy prior to Gama, internal dissensions in the Government of Goa and the failure on the part of the Portuguese to demand the arrears of tribute from Fond Sawant. Fond Sawant strengthened his navy and attacked a Chinese ship and a pal of Daman. He also sold to the English, Negro slaves who had run away from the Portuguese territory of Sawantwadi. The selling of Negro slaves was contrary to the previous peace treaty between the Portuguese and Fond Sawant. The Sawants had accepted the position of feudatory under the Portuguese as early as A.D. 1699. Throwing all these understandings to the winds, Fond Sawant imprisoned some of the Christians and captured a vessel belonging to the Portuguese subject. The Government of Goa, however, had no difficulty in putting him down, by making use of his son Nag Sawant against him.

In this rebellion of Nag Sawant against his father, the Portuguese made use of him though they never trusted him fully. He often played loose and fast with them. As observed, the political situation of 1728, was not favourable to the Portuguese to wage a prolonged war with Fond Sawant as the territory in the north was threatened by the Marathas. It seems that no agreement was reached between the father and the son. They used him suitably as their partisan when Jairam and Ramchandra Sawant, his nephew and brother attacked Bardesh in 1739, as allies of the Marathas. This was what actually the Portuguese desired. The next chapter discusses in detail the role played by Nag Sawant on the one hand and Jairam and Ramchandra Sawant on the other hand during the Maratha-Portuguese war of 1737-1739.

4

JAIRAM SAWANT AND RAMCHANDRA SAWANT BHOSALE (1738-1755)

On 2 January 1738, Fond Sawant died. With his death, Jairam Sawant and Ramchandra Sawant jointly succeeded to the gadi of Sawantwadi. Ramchandra Sawant was the son of Naroba and the grandson of Fond. As Naroba was killed by Fond when he rebelled, Fond had promised his wife that is, Naroba's mother that he would place her other son Ramchandra on the gadi after him. Accordingly, Ramchandra sat on his father's gadi. But he was to carry on the administration of the state with Jairam Sawant his uncle. The joint rule of Jairam Sawant and Ramchandra Sawant continued up to 1753, the former's death. Important treaties, correspondence and other administrative papers were signed both by Jairam Sawant and Ramchandra Sawant as joint rulers. However, reasons for this joint rule are not satisfactorily explainable from the records. Physically Jairam Sawant was a giant having an extraordinary structure and was known for his herculian strength. He was also known for his intellectual capacity.

Several important events took place during the decade of the joint rule which enhanced the prestige of the Sawantwadi State both internally and externally. Army and naval establishments were reorganised and strengthened with a view to prevent the external threats.

At the commencement of the joint rule the Portuguese were pitted against the Marathas in a life and death struggle to retain their northern possessions—Bassein territory. The Marathas, in order to stop succour coming from Goa to Bassein by sea, attacked Goa itself. Their forces under Dadaji Bhave Nargundker, Venkatrao Ghorpade and Jivaji Shinde crossing the Dighi Ghat attacked the Portuguese territory of Salsete on

23 January 1739. Excepting the forts of Rachol and Marmagoa, the entire territory of Salsete came under the occupation of the Marathas. Taking advantage of this calamitous situation in which the Portuguese were involved, the Bhosales attacked Bardesh. They took possession of it, entered into a treaty with the Portuguese, and again lost it to the Portuguese in 1741. The Portuguese advanced as far as Reddi. Later, Jairam Sawant attacked Tulaji Angre forcing him to retreat with heavy loss. In 1753, Jairam Sawant and Ramchandra Sawant quarrelled breaking the joint rule. For sometime Sadashivrao Peshwa was negotiating with the Sawants in connection with the rulers of Sunda, and the Portuguese. Jairam Sawant and Ramchandra Sawant fought wars and tried to play a diplomatic game in a manner that was advantageous to them with the Portuguese, the Angres, the Marathas and the rulers of Sunda. At the beginning of their joint rule, their first concern was Bardesh.

BHOSALES ATTACK BARDESH

The Bhosales were on good terms with the Portuguese when the Marathas attacked Salsete as part of their Bassein campaign. This is discernible from the letter of thanks from the Viceroy Sandomil to the Wadi rulers on 16 February 1739, for not co-operating with the Marathas in their war with the Portuguese. In the beginning of March, the Sawantwadi rulers informed the Portuguese that Bajirao I was pressing them to attack the territory of Bardesh, and if the Portuguese desired that the State of Sawantwadi should not help Bajirao I, they should surrender to the Bhosales the islands of Kharjuvem and Paneli and also exempt the tribute of Rs. 1000 payable annually to them by the Bhosales. Besides this, the expenditure which the Bhosales had incurred for more than two to three months to safeguard the territory of Bardesh from a possible attack of the Maratha forces should be paid to them. The demands of the Wadi rulers were unacceptable to the Portuguese Government and were rejected.

While the above negotiations were being conducted with the Portuguese, the Wadi rulers began concentrating their troops at Alorna. The Portuguese, suspecting danger, enquired about it with the Wadi rulers. They, however, contended that the concentration was made for the security of their territory and thus kept the Portuguese in the dark about their future designs. While the Wadi Darbar maintained secrecy, their Karbhari, Deoba Vishram Sabnis, divulged the secret to the Portuguese. The Portuguese used to consider Sabnis as 'demosthenes' of the Bhosales. Minu Shenvi, brother of Deoba Sabnis was a businessman and was carrying on his trade in the Portuguese territory of Divar. This Minu was the son-in-law of Santoppa Naik, a rich merchant of Goa. The Hindu merchant community at the time was always in good terms with the Portuguese to protect their trade interests. So the Viceroy of Goa had established good conduct indirectly with the *Karbharis* of Wadi through the Goan traders. Thus, though Sawantwadi rulers kept their design a top secret, Deoba Vishram Sabnis through his brother in Goa leaked out the design of the Wadi rulers to attack Bardesh and sent a detailed information about the time of the impending assault. But even after receiving the information well in advance, the Government of Goa was not in a position to safeguard the territory of Bardesh and defend it from the Bhosale's attack. Militarily, the Portuguese were losing hold and were facing troubles on all the frontiers in Goa and Bassein against the Marathas. There was only a company of sixty grenadiers and a company of a light infantry, a very small force indeed for the defence of such a territory. Actually the province of Bardesh was less exposed to enemy attacks but the Viceroy of Goa failed to protect it from the Bhosales. Several precautionary measures were introduced there and necessary instructions were issued to the General of Bardesh.

While these safety measures were being introduced by the Portuguese Viceroy, the Sawantwadi rulers were strengthening their positions. At last, the Bhosales attacked Bardesh in the early morning of 5 March 1739. The details of this development have been lengthily narrated by Dr. Pissurlencar, and are available in its English translation by P.R. Kakodker (*The Portuguese and the Marathas*).

The occupation of Bardesh by the Bhosales was viewed seriously by the Portuguese authorities in Goa and Lisbon. Several arrangements were planned for a fresh attack to reconquer Bardesh.

PORTUGUESE SEEK ALLIANCE OF NAGOBA SAWANT

Nagoba Sawant Bhosale had an uncompromising ill-will towards his father, the late Fond Sawant Bhosale. After his father's death, he was at cross with his brother Ramchandra Sawant, and his nephew, Jairam Sawant, who succeeded to the throne. It is evident from one of his letters addressed to the Portuguese Secretary of State, how strongly he was opposing the Sawantwadi rulers. He writes, "your honour knows that the Wadikars (Jairam Sawant and Ramchandra Sawant) are brothers and would unite on this occasion, though in fact they are worst enemies of each other as proved on many occasions. Knowing this well, due action should be taken against them. I shall remain faithful to you and never break the promise I give as the Bhosales are known for keeping the pledge they give. I shall observe this as much as my religious duty. Should I swerve from this, I could be called not a true son of my father. Nag who had earlier helped the Portuguese against his father Fond Sawant, renewed his allegiance to the Portuguese to remove his brother and nephew from the Province of Bardesh.

In October 1739, the Viceroy of Goa, Count of Sandomil sought the alliance of Nagoba Sawant Bhosale for the reoccupation of Bardesh. The Portuguese had no faith in Nagoba, but now sought his alliance against the Sawantwadi rulers. A plan of adjustment was thus concluded with him on 12 October 1739. The important points involved in this adjustment were the request from the Portuguese to Nag Sawant Bhosale for troops, against Jairam Sawant and Ramchandra Sawant and also help from him to oppose Bajirao's forces in the event of his coming to the support of the Bhosales.

Naro Ram helps Bhosales against Nagoba Sawant

Naro Ram Mantri, a minister of Shahu Raje, was a Saraswat brahmin and a *Mahajan* (devout member) of the temple of Shantadurga of Kavlem. In the beginning of 1740, Naro Ram started from Miraj and reached Sawantwadi to proceed to Phonda for the *darshan* of Goddess Shantadurga. Jairam Sawant and Ramchandra Sawant accompanied him from Sawantwadi to Dicholi. This was a golden opportunity for the Sawantwadi rulers and they successfully sought the help of Naro Ram troops to fight against Nagoba Sawant. These developments made the condition of the Portuguese more difficult because they were afraid that they would have to face a bigger enemy than what they had expected. The Portuguese who had used Nag Sawant as a puppet saw the necessity of bringing to an end the age-old conflict of Nag Sawant with his brother and nephew, because it was affecting the Portuguese state. The Portuguese, therefore considered it necessary to avail of the opportunity of the presence of Naro Ram Mantri in Goa.

It is to be noted that the Portuguese were not the only state which was using Nag Sawant against their enemies. Nag Sawant was related to Hindurao Ghorpade on his wife's side and the state of Kolhapur was against the occupation of the Portuguese territory of Salsete by the forces of Bajirao Peshwa, and claimed those territories by virtue of the Varna treaty of 1731. Nag Sawant was supplying all the news about the Marathas to the Portuguese and also about the political developments in the neighbouring states. The news supplied by Nag Sawant was reliable and it helped the Portuguese to safeguard their territory against any attack from the enemy. For few years Nag was in possession of the territory of Chandgad.

Kolhapur rulers too were using Nag's forces against the Marathas. However, they knew the strength of his army. This is what Hindurao also hinted. With the help of Nag Sawant, the Maharaja of Kolhapur made several attempts to recapture the Portuguese territory lost to Peshwa Bajirao I, but could hardly achieve any success where Bajirao was fully triumphant.

It is thus evident that Nag Sawant Bhosale was a source of menace to his brother and nephew and he remained their enemy till his death on the *Ghats*. Lakham Gauda Sardesai of Khanapur also made some attempts to help the Portuguese by joining hands with Nag Sawant. Though the Portuguese government made an alliance with him, they could not get any benefit out of it. On the contrary, they incurred heavy expenditure. Nag Sawant could achieve whatever he desired through the Portuguese, making the Portuguese position so critical that they had to struggle hard to bring about a settlement between him and the Wadi rulers.

Nag Sawant had a good cavalry and was a military strategist in a limited way. He was a tool in the hands of the Portuguese by which they could interfere in the internal affairs of Sawantwadi to their own advantage. In the Bardesh affair, just discussed, he proved to be a nuisance to the Portuguese and they had to compel him to leave the Portuguese territory. Had they not done so, the Portuguese themselves would have drawn on themselves the wrath of the Bhosales on a greater scale.

While the forces of Nag Sawant and Naro Ram clashed for more than thirty hours at Narva, the Portuguese approached Naro Ram Mantri to bring peace. Mediation by Naro Ram and the pains taken by the Portuguese helped to avoid the crisis. Nag was ordered to go back with his forces, and he left the camp on 7 March 1740. After prayers, Naro Ram left Kavlem for Satara at the end of February 1740. With the departure of Naro Ram, the Portuguese Viceroy, Count of Sandomil sent Bahugun Kamat Wagh and Vitholi Sinay Dhume, the interpreters of the State to resume negotiations with the Sawantwadi rulers. These interpreters succeeded in overcoming all the obstacles and finalized a treaty of peace at Dicholi on 28 February 1740. By virtue of this treaty lieutenant Diogo Prestas de Abreu was chosen to remain in Dicholi as a hostage on behalf of the Portuguese State. This treaty was brought into force on 12 March 1740, and accordingly the Sawantwadi rulers surrendered to the Portuguese the territory of Bardesh. The Portuguese gave the village Pirna to the Bhosales in exchange for the island of Paneli ; the Bhosales also secured the island of Kharjuvem. The Portuguese promised to provide Sawantwadi rulers gunpowder and bullets for a just price whenever necessary. They also promised free shipping. The treaty was more beneficial to the Bhosales than to the Portuguese.

According to the agreement of May 1739, discussed previously, the Marathas gave up the entire province of Salsete except the villages of Kunkali and Assolna. The Viceroy of Goa knew well that unless a new treaty was concluded with the Marathas, they would not give up the above villages. In view of this, the Viceroy sought the mediation of the English and succeeded in his attempt to conclude a new treaty on 18 September 1740, with the Marathas whereby the Maratha chief Balaji Bajirao surrendered to the Portuguese the said villages. Article 13 of the treaty pertained to the dealings with the Bhosales and reads thus :

> The treaty of Peace effected between Sawant and the Portuguese will be implemented in the manner agreed upon. In case the treaty of peace is violated by Sawant Bhosales, we shall side and assist the Portuguese. In case it is violated by the Portuguese, we shall side and assist the Sawants.

BHOSALE'S PLAN FOR AN ATTACK ON THE FORT OF AGUADA

The rulers of Sawantwadi were not satisfied with the gains of the treaty they had signed with the Portuguese on 28 February 1740. They were also unhappy over the terms of the Poona treaty of 18 September 1740. While the Portuguese tried to prevent armed conflict, the Wadi rulers maintained an aggressive policy, politically and militarily, knowing fully well the weakness of the Portuguese. Jairam Sawant and Ramchandra Sawant knew that Venkatrao Ghorpade would help them in their design to attack once again the Portuguese territory. But they could attain success only before the Goa Government could receive succour from Portugal or its overseas territories. The Wadi rulers were so confident of their victory against the Portuguese that they were planning to attack Salsete and even the island of Goa with the help of Venkatrao Ghorpade. The Bhosales even promised Venkatrao Ghorpade of capturing Goa and passing it on to him. Moreover, the Sawantwadi intellectuals used to feel that a Portuguese soldier could face the onslaught of the Vadiker sepoys with ease single-handedly. But now the situation had changed. A Bhosale Sardar now could withstand single-handedly the assault of hundred Portuguese soldiers. As already noted, many of the coward Portuguese soldiers used to seek asylum in the State of Sawantwadi. This situation was advantageous to the rulers of Sawantwadi, who could get all the secrets from such Portuguese soldiers and use them against the Portuguese State. Jairam Sawant and Ramchandra Sawant organized a separate unit of such deserters and gave them full military training. Among such deserters who were in Sawantwadi, captain Jose Francisco de Azavedo was of very much help to the Bhosales. This captain gave a clear picture of the Portuguese land and showed all ways and means to the Wadi rulers for an attack on Goa and the Aguada fort. Thus having collected the information of all the routes, the Sawantwadi rulers made an attempt to attack the fort of Aguada. Vithoji Sinay Dhume who played an important role in the peace treaty of February 1740, frustrated the plan of the Bhosales by leaking the news to the Portuguese in advance of such an attack. This disclosure helped the Portuguese to take strong security measures for the defence of the Aguada fort, whose preservation was equally important from the point of security of the island of Goa. Another reason which prevented the Bhosales from launching an attack, was the arrival of the English squadron at the bar of Aguada. It is probable that the Portuguese might have sought the help of the English to avoid further disaster. The English fleet was of great help to the Portuguese in preventing Bhosale's ships from attacking the fort. It also gave the Portuguese navy free access into the sea by covering the bar of Aguada. The Portuguese could thus scuttle the plan of the Bhosales to attack the fort of Aguada.

Renewed attack on Bardesh

When the attack of the Sawants on Aguada was foiled, the Portuguese immediately moved to take security steps in their territories. The Viceroy kept heavy guard on all the frontiers with whatever force he had. But this job was not easy, considering the strength of the Bhosale's army.

The Wadi troops made a successful entry into Bardesh on 21 February 1741, after landing on the shores near Chapora. The Bhosales also maintained a large army of 1500 men at Dicholi. The entry into Bardesh by Jairam Sawant made him master of the province, excepting the fort of Aguada and Reis Magos. The Portuguese troops were not at all in a position to fight, because they had just been relieved from war. At Aldona, the Bhosales slaughtered four companies of Portuguese troops. This created panic among other Portuguese troops who watched the situation helplessly and waited for the arrival of fresh succour from Portugal. The Bhosales inflicted heavy loss on the Portuguese by plundering their territory.

Bhosales plan for an attack on Goa

Jairam Sawant who had kept his reserve force at Dicholi and ships or little Chinese type boats in the coastal areas near Goa, decided to launch a surprise attack on the island of Goa through Kumbarjuva, as he was aware that many of the Portuguese ships were away from Goa. But the timely arrival of the English Squadron boosted the morale of the Portuguese troops. With the help of this squadron and their own ships, the Portuguese could prevent Bhosales becoming the masters of the territory of Goa. Had this squadron not arrived, the Bhosales would have successfully executed their plan of conquering Goa island. The developments were disheartening to the Portuguese empire.

The Portuguese Government now was determined to put an end to the rule of Count of Sandomil, whose unfortunate and ill fated Government instead of stopping the unrest of the Bhosales, created more problems to the Portuguese State. This compelled the king of Portugal to send a new Viceroy to Goa. Count of Sandomil governed Goa till 18 May 1741, and was succeeded by Dom Luis de Menezes, Conde de

Ericeira and first Marquez de Lourical. He arrived bringing with him aid from the kingdom of Portugal, four battalions, composed of the contingents of Cascaes, Lagos, Peniche and Porto (all places in Portugal). He brought a large quantity of ammunition and sixteen cannons of the new type, invented by Frederick Weinholtz, a Danish national in the Portuguese service. This new type of cannon could discharge thirty shots per minute. It is to be noted that in order to charge these sixteen guns two hundred and forty persons were needed, but from these three thousand soldiers were benefited. All these war material and European troops were brought by the Portuguese fleet of six ships after a tedious journey of one year and six days. Two of them were commanded by Colonel Dom Luis de Pierrepont with the rank of Lieutenant Colonel and by Lieutenant Colonel Jose Caetano de Matos, both infantry officials and commandants of troops aboard. The former had already distinguished himself by his bravery. Thus the home Government by putting new faces in Goa and arming them with all the powerful weapons and new contingent of troops, decided to punish the troublesome Sawantwadi rulers.

Portuguese attack Bardesh

The advent of the new Viceroy in Goa brought success to the Portuguese both on the political and military fronts. A special arrangement was made by the Portuguese Government to accommodate the new Viceroy in the Palace of Panjim. Usually, the Viceroy's residence was in the College of Reis Magos. This special arrangement was made out of fear of the Bhosales who it was feared would attack and capture Reis Magos. The new Viceroy was governing Goa for the second time, the first time he was governing from 1717 to 1720. Having solemnly resolved to punish the Bhosales, the Viceroy lost no time in making preparations against the rulers of Sawantwadi who were within the confines of the Portuguese territory of Bardesh. In June 1741, the Viceroy gave orders for the mobilization of his armed forces for the reconquest of the province of Bardesh. The Portuguese battalions and one company of grenadiers who had their camp in the island of Chodan immediately attacked the island of Kharjuvem. The Bhosales were taken aback by this surprise attack and were unable to defend themselves, thus, allowing the former to occupy the island under the command of General of Bardesh, Manoel Soares Velho.

After Kharjuvem, the Portuguese troops marched on the fort of Kolvale which was defended well by the Bhosales. After a strong resistance the Bhosales finally surrendered the Kolvale fort to the Portuguese.

Bhosales seek Peshwa's help

Having lost the important forts of Kharjuvem and Kolvale to the Portuguese forces, the Sawantwadi rulers, Jairam Sawant and Ramchandra Sawant, now saw the necessity of seeking the help of the Peshwa Balaji Bajirao. No sooner had the Bhosales approached the Peshwa, than the Portuguese drew the attention of the Peshwa Balaji Bajirao to the terms of the treaty the Peshwa had signed with them on 18 September 1740, at Poona. One of the terms of the treaty stated that "the treaty of peace effected between Sawant and the Portuguese will be implemented in the manner agreed upon. In case the treaty of peace is violated by the Bhosales (Sawants) the Peshwas shall side and assist the Portuguese. In case it is violated by the Portuguese, the Peshwas shall side and assist the said Sawants." The Peshwa bound by this treaty could not go to the rescue of the Bhosales.

Peshwas help the Portuguese

Peshwa Balaji Bajirao saw the weak position of the Bhosales and considering that they had violated the treaty, offered help to the Portuguese which made the position of the Bhosales critical. Therefore, Jairam Sawant thought it would be unwise to carry on the resistance any further and ordered his forces to abandon the forts in their possession.

Lt. Colonel Dom Luis de Pierrepont who had bravely captured the forts of Kharjuvem and Kolvale from the Bhosales immediately marched to the abandoned fort of Chapora and occupied it. Soon after, the Bhosales also abandoned all other forts, which were later occupied by the Portuguese, without much difficulty. Thus in a day the entire province of Bardesh was seized from the hands of the Bhosales by the Portuguese.

The defeat of the Bhosales forced them to enter into a treaty with the Portuguese which they signed on 11 September 1741.

This treaty incorporated all the provisions of the previous treaty signed on 7 April 1712, and imposed fresh conditions on the Bhosales.

This treaty was supposed to be a permanent arrangement to be ratified by the Home Government. Failure on the part of any one of the parties to observe the terms, enabled the other to give notice to the offended party, which in due course was free to take action which it deemed fit.

The Viceroy, Marquez de Lourical, in a representation had felt the need to sign a treaty with the Bhosales, who repented for their past acts and pleaded for peace. Therefore, he authorised Manoel Soares Velho, General of Bardesh, to sign treaty with the Bhosales. He also insisted that the treaty should be countersigned with the seals of the Bhosales.

With the defeat of the Bhosales, the Portuguese could gain whatever they had surrendered to them in the treaty they had signed with them at Dicholi, a year and a half ago. Also, they were now in a position to impose severe terms on the Bhosales. The news gladdened Nag Sawant Bhosale who bore an uncompromising ill-will towards his father and after his death towards Jairam Sawant and Ramchandra Sawant.

Bhosale's help sought by Anaji Prabhu

Interestingly one of the clauses of the treaty of 1741, forbade the Bhosales from interfering with the lands of Phonda. Sawantwadi rulers always had an eye on the territory of Phonda and were waiting for an opportunity to capture the said area. On 12 May 1742, Govind Pant Thakur a Sardar of Peshwa Balaji Bajirao who had for sometime joined Kolhapur crossed the Ghat with 3000 horse and 3000 infantry and entered Sanguem. The forts of Sanguem and Phonda were, however, captured from Kalpaya, a General of Sunda, by Anaji Prabhu a Commandant of Sambhaji Raje by deceit, immediately after the death of Naro Pant, a Sardar of Peshwa. Anaji Prabhu wanted to liberate the forts of the districts of Phonda from the Peshwa. When the forces of Govind Pant reached

Sanguem, Anaji Prabhu was already in the fort of Mardangad. The former sent a message to Anaji Prabhu. When Prabhu reached Sanguem, Govind Pant imprisoned him, and also demanded from him the forts of Sanguem and Mardangad. Anaji Prabhu could not reject his demand before his powerful forces and handed over the fort of Mardangad, on 15 May 1742. Govind Pant requested the Portuguese to send their official for talks with him but since no reply could be received by him, Govind Pant attached Salsete, plundered it and threatened the inhabitants, that if they fail to pay Rs. 40,000 pardaos they would suffer heavily. The said amount remained unpaid during the time of Count of Sandomil. Govind Pant remained in Salsete for 14 days and then immediately returned to Sanguem on hearing the news of the capture of Mardangad by the forces of Kalpaya, General of Sunda. Actually the Peshwa was supposed to issue orders for giving the forts of Sanguem and Phonda to the king of Sunda. The political situation took a new turn when Kalpaya captured Mardangad. Anaji Prabhu requested the Sawantwadi rulers for help. This was an opportunity for them to fulfil their long-cherished wish to secure Phonda. The troops of the Bhosales rushed on the scene to drive away the army of Sunda. Bloody clashes took place between the forces of Kalpaya and the combined forces of Anaji Prabhu and the Bhosales in which they defeated Sunda, took possession of the fort of Mardangad and forced their army to take shelter in the Portuguese territory of Salsete. Kalpaya himself took refuge in Salsete. But the presence of Kalpaya in Salsete was found to be more dangerous by the Portuguese and they ordered him to leave their territory immediately. After repeated requests, he finally left the place and went to Cape of Rama.

Anaji Prabhu could not pass the fort of Mardangad to the Bhosales, but for the help rendered, the Bhosales received from him the fort of Dumengad, located in the same territory. This was an important point for commerce from Balghat.

Portuguese attack Sanguem

When Anaji Prabhu was imprisoned by Govind Pant, eight hundred sepoys and the principal captains of his army had come to the service of the Portuguese. This was an important asset to the Portuguese who could use them against the invading forces. On 8 June 1742, making use of these forces, and with 600 Portuguese Europeans, 1,500 natives and with artillery under the command of General Manoel Soares Velho attacked Sanguem and the fighting that ensued for three hours brought victory to the Portuguese. Govind Pant was defeated and fled up the ghats. About 200 horses and one elephant of the forces of Govind Pant were killed with no loss to the Portuguese.

Attack on Phonda

With the Portuguese victory at Sanguem, Kalpaya, the Sunda General joined Portuguese forces at Sanguem with more than 1000 forces. On 11 June 1742, the combined forces of the Portuguese and Sunda attacked the forts of Mardangad and Dumengad which were in possession of Anaji Prabhu and the Bhosales respectively. Anaji Prabhu had hardly 100 soldiers with him. The position of the Bhosales was also not better. Thus the defeat of both was almost a certainty and, therefore, they surrendered the forts to the Portuguese. The Portuguese in turn handed over the fort of Mardangad to Sunda king on 12 June 1742, but the fort of Sanguem was demolished. Anaji Prabhu was imprisoned by the Portuguese and was kept in the fort of Aguada, where he remained for 28 days before he fled from there.

In 1743, the Bhosales captured some of the Portuguese galbats, thinking that they were of the merchants of Karnataka. Actually the galbats belonged to the Portuguese and they were returned to them as they were friendly.

Meanwhile, the army of the Bhosales numbering 5,000 to 6,000 pitched its camp at Ussagaon. The king of Sunda sought the Portuguese help to attack the Bhosale's army and also requested them to take defensive measures at Mashel, Bori and Raichur which the Bhosales were now planning to attack. However, they could not succeed in attacking neither Sunda nor the Portuguese.

Viceroy Marquez de Lourical died at Paneli on the night of 13 June 1742. In his very short reign of nearly 13 months, he had many heroic deeds to his credit which brought back the lost prestige to the Portuguese.

With the death of Marquez de Lourical, a commission was appointed to look after the administration of Goa which ruled over two years. The commission included Dom Lourenco de Noronha, Councillor of the State, who was the Governor for Mozambique, Francisco de Vasconcellos, Bishop of Cochin and Dom Luis Caetano de Almeida, who was the only one to take charge of the Government on the death of the Viceroy, and who carried on the administration, first in conjunction with Dom Francisco de Vasconcellos, and subsequently with Dom Lourenco de Noronha.

On 24 September 1744, Dom Pedro Miguel de Almeida e Portugal, Conde de Assumar, first Marquez de Castello—Novo, and afterwards of Alorna, succeeded the provisional Governors. The arrival of the new Viceroy was welcomed by the Wadi rulers and requested him to maintain friendship with Sawantwadi. The administration of the Marquez de Alorna was very important from the point of view of the Marathas and the Bhosales. He was highly successful in checking the advance of the power of the Bhosales. He punished them by expanding the limits of Goa at the cost of the neighbouring power that is Sawantwadi.

Attack on the Fort of Alorna

In 1746, the Portuguese Viceroy decided to wage a war against the Bhosales. The Portuguese also sought the help of the king of Sunda who was not in good terms with the Sawantwadi rulers. Naturally, Sunda king came forward to help the Portuguese against the Wadi rulers.

Having made up his mind to punish Wadi rulers, the Viceroy concentrated troops for an attack on the fort of Alorna which lay on the north-eastern limit of Pedne and on the right bank of the Chapora or Kolvale. It had four guns, and was one of the important stronghold of the Sawants.

The attack on the fort was not an easy task, and the Portuguese had to face hardships in transporting war material. The Portuguese forces were under the command of M. Pierri Pont (a Frenchman). There were six companies of grenadiers and seventeen companies of light infantry, in all about 4,000 men. Besides there were 80 horses, 150 artillerymen, 1,000 sepoys, and a company of sharp shooters. The forces made their concentration on the heights of Revora, a village four and half league from new Goa. In addition, to these land forces, the Portuguese also made preparations for a naval attack and kept their vessels alert. More than 27 vessels of various sizes were plying in the waters of Kolvale. The Portuguese Viceroy used brilliant tactics for an attack on Alorna. In the early hours of the 5 May 1746, the Portuguese forces attacked both by land and sea the fort of Alorna. The onslaught created panic in the Bhosale's camp. The Portuguese forces advanced silently and by making use of a weapon named 'Petardo' blew up the big, strong door of the fort and entered the fort facing heavy fire from the Bhosale's muskets. The loss on the Portuguese side in men and material was enormous. However, the Portuguese repulsed the attack with the powerful weapons which the Bhosales forces did not possess. The fight continued for several hours as the Bhosales resisted with firm determination. The Subhedar of the fort of Alorna, Goma Sawant, defended the fort with bravery and courage so much so that he made the Portuguese victory difficult. The Portuguese commander sent him the message for the surrender of the fort if he wished his life to be spared. But the Subhedar of the Bhosales flatly refused and informed the Portuguese commander that he would give them the same kind of reception which they had given him at Alorna before.

No sooner did the Portuguese commander receive his reply, than he redoubled the attack. The Subhedar of the Bhosales too countered the attack with equal zeal resulting in several reverses on the Portuguese side. Fearing renewed attacks of the Bhosales, the Portuguese forces began to disperse. There was uncertainty of victory. Almost all the Portuguese soldiers were killed or mortally wounded. But the situation did not remain for long as sergeant-Major Pedro Vicente Vidal instilled a new spirit in the minds of the Portuguese soldiers. By placing a bomb near the castle gate, he blew it to pieces. The Bhosale's troops who were in the tower of the castle were killed and the Portuguese made their entry followed by a face to face fight. The Portuguese troops still could not attain victory, because there was still a stronger gate which was a real obstacle to them. The Portuguese once again made use of 'Petardo' to break open the gate, their forces along with those of the Sunda made their entry into the fort. The Portuguese first had made use of 'Petardo' against the Bhosales in 1741. The weapon was unknown to the Bhosales and they thought that it was a magic. The Subhedar of the Bhosales however, fought heroically and even the Viceroy of Goa who was personally present at this expedition praised his gallantry. Thus after five hours of fierce fighting, the Portuguese succeeded in capturing the stronghold of Alorna from the Bhosales. The Portuguese soldiers gave it the new name as Santa Cruz de Alorna and erected there a cross in front of the castle gate to mark the memory of the victory. Soon after the victory, the Sunda forces acting on the orders of the Portuguese burnt the village of Ussagaon and nearby places of the Bhosales. The Sunda forces arrested some persons, who were later killed by them, they were also planning to burn Dicholi and Mayem.

The fort of Alorna which was damaged in the war was immediately repaired and left under the command of Lieutenant Colonel Jose Lopes.

When Alorna won his victories over the Bhosales, Tulaji Angre decided to woo him with peace overtures, suggesting that they ally themselves against the 'common enemy'. Alorna politely refused, while grateful for the respite from piratical attacks.

The capture of Alorna formed an important landmark in the tenure of office of this Viceroy, who was held in esteem for the brilliant success during the declining years of the Portuguese power in India. The victory enhanced his prestige and the king gave him the title of Marquez de Alorna.

Attack on Dicholi and Sakhali

After the capture of Alorna, the Viceroy Marquez de Alorna, on 18 May 1746 marched on to Dicholi which was destroyed by Bhosales before being abandoned. They set on fire many of the villages of Dicholi Province and left it undefended only to be taken by the Portuguese who handed it over to their allies, the Sundas. The Portuguese General informed the General of Sunda that he should guard the province till his arrival. Later, he ordered the captain of sea and war Francisco Xavier to take charge of the province of Dicholi and the Sundas evacuated their forces. Once the province of Dicholi came under the occupation of the Portuguese, they issued an ordinance in Marathi requesting the Desais to come back and stay in their respective places. The Desais of Sakhali, Keri and Maneri were in friendly correspondence with the Portuguese before this incident. Being afraid of the Sawantwadi rulers they did not dare to show openly their allegiance to the Portuguese. Therefore, they made a show that they were compelled by the Portuguese to surrender so that they should not incur the wrath of the Bhosales for surrendering to the Portuguese. The skirmishes that took place between the Desais and the Portuguese were just sham. Under the orders of the Marquez de Alorna, the Portuguese troops who had now attacked Sakhali took utmost care not to destroy Sakhali fort and town which were under the Desais. On 21 October 1746, various Desais, such as Satroju Rane of Sakhali, Manerikar Gaons Raghunath Prabhu of Dicholi, Kushtoba Desai of Advai and others accepted Portuguese sovereignty by turning their backs against the Wadi rulers. Satroji Rane in order to show his allegiance to the Portuguese even attacked the forts of Avade, Morle and Sattari and on capturing it handed it over to the Portuguese.

The Desais were permitted to have all the rights and privileges which they enjoyed under the Bhosales ; the Portuguese were to pay for the 800 sepoys who were to serve the Desais, at the rate of four rupees per sepoy *per mensum* and for ten officers at the rate of thirty pardaos *per mensum*; all were to qualify themselves duly and to be at the service of the Viceroy, whenever they might be required. The Desais were at liberty to maintain their *Pagodas* (temples), and to worship in accordance with the rights of their religion, provided they did not interfere with the Portuguese missionaries, or the erection of churches within their territories. The Viceroy further undertook that no cows should be slaughtered, either in the temples or in the grounds adjoining them. The Desais were to have no understanding with the Bhosales without the permission of the Portuguese ; and all the "foros" custom dues, revenue from tobacco, etc., of the Desais' estates were to be paid into the treasury of the Portuguese Government.

It is significant to observe that the Desais were not only free to follow their religious practices, but cow slaughter was prohibited in the region adjoining their temples.

These declarations were obviously made to win the Desais of the said territories and to keep them away from the Bhosales.

The advent of the monsoon brought the war to a sudden halt. This respite also gave the Portuguese enough time to concentrate their forces and keep them ready for fresh attacks after the monsoon.

Attack on Terekhol

As soon as the rainy season was over, the Portuguese began to mobilize their army and navy for an attack on the fort of Terekhol. This fort is situated six miles from Chapora, and stands on the brow of a hill on the right bank of the river Chapora, from the northern boundary of the territory of Goa. The fort had twelve guns, a barrack and a Chapel.

On 16 November 1746, the Portuguese Viceroy arrived with his fleet in the river of Kaisuva. The fleet consisted of ten pals each having fifteen to twenty guns, seventeen galbats, three batelas, a war machuva, four parangues and many small crafts. The Bhosales too had a strong fleet guarding their sea frontier in the creek of the fort of Terekhol. The creek of Terekhol often protected the Bhosale's ships and as such was a haven for them.

Heavy fighting broke out between the two fleets. The commander of the Bhosales displayed bravery and courage by making surprise attacks on Portuguese war machuvas, and many of the Portuguese crafts were sunk. The Portuguese too launched a heavy attack on the ships of the Bhosales sinking and capturing a number of them. Their navy being defeated, the Bhosales left the sea clear to the Portuguese who attacked the fort of Terekhol from the shores with great vigour. The Portuguese battleships were well manned and heavily gunned and ultimately overpowered the ships of the Sawants. After several skirmishes, the Bhosales finally surrendered the fort of Terekhol to the Portuguese on 23 November 1746.

This naval battle though fought on a small scale is significant because the Bhosales often depended more upon their land forces than navy. But in the battle of Terekhol, the Sawants had to bring their navy into action as they could not avoid an attack on the Portuguese ships. A list of the captured ships given in the Assentos dos Concelhos do Estado (*Proceedings of the State Council*) enables us to know the strength of the navy of the Bhosales. It seems that the Bhosales had kept a sizable navy of battleships, big and small in the creek of Terekhol. The Portuguese captured and carried to Goa : Ten pals, of which seven were taken to Goa and the three were ordered to be burnt ; one pataxo, one *batela* (later burns), seventeen galbats, out of which ten were taken to Goa and seven were burnt ; one new galbat, which was later sent to shipyard ; four parangues, one small batela, two small boats, 225 pieces of various calibres, three mason of bronze and 15 of iron. It is well known that the pals were the biggest warships of the Marathas. Next in size and importance were the gurabs and galbats. Among the smaller crafts were parangues. Machuvas were very useful for quick movements in shallow waters. (The Raja of Sunda conveyed his happiness to the Portuguese for defeating the Bhosales. The Bhosales were getting an annual income of Rs. 1,22,885 i.e., 73,731,000 moedas from Alorna, Dicholi and Sakhali).

Attack on Fort Reddi

The victorious Viceroy could not remain silent only with these gains. After making necessary preparations, four Portuguese battalions embarked on two ships, four galleys and 10 galbats sailed towards the fort of Reddi for an attack. The fort stood on the southern bank of the river guarding its mouth where it meets the sea. A good part of the navy of the Sawant was anchored in this river. It was perhaps next in importance to Karli and Terekhol. The Portuguese now sought the help of Sunda king to prepare for an attack on the fort of Reddi. Thus the combined forces of the Portuguese and the Sundas jointly attacked the fort at the end of November 1746. The Bhosales resisted the heavy attack of the combined army with great difficulties and retreated within a few days. On 3 December 1746, the fort was occupied by the Portuguese.

Resentful of the Portuguese action, the Bhosales charged the Portuguese that the fort of Reddi was captured from them by deceit and requested the Portuguese to hand over the fort, but the Viceroy informed them that the fort would be handed over only on the advice of the king of Portugal.

The Peshwa's interference

The victory of the Portuguese Viceroy over the Sawantwadi rulers could not keep the Peshwa silent. He immediately sent his envoy to hold talks with the Portuguese. Mahipatrao Chando, the envoy of the Peshwa arrived in Goa with the mission of mediating a treaty between the Bhosales and the Portuguese. He stayed in Goa for many days and tried his best to bring about an understanding between the two states but met with no success. At last the Peshwa requested Sadashivrao Bhau to undertake this task and he was sent with a heavy force to Karnataka. The Bhosales also began to incite Nanasaheb Peshwa by rousing his religious feelings.

Meanwhile the troops of the Bhosales attacked the fort of Supa and Medda. The king of Sunda, on receipt of the news, despatched his forces from Sanguem and Jambaulim. The Sunda forces under the Subhedars Gharoji Pawar, Nagba Desai and Vassudev Pant left from Dighi and Kundal Ghat. They also sought early Portuguese help, on receiving which they succeeded in driving out the Bhosales.

In March 1747, the army of Nanasaheb Peshwa composed of 30,000 horses and an huge infantry, arrived at Supa and were joined by the forces of the Bhosales. Their main objective was to land on the ghats and attack the Portuguese territory of Salsete. At the news of their movement, the Portuguese sealed all the ghats as well as rivers with their war vessels. It is significant to note that Portuguese spies, actively working in the army of Nanasaheb and in the Maratha *Darbar*, were able to supply information in advance to the Portuguese at Goa. Fearing the arrival of the combined forces of the Bhosales and the Marathas, many residents of Salsete left the province and the sepoys of Sunda and the Ranes who were guarding the *ghats*, left their posts. The Portuguese soldiers would have followed suit, but they were sternly threatened with severe consequences if they left the ghats undefended.

The aim of the Peshwa in helping the Bhosales was to keep the Portuguese away from attacking the Maratha territories in the north. The Marathas were afraid of the successful Portuguese army penetrating into the Bhosale's territory. While many of the potentates of Asia bowed down before Sadashivpant, the Portuguese at Goa did not pay much attention to him probably because he did not desire the conquest of Goa. On 8 March 1747, the Karbhari of Sunda met Sadashivpant at Khanapur. Sadashivpant informed him of his designs to attack Goa because of the aggressive activities of the Portuguese carried up to the fort of Reddi and requested to hand over the fort of Mardangad and further asked the help of Sunda to bring down the Peshwa's army from the ghats. The Sardar of Sunda, Hangal appealed to the Peshwa not to attack Goa and desired to pay him one lakh rupees as a tribute. It is to be noted that the king of Sunda had entered into an agreement with Shahu to pay Rs. 40,000 in connection with Phonda and Jambaulim territories as a tribute. Sardar Hangal promised Sadashivpant that the Sunda will honour the agreement entered into with Shahuraje. He also bribed many of the Maratha soldiers. Sadashivpant also discussed with him about the fort captured by the Portuguese.

Though the Portuguese were not afraid of the Marathas in order to avoid armed action they moved the Peshwa Court to recall their forces. The Viceroy informed Nana, that the Portuguese had no desire to reoccupy the Province of the North. But the Portuguese were not ready to surrender the forts of the Bhosales occupied by them. The Viceroy expressed his desire to conclude a new treaty with the Bhosales and also showed his willingness to discuss things with the Peshwa's envoy. The Peshwa tried his utmost to get back for the Bhosales, the sea forts of Terekhol, Alorna, and Reddi because of their key positions. However, on getting half of the tribute from Sunda, Sadashivrao shifted his camp towards the boundaries of Canara on 10 March 1747.

The Bhosales try to capture Fort Reddi

The destruction of the major portion of the territory of Sawantwadi and the capture of the sea forts was a serious setback to the Sawantwadi rulers. There was no hope of regaining the lost territories without aid from a friendly power, and the prospect of such aid was very dim. In this situation, the Bhosales in July 1747, tried to win over captain of the fort of Reddi, Raghuji Naik, appointed by the Portuguese. The Bhosales succeeded in winning him over and even fixed a time for handing over the fort. Hearing about this from a trader (Rama Kamat) and a soldier (Pokya Naik), the Viceroy ordered the arrest of the captain before the actual transaction. A commission of enquiry was appointed by the Portuguese to investigate the charges against the captain Raghuji Naik, which being proved, he was hanged for treason. As a token of gratitude and favour, the Portuguese offered Rama Kamat some money. Pokya Naik too was given a prize of 300 pardaos.

Thus having failed in their plot, the Sawantwadi rulers once again made an attempt in August 1747, to take back the fort of Reddi. The Bhosales now planned a dirty trick. They arranged to sell poisonous dry fish to the soldiers of the fort through their spies. The Portuguese soldiers fell sick after eating it. Seizing the opportunity, the Bhosales suddenly attacked the fort. The Portuguese Viceroy who had kept forces ready immediately retaliated vigorously and compelled the Bhosales to retreat. The Portuguese thus succeeded once again in thwarting the plan of the Bhosales in capturing the fort.

Attack on the Fort Nivty

In September 1748, the home Government sent to Goa powerful military weapons and other war material along with 752 soldiers headed by brilliant captains. Besides, a fleet from Lisbon joined the navy at Goa. Thus the Portuguese Viceroy, being encouraged by the reinforcement, once again decided to attack the strongholds of the Sawantwadi rulers. One of the strongholds of Bhosales that had remained untouched by the Portuguese, was the fort of Nivty. This important fort was in the village of Kochra, six and half miles south of Malwan and eight miles north of Vengurla. Now in complete ruin it stood 150 feet high at the mouth of a small creek in rather a striking bay.

On 2nd December 1748, the Portuguese forces attacked the fort and after heavy fighting successfully captured it. One of the captains of the Portuguese army, Ismail Khan proved his skill and valour by inflicting heavy loss on the Bhosales. Ismail Khan, who previously served in the army of Sambhaji, Angres, Sawantwadi rulers, Hari Pant Fadke and the Sundas was now with the Portuguese. He had full knowledge of the important places of the Bhosales which now proved helpful to the Portuguese. Ismail Khan who, though not Goan by birth, adopted Goan land and its Government defence service from 1746. He displayed bravery in the war with the Bhosales and he was the first Indian to become a Capitao de Mar e Guerra that is, Captain of the Sea and War. His appointment in 1756, was followed by a grant of lands in the New Conquests, where he settled after active service, training his son Daud for a soldierly career by putting him in charge of the sepoy company raised there.

Bhosales fleet destroyed

The capture of the Nivty fort was a great blow to the Wadi rulers. Realizing the gravity of the situation, the Bhosales began to prepare for a naval expedition against the Portuguese who were now in possession of important strongholds of the Bhosales. In the Karli river, the Bhosales started constructing more ships to add to their existing naval force. Heavy guns were mounted on the bank of the river Karli and care was taken to keep the construction of ships a close secret. In spite of this, the Portuguese received reports from their intelligence service about the construction of ships. At this time, the Portuguese Viceroy Marquez Castello de Novo was in the fort of Nivty. Captain Ismail Khan of the Portuguese on receiving orders from the Viceroy attacked and burnt all the ships under construction. The Bhosale guns mounted on the bank unsuccessfully tried to counter the attack. This victory earned a great name for Ismail Khan whose daring action caused heavy loss to the Bhosales both militarily and economically.

Attack on Fort Vengurla

Immediately after the capture of Nivty the victorious Portuguese fleet proceeded to attack the fort of Vengurla built by the Dutch and extended by the Bhosales. This fort was strategically important for the Bhosales who, on receiving the news that the Portuguese naval fleet was heading towards Vengurla, rather than let it fall into their hands major part of the fort and withdrew their forces. The Portuguese naval fleet on arriving at Vengurla, destroyed the remaining part of the fort as well as the territory around it. Meanwhile, the Portuguese Viceroy having to attend to some urgent matters in Goa left the place with his naval fleet in a hurry. But before leaving, he caused maximum destruction for the Bhosales.

The king of Sunda on learning of the successful mission of the Portuguese Viceroy against the Bhosales, expressed happiness through his Pradhan Krishnarao.

ROLE OF KOLHAPUR IN THE PORTUGUESE-SAWANT CONFLICT

The rulers of Kolhapur were never friendly with the Sawantwadi State and were supporting the Portuguese at this time. When the Portuguese were busy attacking the strongholds of Sawantwadi rulers, the Chhatrapati of Kolhapur at the end of 1747 sent his envoy to Portuguese Viceroy with the aim of providing necessary help. Meanwhile, Kolhapur was mobilizing its army. It seems that the Portuguese restrained the Kolhapur ruler from attacking Sawantwadi as they were capable of facing the Bhosales. In the conflict that ensued between the Portuguese and the Sawants, the latter were defeated by the Portuguese in 1748. Taking note of the defeat of the Bhosales the Chhatrapati of Kolhapur again showed his willingness to crush the Bhosales by joining the Portuguese. In January 1749, the Portuguese learnt that the Poona *Darbar* was discussing the collection of revenue of Sawantwadi State through their agent Ramchandra Malhar. The Portuguese feared that this arrangement would extend the sway of the powerful Peshwa Nanasaheb as far as Sawantwadi. In order to avoid this, the Portuguese Viceroy asked the Secretary to inform Chhatrapati Shahu and his ministers, that the right of collecting revenue in Sawantwadi, if given to the Peshwa, would be detrimental to Chhatrapati Shahu.

In March 1749, Sambhaji Chhatrapati of Kolhapur reached Sindhudurga. At this time, he deputed his envoys by name Tuko Shamji and Maloji Malda to the Portuguese, and informed them of his desire to work as a mediator in the Bhosale-Portuguese conflict. But the Portuguese turned down his request, as Sambhaji wanted that the Portuguese should bring to an end their conflict with the Bhosales by returning to them the forts captured in the war. Later, in April 1750, Sambhaji of Kolhapur again deputed his envoy to the Portuguese Viceroy, suggesting that the Portuguese should hoist the flag of Kolhapur on the forts of the Bhosales captured by the Portuguese. The Portuguese again turned down his request and made it clear to him that they would only hoist the flag of the king of Portugal on the forts captured from the Bhosales.

The Viceroy of Goa was also trying his best through his envoy at the Court of Shahu Chhatrapati that they should not provide army to help the Bhosales. Under the circumstances, the only friend through whom the Bhosales could muster support was Nanasaheb Peshwa. But, at this time, the political situation was not favourable to the Peshwa as he was engrossed in many important problems which prevented him to send armed forces, to help the Sawants against the Portuguese. He could only offer monetary and moral support to the Bhosales.

The Sawants were at war with the Portuguese for nearly three years bearing heavy losses. Yet they admirably continued the war and did not surrender to them.

Viceroy Dom Pedro D'Almeida e Portugal Marquez de Alorna before departing to the Kingdom drew up an important document in which he left valuable instructions to his successors and also a lucid account of the state of affairs in India during his viceroyalty. The instructions regarding the Portuguese policy towards the Sawants run as follows :

> Before proceeding any further I will give you my reasons for not prosecuting the conquest of the whole dominions of Kudal Desais. It is my opinion that all incursions into such territories of the enemy, which have no sea board, are useless, and if I captured Alorna it was for two reasons: The first was that it was accessible by means of a winding

> river; the second being that it was a stronghold in the very heart of the country, and I considered that if it was once captured, it would almost mean a death blow to the Bhosales.
>
> Should the Bhosales come to terms and agree to surrender the district from Sakhali to the Araundem rivers, with the fort of Terekhol, we shall be satisfied and prepared to cede him Reddi and Nivty, which are on the coast, and will therefore, always be at the mercy of our fleet in the event of the enemy becoming aggressive.

The policy regarding conquest of any territory outside the area of New Conquests is explained clearly by Viceroy Alorna in his instructions. It was easily possible for him to conquer territory as far as Kudal but, Kudal being landbound, it was not easy for the Portuguese to keep it under control because it was not approachable by their navy. He insisted that Alorna and Terekhol should be retained by the Portuguese because of their strategic importance. If the Sawants were agreeable, he further stated that they should be allowed to hold Nivty and Reddi leaving to the Portuguese the district from Sakhali to the Araundem river, with the fort of Terekhol. Terekhol was an important river for naval anchorage. Its possession by the Portuguese was therefore, bound to deprive the Sawants of its use, making them weak at sea. In the war of 1746, the Portuguese carried a good part of the navy of the Sawants from this very river to Goa. Allowing the Sawants to keep Reddi and Nivty was not a problem to the Portuguese as they could launch an offensive with their fleet at any time they liked.

It may be observed that a part of this very policy was pronounced as early as 1510, by Afonso de Albuquerque, taking into consideration the strength of the Portuguese on land and sea against the powers that surrounded Goa.

About four years after Marquez de Alorna this policy was once again emphasized by Marquez de Tavora. For his strategy and correct policy and able generalship, the king of Portugal bestowed upon him the title of Marquez de Alorna, his former name being Dom Pedro Miguel de Almeida e Portugal, Count of Assumar and first Marquis of Castello Novo. His policy went a long way in deciding relations between the Portuguese and the Sawants as beneficial to the Portuguese Government.

War with the Angres

The Angres were a constant source of menace to the Sawantwadi State. While the Sawants were facing opposition from all those who were aiding the Portuguese, the Angres were also trying to finish Wadi rulers with the help of the Portuguese.

The political situation in the state of Sawantwadi was not favourable to the Wadi rulers to attack the Angres as they were without any friends from whom they could expect support. Their naval squadron at Karli was burnt down by Ismail Khan, and the one in the creek of Terekhol was partly destroyed and partly carried away to Goa. At the same time, the Sawants were making unsuccessful attempts to construct new ships in the Karli river. Even in this weakened condition, the Sawants systematically attacked Govalkot, Anjanvel and the fort of Mudagad in February 1748, which was in the possession of Tulaji Angre. The Angres were forced to retreat and the Bhosales successfully occupied the fort of Mudagad. The Portuguese were informed of this and requested to assault the Angres. The ruler of Kolhapur who had sometime back turned against Sawants, now again offered financial help to the Portuguese, offering them dress and honour. Now, the Angres attacked the fort of Bharatgad. This strategically important fort was on the south-west of the Kalavali creek on a hill commanding the Malwan village of Masura. In 1680, Fond Sawant, being afraid of its falling into the hands of a chief named Bavdekar, had out a great wall through the rock, and finding water, built the fort in 1701. While the attack was in force, the Sawantwadi rulers were negotiating with Tulaji Angre to desist from the attack. But Tulaji Angre stuck to his gun and continued his attack vigorously. As negotiations could not produce any effect, the Sawants stepped up the attack under Vithal Vishram. After several skirmishes, the Sawants finally forced the Angres to evacuate the fort. The Angres suffered heavily both in men and material.

In 1749, the forces of the Bhosales attacked the fort of Masura which had been occupied by the forces of Tulaji Angre sometime back. This strategically important fort lies in the village of Masura. Masura is halfway between Malwan and Maland or Milandi on the Kalavali creek and is identified as the Muziris of Ptolemy and Periplus. The Bhosales, by joining hands with some of the Angre officers who were defending the fort, suddenly attacked it. There was heavy fighting between the Angres and the Bhosales. The Angres defended the fort for nearly five days when the necessities of life began to get exhausted and they began to face scarcity of water. Meanwhile, Tulaji Angre learning the situation, moved with his forces to Masura. But before he could reach there, the Sawants had taken the fort. Tulaji did not feel the necessity of pursuing the fight against the victorious army of Sawants as he was doubtful about a victory and requested the Portuguese for help against the Bhosales. He deputed to Goa Rudraji Dhulap to negotiate for help. The talks continued till May during which the Portuguese showed their willingness to help. In fact, the Portuguese were reluctant to help the Angre against the Bhosales because they did not want Angres coming closer to the Portuguese state and endangering the security of Goa. Therefore, the desire expressed at the talks to offer help to them was only an eye wash.

After securing success at Masura, the Bhosales concentrated 4000 infantry and 500 horses for an attack on Sakhali, Phonda and Jambaulim. The king of Sunda, fearing the attack sought Portuguese help. However, no attack was carried by the Bhosales as the idea was dropped.

Tulaji Angre a servant of the Chhatrapati of Satara next took away some ships from Malwan to his own port by deceit. Enraged at this, the Chhatrapati of Kolhapur requested the Bhosales of Wadi for help against the Angres. At the same time, Bhosales asked the Portuguese whether they would come to their help in the event of the attack on the Angres by the joint forces of Kolhapur and Bhosales. Meanwhile, the Portuguese having received succour from Portugal, the Viceroy ordered concentration of troops at Kolvale bordering the Bhosales territory.

After the monsoon Tulaji Angre with his fleet of six big pals and fifty galbats made an attack on Mangalore carrying away a rich booty from that city. A Portuguese factory was also looted by them. This attack on the factory was viewed seriously by the authorities in Goa who lodged a protest with Tulaji and demanded compensation for the loot. The betrayal of friendship on the part of the Angres was a good opportunity for the Portuguese not to assist them against the Bhosales. Thus for the time being, the Angres lost all hopes of securing any help from the Portuguese against the Sawants.

Bhosales-Marathas attack Angres

Like the Sawants of Wadi, the Chhatrapatis of Satara too were attacked by Tulaji Angre. Therefore, they were also eager to end the menace of Tulaji and accordingly requested the Sawants to help them. The situation was also favourable for the Satara Darbar to pursue this plan. Representative of Sawantwadi, Sultan Rayjade was at the court of Satara to discuss with them some important political problems that the Wadi rulers were facing. He with the Chhatrapati arrived at the decision to attack the Angres jointly. The Marathas were also planning a joint attack with the Bhosales on the Sunda and the Goa territory. Jairam Sawant and Ramchandra Sawant also informed the Portuguese about their decision to attack the Angres with the help of the Marathas and requested the Portuguese to send military help. The Maratha forces numbering 4000 to 5000 pitched their camp at Masura and carried talks with the Angres. They demanded that the Angres should hand over three lakhs and seven places occupied by them. The Angres were willing to give three lakhs but refused to surrender seven places. It is not known which of the seven places the Marathas were demanding from the Angres. At last, at the end of the year 1749, the forces of the Bhosales and those of the Marathas under the command of Bhagvantrao Pandit, attacked Tulaji's territory and captured important places as far as Lanja. The Angres in this situation appealed to the Portuguese for help. The latter reminded Tulaji of his attack on the Portuguese factory at Mangalore sometime ago and rendered him no help.

Viceroy Marquez de Alorna returned to the kingdom on 27 September 1750, and a new Viceroy was appointed in his place by name Francisco de Assis de Tavora who followed the footsteps of his predecessor, during his regime. Taking note of the change of administrator in Goa, the Maratha Sardar, Venkatrao Ghorpade, in charge of the forts of the border of Goa territory, requested him to return to the Bhosales the *talukas* of Pedne and Dicholi. However, the Portuguese did not respond to his request.

Tulaji again attacks Sawantwadi

Tulaji Angre once again raised his head in 1750. Taking advantage of the strained relations between the Bhosales and the Portuguese, he attacked Bharatgad and Sidhagad. He was successful in capturing the fort of Bharatgad. Jairam Sawant on hearing this news moved immediately with his forces to Masura. He persuaded *Naikwadi* (the people inside the fort were called Naikwadi) to surrender the fort of Bharatgad to him without a war.

Now Tulaji Angre with his navy proceeded to attack Kudal, the capital of the Sawants. The forces were under the command of Rudraji Dhulap numbering 3000. Tulaji starting from Assyamath reached Bambarda via Talegaon and made Bambarda his headquarters with heavy concentration of troops. The Wadi rulers were intimated about this by Shivaji Londe. Jairam Sawant alerted his troops and issued orders to the Hewalkars, Usapkars and other prominent Sardars to report immediately with their forces to defend Kudal. Meanwhile Angre's forces attacked Kudal and Karli and inflicted much loss to the Bhosales. Bhosales now appealed to the Portuguese for help. They also rebuilt the fort of Kudal which was destroyed by the Angres. The ruler of Sunda was in constant touch with the Portuguese and preferred Bhosales as good neighbour to the Angres.

Tulaji now renewed his attack vigorously. The forces of the Bhosales in the early part received setbacks. Jairam Sawant, well prepared, riding on his beloved mare (Bormanaki) was inspiring his forces. The mare which had always brought him success died while jumping over a bunker. Jairam Sawant took this as an ill omen. He appealed once again to the Portuguese to provide succour. Both the Angres and the Bhosales were constantly in touch with the Portuguese authorities to secure their help. The secretary of state sought opinion of different members of the council whether aid should be given to the Angres or the Bhosales. It was the Viceroy's opinion that both the Angres and the Bhosales were following the same method and were holding the same intention in seeking Portuguese help. Tulaji did not wish his expedition to be embarrassed by the Portuguese, while the Bhosales wanted that the Portuguese should not help the Angres. The Portuguese did not consider either the Angres or the Bhosales to be trustworthy friends. It was their experience that both the Angres and the Bhosales were enemies in disguise and respected treaties of peace as long as it was convenient to them. The Portuguese regarding the Bhosales, the Angres and the Marathas as potential enemies on the sea, desired that no help should be provided to either of them, unless they were sure that the aid given to any of them was beneficial to the Portuguese.

The Viceroy further stated, considering the proposal made by the Angre, that the Portuguese should not disturb the existing friendly relations with Tulaji as he was very powerful, especially on the sea, and was liable to cause loss to Portuguese shipping. He therefore, felt that the Portuguese should prolong negotiations with him and treat him in such a way that a treaty was not concluded unless terms were favourable to the Portuguese. In order to please Tulaji, the Viceroy suggested that as the river and the territory of Karli belonged to the Portuguese by the right of conquest after a just war with the Bhosales (where actually Tulaji was now preparing to attack) they would not put up any opposition to him nor embarrass him, to let him know that they wished to have harmonious and good relations with him. But the Portuguese, however, would take care and see that Tulaji did not strengthen the said territory and the entrance to the said river. The Viceroy also felt that Tulaji should not interfere with the sea-side territories, which the Portuguese had acquired through force of arms, but he was free to attack the Bhosale territory which the Portuguese had not conquered. If Tulaji agreed to this proposal, then he could send his conditions and privileges in order to get the desired aid from the Portuguese, which he could get if the conditions were favourable and beneficial to the Portuguese state.

The Viceroy stated that the Portuguese ships anchored in front of Aguada with provisions be shifted to near places, closer to places of embarcation, so as to make Tulaji feel that the Portuguese were ready to give him help at first notice. He felt that though he considered the neighbourhood of Bhosales as bad, that of Angres was worse. In comparison with the pride and unfaithfulness of the Bhosales, the Angres were superior in forces, extension of dominions and in securing valuable help of the Marathas as experienced by the Portuguese in their campaign of Kulaba. This was, in his opinion, the only reason behind their seeking the Sunda and even the Bhosales to be Portuguese neighbours, without allowing more powerful neighbour to take their place. The same position the Portuguese had maintained in regard to the northern provinces that is, Bassein. The Nawab of Kalyan and others, served as barriers to the Portuguese territory to defend themselves, and, had they been conquered by the Marathas, the Portuguese would have lost that province.

As regards the Bhosales, he felt that though they were not worthy of any compassion on the part of the Portuguese, they should be made to entertain the hope of getting Portuguese help, in order that they may not be disheartened in the war waged against them by the Angres, getting at the same time weaker both in forces and money. Lastly, the Viceroy suggested that both the Angres and the Bhosales should be advised to send a learned man, to deal with this grave matter, with the conditions they were willing to offer and which the Portuguese should accept only if they are beneficial to the state.

Meanwhile, both the Angres and the Bhosales deputed their envoys to Goa to hold talks with the Portuguese. The Portuguese informed the envoy of the Bhosales that without discussing the conditions of peace, it would be difficult for them to provide succour. The conditions were also not favourable for the Portuguese to help the Bhosales as there was paucity of troops to defend the Portuguese territory. The Portuguese authorities considered Angres to be lacking in fidelity and they stood as a friend only when they were in need of help. In general, the Portuguese considered Asiatic people as opportunists. However, they preferred Bhosales to the Angres who in the event of defeating Bhosales would rise as a powerful enemy to the Portuguese territory. The authorities diplomatically tackled the issue. They treated the envoys of Angres and the Bhosales with all respect. However, the Portuguese maintained neutrality in the Angre-Bhosale conflict. Meanwhile, Jairam Sawant rallied his forces and launched the vigorous counter attack on Tulaji Angre compelling him to retreat with heavy losses. Never before had the Angres suffered such a defeat at the hands of the Bhosales. The battle drum which Tulaji had brought with him was captured by Jairam's men and was kept at the entrance of his palace as a trophy of his victory over Tulaji. One of the most brilliant soldiers of Tulaji Angre known as Manaji Fankade died in this war. On the side of Jairam Sawant, the well known Rajput Sardars Navasingh and Angoli Patya fell fighting. The battle of Kudal is considered memorable in the Sawant-Angre conflict.

The fleeing army of Tulaji Angre was chased by Jairam's armymen upto Lanja, Devruk, burning many villages on the way. The victory over the Angres raised the status of Jairam Sawant in the eyes of the neighbouring powers. The Bhosales became more influential than before in the Satara Darbar. At last, peace was adjusted between the Angres and the Bhosales and the Portuguese on receiving intelligence that the Bhosales had concentrated an army of 2000 strong, made preparations in the event of their attack on Goa. However, no such attack was carried out by the Bhosales.

Attack on Sunda

In 1752, the Portuguese attacked Sunda territory. Ramchandra Sawant desired that the Portuguese should have informed him of their design so that he would have joined them. He promised to send his army and asked the Portuguese from where he should transport them. He even concentrated his forces at Sakhali and informed the Portuguese that as soon as his galbats returned from the expedition, he would deploy his navy to help the Portuguese. He was confident of the Portuguese victory and promised them sea facilities. The Portuguese defeated Sunda and captured two forts, one of which was Kholgad. Ramchandra Sawant, on hearing the news expressed his happiness to the Portuguese. Though he had promised to help the Portuguese, he was not able to send his forces as he was now engaged in a family feud at home.

INTERNAL DISSENSIONS IN THE WADI COURT

For thirteen years the joint rule of Jairam Sawant and Ramchandra Sawant was very successful but internal dissensions became inevitable when differences between the two began to increase. Several reasons are attributed for the differences of Jairam Sawant and Ramchandra Sawant. For many years Ramchandra Sawant had no male issue to succeed him. The son born to Ramchandra in 1749, made Jairam realize this would reduce his importance and strained his relations with Ramchandra. Another reason for the difference between Jairam and Ramchandra was about the use of a huge quantity of precious teak in the state. Ramchandra Sawant wanted to build a stately edifice for himself out of this teak whereas Jairam Sawant was of the opinion that the teak should be utilized for shipbuilding which would strengthen the position of the state. The Portuguese source says that Ramchandra being the eldest son in direct line was heir to the Sardesai title. But his uncle Jairam Sawant, a person of proud restive character who commanded more respect and obedience than his peace-loving nephew in the territory, also claimed the title. The differences between them went on increasing despite efforts at mediation by number of well-wishers. Peshwa Balaji Bajirao too tried to reconcile Sawant brothers with each other but could not succeed. He had sent a clever envoy, Ramchandra Bava Sukhtankar, to bring about an understanding between Jairam Sawant and Ramchandra Sawant. He had put forth a proposal that Ramchandra should rule at Wadi with the help of Jivaji Vishram while Jairam Sawant with his sons should stay at the Poona court. These proposals were not acceptable to Jairam Sawant. In order to patch up the differences, Vithal

Vishram Sabnis, a brother of Jivaji Vishram Sabnis who was in Poona addressed a letter to Ramchandra Sawant pointing out how the differences between the two, that is, Jairam Sawant and Ramchandra Sawant were harmful to the state, and how the Portuguese were bound to make capital of it on a suitable occasion. The letter reads :

> There is no dearth of small men who would poison your ears. You are likely to believe what such people tell you, but in consequence it will harm whatever good has been done so far. Outsiders will be in the state and we would have to watch things helplessly. Any attempt to amend matters would then be useless. I am writing this to you in detail after discussing the matter with Ramchandra Baba. It is hallucination to suppose that the firinguis are supporting us. I state this because I know things well as I am here. I may be excused for writing this by going a little beyond the limits.

As no settlement could be reached, Jairam, joining hands with Tulaji Angre attacked the fort of Vengurla, while Ramchandra's people were engaged in rebuilding the fort. Jairam was successful in capturing the fort of Vengurla and now made preparations for an attack on Wadi. He also gave details of the family conflict to the Portuguese and sought their help to end it. In his letter Antaji Krishna hejib of Jairam Sawant writes accordingly :

(1) Fond Sawant had nine sons. Nar Sawant the eldest rebelled against him and put him in prison. While in prison the father hatched a plot and got Nar killed. Another son Nag, who had also rebelled against his father, was forced to run up the Ghat, where he died.

(2) After the death of Fond Sawant, there was joint rule of Jairam Sawant and Ramchandra Sawant. For all administrative purposes, the names of both were used with the name of Jairam Sawant appearing first. Jairam Sawant gave the state seal to Ramchandra. Things went well between the joint rulers for sometime when there was full

understanding. This condition did not last long and due to some discord, Jairam Sawant demanded from Ramchandra Sawant the State seal which he did not return.

Ramchandra continued to use the seal. The remaining seven brothers and a son of Nag, wanted to use the seal, taking it back from Ramchandra Sawant. Under the circumstances, Jairam Sawant appealed to the Portuguese Viceroy to settle the family dispute and also about the seal. Ramchandra Sawant on receiving intelligence that Jairam Sawant was planning for an attack on Wadi, requested the Portuguese through his administrator Jivaji Vishram, to send in their navy and army against Jairam Sawant who had also captured Vengurla fort. While Ramchandra Sawant sought support from the Portuguese against his uncle Jairam, the latter allied himself with the Sundas against the Portuguese. Both Jairam Sawant and Ramchandra Sawant deputed their envoys to the Court of Goa. To Ramchandra's appeal the Portuguese replied that, since the Bhosales had infringed every peace treaty signed with them, only a personal appearance in Goa would give the Viceroy some surety for his peace declarations. Accordingly, Ramchandra promised to come himself or to send his wife and son, but later he changed his mind, either through fear of his uncle or mistrust of the Portuguese. Jairam on his part did not venture beyond covert hostilities against Goa. In the family conflict of the Sawants the Portuguese were helping militarily Ramchandra, and at the same time were instigating him to act against Jairam.

Ramchandra Sawant Bhosale's intention was to avoid further differences with his uncle Jairam Sawant and with this in mind, he now requested Portuguese to mediate. The Portuguese who wanted to keep Jairam Sawant and Ramchandra Sawant at loggerheads as it was advantageous to them, on one pretext or the other, delayed any adjustment between them. Once the real intention of the Portuguese was known to Ramchandra Sawant, he also changed his policy and informed the Portuguese that the help which he had sought from them was regarding the return of forts and lands and not for the adjustment of the conflict with his uncle. It was obvious that this sudden change in the reason for help was to prevent the Portuguese from interfering in the internal affairs of Sawantwadi. He felt that perhaps the Portuguese might take advantage of their disunity and fish in the troubled waters.

Jairam Sawant, finding that no understanding could be reached with Ramchandra Sawant, left Wadi and started residing at Kudal.

DEATH OF JAIRAM SAWANT

Jairam Sawant was a high-minded person and never compromised his honour and prestige. He was highly successful in bringing back the lost glory to the Wadi State by conquering Bardesh and defeating the powerful Tulaji Angre. The Peshwa's proposal that he should come and stay at Poona was not accepted by him as he felt that it was not in keeping with the dignity of the Bhosale House. Shortly after he shifted his residence to Kudal, he died. His death prevented differences with his uncle Ramchandra Sawant before they took a serious turn.

On 1 September 1754, Marquez de Tavora returned to Lisbon after having handed over the reins to his successor, Dom Luis Mascarenhas, Conde de Alva.

On taking charge as Viceroy, Marquez Alva decided upon an aggressive policy towards the Bhosales. Ramchandra Sawant had sought the help of the Portuguese against the attack of Tulaji Angre. He never agreed to a regular treaty to give away to the Portuguese the territories which they had conquered from him, that is, Terekhol, Alorna etc., during the time of Marquez de Alorna. Viceroy Alva was disappointed with this sort of relationship and attacked Wadi. Ramchandra Sawant was not in a position to defend it, and after a few skirmishes came to terms with the Portuguese and signed a treaty on 25 October 1754. By this treaty, the Portuguese ratified the treaty of 1712, signed with Fond Sawant. The Portuguese surrendered to the Bhosales the outposts of Reddi and Nivty. The Bhosales were to allow the Catholic missionaries to perform the functions of the Catholic religion without impediment. The Desais of Keri, Sakhali and Morli who swore fidelity to the

Portuguese were reputed as vassals of the Portuguese State. The Portuguese exempted the Bhosales from the payment of tribute which they owed since 1739. The slaves and run-away soldiers were to be returned reciprocally. The Portuguese promised protection to Khem Sawant, the son and successor to Ramchandra.

Alva's aggressive policy was successful. After a few months, Ramchandra Sawant died in 1755. He was 43 at the time of his death. He had only one son named Khem and four daughters. Thus the seventeen-year rule of Ramchandra Sawant came to an end leaving his only son to succeed him on the gadi of Sawantwadi.

5

KHEM SAWANT III : (1755—1803)

Khem Sawant III when hardly 6 years of age succeeded to the Gadi of Sawantwadi after the death of his father Ramchandra in 1755. According to Portuguese sources, Ramchandra was poisoned to death by one of his rival relations, probably an uncle, though the name of the relation is not recorded. The Portuguese who had a stake in this matter preferred Khem Sawant III as a successor because he was a minor. In order to put down the rivals of Khem Sawant III, they sent two hundred sepoys and some cavalry to Sawantwadi. They thought that Khem Sawant III as a minor would be favourable to them. The Portuguese were successful in setting Khem Sawant III on the throne; Khem Sawant was hardly six years of age when his father died; his mother Janakibai carried on the administration of the State, with the help of Jivaji Vishram Sabnis who was the first secretary. Janakibai, a capable lady, enhanced the power and prestige of Sawantwadi during her regency which lasted from 1755 to 1763, during which Jivaji Vishram Sabnis played a dominant role. In order to gain recognition for her son Khem, as the due successor to the gadi, Janakibai made a representation to the Portuguese. They on their part deputed Dom Christovão Carcome Lobo, to the Wadi fortress. There, he recognized Khem Sawant as the lawful successor of the state. This was actually done only when the treaty of 1754 was duly ratified by this young successor in 1755.

The political situation in the neighbouring states, at the commencement of Janakibai's regency was favourable to Sawantwadi Darbar. The Peshwas were not on good terms with the Portuguese, constant clashes took place between the rulers of Kolhapur and the Chieftain of Icchalkaranji Venkatrao

Ghorpade. Kolhapur was very much troubled by the petty chiefs of Kagal and Miraj. The Angres were at war with the Peshwas in which the interests of both the Portuguese and the English were involved. The Portuguese supported the Angres while the English offered their help to the Peshwas. Janakibai and her secretary, Jivaji Vishram, took full advantage of the political situation prevailing in the states around Sawantwadi and strengthened its army and naval establishments. The navy, particularly, destroyed by the Portuguese, was reconstructed and organised in the Karli river.

THE DISTURBANCES OF THE PRABHUS

During the reign of Khem Sawant II, the Prabhus who were trying to regain power in Sawantwadi were defeated. Actually Jogan Prabhu was killed and Narayan was forced to flee. Now once again Dadaji Prabhu, the son and successor of Narayan, tried to regain power by seeking help from the Poona Darbar. He sent one of his able envoys to the Peshwa for military help and the Peshwa always eager to fish in the troubled waters sent Naro Trimbak to support the cause of Dadaji with an army of 3000 strong. Naro Trimbak who was then at Dandarajpuri marched to Nerur. Hearing of this, the Sawantwadi Darbar hurriedly deputed their envoy Vithal Vishram Sabnis to Poona to persuade the Peshwa to recall the army sent under Naro Trimbak. The envoy was successful in his mission and the Peshwa ordered Naro Trimbak to withdraw his troops from Nerur in Sawantwadi state. Thus, a confrontation with Naro Trimbak's army was diplomatically avoided and the cause of the Prabhus was defeated. They do not seem to have raised their heads again during the reign of Khem Sawant III.

As Khem Sawant III was a minor, hardly six to seven years old, the credit of avoiding a clash with Naro Trimbak's army, and at the same time eliminating the rebellion of the Prabhus once for all goes to Janakibai and her able administrator, Jivaji Vishram Sabnis.

Marathas attack Phonda (1756)

The Maratha-Portuguese war of 1737-39 was concluded by a treaty between the two powers in 1740. All the northern possessions of the Portuguese with Bassein as the headquarters were surrendered to the Marathas. On the Goa side the territory of Sashti was returned to the Portuguese, and Phonda Mahal was returned to the Sunda ruler. It was Bajirao's desire to retain Phonda in Maratha hands. But nothing could be done as he died a premature death in 1740. Ten years later, his son Peshwa Balaji Bajirao alias Nana, demanded the fort of Phonda from the ruler of Sunda.

For the expanding power of the Marathas, particularly in the south, then commonly called Karnatak, the fort of Phonda was of great strategic importance. Phonda lay on the route from Poona to western or coastal Karnatak. This route, via Phonda, was shorter than the one which passed from the eastern side of the Sahyadri mountains. Moreover, with Phonda in their hands, the Marathas could control the activities of their feudatory, the Sawant of Wadi who was of uncertain loyalty. At the same time from Phonda they could checkmate the Portuguese if they joined any power against the Marathas. With this in mind, Peshwa Balaji Bajirao in 1750 seems to have demanded Phonda from the ruler of Sunda. But under pressure from the Portuguese, the Sunda ruler refused to hand over the fort to the Peshwa. The Peshwa was not in a position to press his demand further either by force or persuasion, as he had a number of other important affairs on hand. However, he took up the matter again in 1756. Now the ruler of Sunda without much hesitation agreed to hand over the fort of Phonda to the Peshwa, on condition that he should treat Phonda as mortgage territory in lieu of which he should pay annually rupees five and a half lakhs to the Sunda state. The Portuguese resented this transaction very much and attacked the fort of Phonda under the impression that the Maratha forces had not yet occupied it. The Maratha forces in the fort repulsed the Portuguese attack. After making necessary preparations the Portuguese Viceroy led an expedition with a large army which camped near the famous temple of Kapileshwari at a very short distance from the fort. The Sawants, being requested by the Viceroy for help, sent their forces. The Portuguese had a special advantage in the "Petardo" a mine which was unknown to the Marathas. Unfortunately, on the day of the attack, the 28th of June, the monsoon burst with all its fury in Goa, dampening the gun-powder and rendering their fire arms useless. This was the proper occasion for the Marathas to swoop down upon the Portuguese. The Maratha commander of the fort, Ram Joshi Hooprikar, sallied forth with a batch of 400 soldiers and swords in hand fell upon the Portuguese with great fury. A good number of the Portuguese soldiers fell to the Maratha sword while the rest took to their heels. The Viceroy, Count of Alva, who was leading the attack fell in the fighting. The Sawants seeing the plight of the Portuguese joined the victorious Marathas, but did not fail to send condolence message to the Goa Government for the death of Viceroy Alva on the battlefield. The victorious Marathas handed over the dead body of the Viceroy to the Goa Government with due honour. Maratha-Portuguese relations more or less remained undisturbed from 1756—1763.

After the death of Viceroy Alva, the Home Government appointed a board of administrators to look after the affairs of Goa and this board continued to administer up to 1758. On 23 September, 1758, Manoel de Saldanha de Albuquerque, Count of Ega, was appointed Viceroy at Goa. At this time, the power of the Peshwa was at its peak. He had a vast army at his command and also possessed a navy on the west coast under his admiral, the Dhulap of Vijaydurga. A year or two earlier the Peshwa had defeated the defiant Tulaji Angre at Vijaydurga with the help of the English. The new Viceroy naturally wanted to establish friendly relations with the powerful Peshwa Nanasaheb, and wrote to the Home Government that in pursuance of this policy the Goa Government should avoid any conflict with the Peshwa. With this in mind, in February 1759, when Nanasaheb was at Vijaydurga, the Viceroy deputed his envoy Tomas Zoje Kodmor with a view to establishing friendship with the Peshwa afresh and to prevent an offensive pact against Goa, between Poona and Sawantwadi. Not meeting him there, Kodmor had to proceed to Poona where he was received cordially. After preliminary talks with the Peshwa the envoy returned to Goa,

Later, the Peshwa sent his envoys to finalise the treaty of friendship. Through one of the envoys Mahadaji Keshav Fadke, the treaty of friendship between the Peshwa and the Portuguese was signed on 20 March, 1760, giving the required security to the latter.

Up to the third battle of Panipat, the Peshwa's power was at its zenith, and he was supreme in the Deccan as well as on the west coast. The Portuguese, therefore, found it difficult to expand their power till 1761. This factor was very favourable to the ruler of Sawantwadi. The Portuguese in order to maintain the *status quo* with the Peshwa, the ruler of Sawantwadi and the Sunda, were friendly with all three. The Home Government had also instructed the Viceroy to avoid any clash either with Sawantwadi or Sunda, with a view to preventing any interference from the powerful Peshwa. It had also cautioned the Goa Government not to allow expansion of the naval power by the ruler of Sawantwadi as being dangerous. The situation continued unchanged till 1761.

Phonda was in Maratha hands since 1756. The Portuguese were ill at ease with this situation. With the disastrous defeat of the Marathas in the third battle of Panipat in 1761, they had an opportunity of recapturing the strategic fort of Phonda. Following the defeat of the Marathas at Panipat, the Peshwa Nanasaheb died at Poona. The Poona Government was occupied with its own problems, internal and external. Seizing this opportunity, the Portuguese signed a secret treaty with Khem Sawant in 1762, for the occupation of Phonda. By one of the term of the treaty, it was decided that the Bhosales should supply to the Sunda ruler nearly one thousand five hundred soldiers, and the latter should keep ready two thousand men for a concerted attack on Phonda. The combined forces of the Portuguese and the Sawants launched an attack on Phonda. They were joined by the Desai of Phonda, Narba Naik Prataprao Sardesai, who was an enemy of the Marathas. At the eleventh hour the Sunda forces do not seem to have joined their allies. It is strange to observe that some of the Maratha soldiers Ramaji Hari, Raghu Sawant Wadikar, Bapuji Pant Majumdar, who were guarding the fort, helped the Portuguese against their own master. As a result of the joint attack and treachery, the Portuguese secured the fort without much difficulty. They demolished it once for all and the entire area of Phonda Mahal went under their possession. In the beginning of January 1764, the Portuguese Government admitted Raghu Sawant, his son and nephew, as their vassals and granted them some privileges.

In this struggle of Phonda, Jivaji Vishram the administrator of Sawantwadi was of great help to the Portuguese. He was instrumental in signing the treaty of 1762, with the Portuguese, and seems to have been successful in bribing some of the Maratha soldiers in the fort to desert the cause of their master.

NARO TRIMBAK ATTACKS BHOSALE'S TERRITORY—BHARATGAD, MASURA, VENGURLA, KUDAL, CHEDVAN, NIVTY AND KARLI

In 1757, Naro Pant, the admiral of the Peshwas, having entered into an understanding with the Queen of Kolhapur, arrived with a fleet in the Port of Malwan, consisting of two parangues, some gurabs and 20 small and big galbats. He had also transported a force of 1500 to 2000 strong and 300 horses. His intention was to attack the key forts of Bharatgad, Masura, Karli and Nivty. The fort of Karli guarded the creek of the same name where the Bhosales usually had their navy. The exact reason of this attack is not clear from the Portuguese documents. Jivaji Vishram calls this attack by Naro Trimbak an act of treason, though this is not corroborated by the published documents either in the Peshwa Daftar or in the Kolhapur Papers. Naro Trimbak, it seems was also in touch with the English. The arrival of Naro at Malwan was reported by Jivaji Vishram, the administrator of Sawantwadi to the Portuguese at Goa, and he asked for their help. The Portuguese in their own interest offered help to Jivaji Vishram against the forces of Naro Trimbak. It is not known whether Naro Trimbak was given military help by the Rani of Kolhapur though she had allowed his forces to land in the Port of Malwan. Naro Trimbak's forces attacked Bharatgad and Masura situated to the north-east of Malwan, and Karli to the south of Malwan, along the coast. Naro Trimbak's attacks on Bharatgad and Masura were repelled by the Sawants who were supplied ammunition and cannon balls by the Portuguese. Karli and Nivty fell into the hands of Naro Trimbak, but were wrested from him when the Portuguese helped the Sawants. Repelled from Nivty and Karly, Naro Trimbak unsuccessfully tried to secure Vengurla, Kudal, Chedvan and Valavali. The port of Vengurla was a naval station of the Sawants, guarded by a fort. Naro Trimbak attacked Vengurla by land and sea, and the engagement lasted three days. Naro Trimbak had to retreat having lost about two hundred persons, among whom were a few distinguished soldiers. Some of Naro Trimbak's men were arrested and beheaded. Though dogged by defeat, Naro Trimbak undauntedly launched a vigorous attack on the fort of Sidhagad and was successful in securing it. This was the only notable victory to the credit of Naro in his attacks on the territory of the Sawants. In the agreement between Naro and the Sawants, the former was allowed to retain the fort of Sidhagad which remained in the possession of the Peshwas till 1795.

The Portuguese helped the Sawants in this short warfare according to the treaty of 25 October, 1754, which they had signed with Ramchandra Sawant.

The Portuguese power was definitely on the decline after their defeat by the Marathas in the battle of Bassein in 1739. Yet on suitable occasions, throughout the 18th century, they did not fail to add a few districts to their old conquests. The districts which they added are known in history as the New Conquests. This expansionist activity in the provinces adjacent to the Old Conquests continued up to 1783. The new conquests added to the Portuguese territory the districts of Dicholi, Sakhali and Pedne. These districts, however, changed hands between the Portuguese and the Sawants, even a few years after the completion of New Conquests in 1783.

The district of Pedne and Dicholi were in Portuguese hands as decided in the treaty of 1754. The disaster of Phonda (1756), was a pretext for the Bhosales to try and recover the territories of Pedne, Dicholi and Sakhali. With the open quarrels going on among the Goa Governors, the Wadi rulers were tempted to make a bid for their former possessions. At this time that is, in 1758, the economic condition of the

Portuguese being bad, they collected taxes forcibly from the people of Pedne, and to raise money compelled them to buy tobacco only from Goa. The Sawants resented this and instigated the Desais of Pedne to rise in rebellion. Domingo Branco, who was in command of Pedne, was arrested by the Sawants and the district taken. Further, the Sawants raided a fair at Mhapsa and carried off much loot. The fair of Mhapsa, a well-supplied and well-attended weekly fair, had already attained wide local fame. Next, they attacked Bardesh. The Portuguese Governor sent two companies of grenadiers and one of artillery against the Bhosales but the Portuguese forces were repelled.

Maneri in the district of Pedne was in the next target of the Sawant's attack. It fell without much resistance as it had water shortage. The strategically important fort of Alorna was also besieged by the Bhosales. Sioli, an outpost of Bardesh and Santo Estevam or St. Stephen island, fell easily to the Bhosale's attack.

A furious battle between the Portuguese and the Sawants was fought when the latter attacked Dicholi. The Portuguese forces consisting of six companies of grenadiers, seven of light and two of artillery were under the command of General Joao Manoel de Lacerda and commander Ignacio de Souza. The artillery was under Lieutenant Colonel Manoel Garlez. Both sides fought desperately. The loss on the side of the Sawants was heavy. About 600 of their soldiers died, while the loss to the Portuguese was comparatively slight. Their captains of cavalry and infantry were seriously wounded. Finally the Portuguese succeeded in taking possession of Dicholi. In this battle fought for Dicholi, the defeated soldiers of the Bhosales who, it seems were not paid for a long time, desperately attacked a few villages in the neighbourhood of Dicholi and looted them. Among these soldiers were a number of Pathans in the service of the Bhosales.

Retreating from Dicholi, the Sawants launched an attack on the fort of Terekhol. It was well guarded and well supplied with ammunition. The siege of the fort by the forces of Sawant lasted for three weeks, after which they were compelled to retreat. After Terekhol, the Sawants fell upon Morgim at night during winter, and killed the canarins, soldiers of the Portuguese. With this, the Sawant-Portuguese battle for Pedne, Dicholi, Terekhol, Alorna and Morgim seems to have come to an end in August 1758. Such wars at these places were a matter of common occurrence between the Portuguese and the Sawants.

The new Viceroy who took charge on 23 September, 1758 was very eager to recapture the territory lost to the Sawants the previous year. He visited the warehouses and despatched provisions to the fort of Alorna under the command of Lieutenant Colonel Ignacio de Souza, as the Bhosales were planning to attack it. The Portuguese troops wanted to proceed further from Alorna, and attack the fort of Reddi, but were prevented by the Viceroy. At this time, a small group of soldiers led by Atmaram, brother of Jairam Sawant, offered their help to the Portuguese. The Portuguese took the village of Pilgao near Dicholi. The Viceroy having received intelligence that the Bhosales were constructing a fort at Amona, ordered two companies of grenadiers and six of soldiers to march to Amona. Amona was easily taken and the fort under construction easily demolished.

The Viceroy next collected his forces at Kolvale consisting of seven companies of grenadiers, four light companies, twenty gunners, 2000 soldiers and seventy horses munitioned with two artillery pieces of 24, four mortars, gun-powder and carriages, and attacked Pedne. By January 1759, Viceroy Ega won back Pedne from the combined Bhosale-Maratha army, after a severe fight. The Portuguese records report that the Sawants lost as many as 800 soldiers, whereas the Portuguese lost a few officers and soldiers. In the month of August, the Bhosales made a surprise attack on the Portuguese church at Kerim (Pedne) and carried away a safe containing the consecrated Host with the Holy form. Finally, the Sawants appealed to the Portuguese for a settlement. The Peshwa who was at this time at Vijaydurga, sent his envoy Mahadaji Keshav Phadke who helped the Sawants in bringing about the treaty. Khem Sawant, on this occasion, sought the help of Suba Kamat of the famous historic Mhamai Kamat family of Panjim as a mediator. Originally, this family hailed from the village of Guirdolim of Chandor. After the Portuguese initiated the conversion drive in Goa in 1541, the Mhamai family members fearing religious persecution, fled with the images of their deities to the neighbouring hills of Antruz, which were then under the rule of the Hindu Prince of Sunda. It was only at the close of the 17th century, that the family came back to the Portuguese territory and settled at Panaji, which was then a suburb of the Old Goa city inhabited chiefly by fishermen and artisans, having country houses of the Portuguese grandees and some native merchants. The commercial interests of the Mhamai family are traceable in the family records as far back as A.D. 1759. Unfortunately, most of the earlier records have been very badly damaged and are no longer in usable condition. The records which are in good condition reveal that the family had trade dealings with the colonies of the French in India, and the Portuguese overseas colonies. The Mhamai family had its own ships. The Kamat Mhamai family was one of the leading families engaged in trade and commerce with the neighbouring coastal powers including the Sawants of Wadi. They also wielded influence at the Portuguese court and, therefore, were best suited to play their role in the negotiations between the Portuguese and the Sawants. At last, with the mediation of Suba Kamat and Mahadaji Keshav Phadke, a treaty was concluded between the Portuguese and the Sawants on 26 July, 1759. By this treaty, the Portuguese, taking into consideration as usual the repeated assurance of repentance on the part of the great Sardesai Khem Sawant, accepted him as their friend and renewed the treaty of 1754. They agreed to the mutual exchange of prisoners and deserters ; the territories of Pedne, Dicholi and Sakhali were leased to the Bhosales on an annual payment of 50,000 xerafins ; the Bhosales were permitted to collect taxes connected with justice ; distributions and administration from the said provinces and were to pay an annual pension of Rs. 2,000 to Krishna Sawant Bhosale serving the Portuguese. The Viceroy also undertook by a secret agreement to recommend to the King of Portugal to restore to Khem Sawant all or a portion of the provinces which he, the Bhosale, had ceded to the Portuguese under the treaty of the 25 October, 1754. Some years later, Marquez of Pombal blamed

Count of Ega for the miserable treaty of 1759, which had robbed Goa both of income and its buffer provinces against northern provinces.

Up to 1761, the power of the Peshwa Nanasaheb was at its zenith. Taking advantage of this, Khem Sawant demanded from the Portuguese the transfer of the territories of Pedne, Dicholi, Sakhali and the fort of Terekhol. The Portuguese refused to grant his demand and closed the Ghats between their territory and that of Khem Sawant. The Sawants, however, marched on the Portuguese territory and the Viceroy of Goa on the advice of the King of Portugal concluded a treaty with Khem Sawant on 24 December, 1761.

It is strange to see that the Viceroy who had acted on the advice of the King of Portugal, was highly criticised later on, because of the Bhosales repeated infidelities, and the wastage of Portuguese blood in taking the said forts and provinces, without any subsequent benefit to the State. On this occasion the Portuguese it seems preferred to avoid a conflict with the Sawant as they were likely to be helped by the Peshwa.

Janakibai who was working as regent during Khem's minority seems to have entrusted the administration of the State to him in 1763 when he was 14 years of age. According to the custom he was now of marriageable age and the elders at the Wadi Darbar considered the proposal for a spouse coming from the Shindes of Gwalior. The Gwalior Darbar was in search of a suitable bridegroom for Laximibai, the daughter of Jayappa Shinde. Jivbadada Kerkar who hailed from Pedne Kerim, was by this time an influential person in the service of the Shindes, holding the rank of Senapati. At his instance the Shindes deputed some persons to Sawantwadi for a preliminary talk regarding the marriage of Laximibai with Khem Sawant. Jivbadada as a matchmaker between the two royal houses of Sawantwadi and Gwalior, played an important role as he knew both the parties very well and was also respected by them. The proposal was accepted and it was decided to celebrate the marriage at Srigonda, the original place of the Shindes' Jahangir. The marriage was performed with all pomp and Show in 1763.

Khem the III informed the Portuguese of his departure for Srigonda for the celebrations of his marriage and also of his return to Sawantwadi after the performance. In all probability Khem must have invited the Portuguese Viceroy for his marriage, though the invitation letter or the reference regarding the same are not traceable in the records.

END OF JANAKIBAIS REGENCY—KHEM ASSUMES CHARGE

The regency of Janakibai came to an end in 1763, and Khem Sawant the III succeeded to the gadi. Sawantwadi-Portuguese relations hereafter fall under his rule. When Khem took charge of the administration regularly in 1763, he was keen to maintain friendship with the Portuguese. However, he did not remain favourable to them throughout his rule as they had expected at the beginning. The next year that is, in 1764, Madhavrao Peshwa, planning to proceed to Karnataka in one of his four campaigns against Haider Ali (1764—1772) demanded the surrender of Mardangad and Phonda area to him as they lay on the route to Karnataka and also demanded that the Portuguese reconstruct the fort of Mardangad which they had demolished, before handing it over to him. But all this was to be secured by negotiations. Khem Sawant was asked by Madhavrao to render all help to the Maratha army proceeding to Karnataka. In the month of October the Peshwa forces under Janoji Dhulap arrived at Sakhali. Khem informed the Portuguese of this stating that the real aim of the Marathas was to attack the taluka of Mardangad on the pretext of their march to Karnataka. Khem Sawant collected his forces and guarded all important points on the border. He, had no intention of rendering any help to Madhavrao as he did not want to disturb his relations with the Portuguese. He, therefore, tried to misrepresent the Maratha demand to the Portuguese in his own interest. Madhavrao asked from the Portuguese the fort of Mardangad and the Phonda region not on the pretext of proceeding to the south but because of their importance and position on the way to Karnataka.

In March 1768, the Portuguese learnt that the Peshwa had sought the help of Khem for a campaign on Phonda. He had kept his forces ready under the command of one Yesajiram for an attack on Mardangad Taluka, which it seems actually never materialized. However, the Portuguese Governor in order to bring Khem closer to them entered into an agreement with him on 14 October, 1768 ratifying the earlier treaty of 24 December, 1761.

THE PESHWAS ASK PERMISSION FROM THE PORTUGUESE FOR A PASSAGE TO KARNATAKA VIA PHONDA

Peshwa Madhavrao had been asking the Portuguese to give passage to his army proceeding against Haider Ali through the Phonda region. The Portuguese denied this permission as observed previously. In the beginning of January 1771, the Peshwa concentrated his forces numbering about 10,000 at Masura, Kudal and Banda under the command of Visaji Pant Lele. A naval squadron consisting of 17 pale and 85 galbats lay anchored in the Karli creek. The forces of Khem numbering about 2,000 under the command of Som Sawant and Krishna Sawant, were to join Visaji Pant Lele. When all arrangements were ready, the combined forces of the Peshwa and Khem Sawant were to attack Haider Ali's territory. For this the Peshwa Madhavrao asked the Portuguese to grant permission to the combined armies to pass via Phonda. The Portuguese brought to the notice of the Peshwa through their envoys Vithal Gorkhe Valavalkar and Prabhakar Dikshit Sotri that the grant of passage via Phonda would make Haider Ali hostile to them, bringing their territory into danger. An envoy of Haider Ali at the Portuguese Court was reporting to his master the events taking place in the region of Sawantwadi. Knowing well the superiority of the combined armies of the Peshwa and Khem Sawant the Portuguese could not flatly deny passage to them. They, however, guarded their frontiers as a precautionary measure. In the war between the Peshwa and Haider Ali, they were caught in a dilemma ; straight denial of passage to the Peshwa was dangerous when his army and navy were in the Sawantwadi region and grant of passage meant drawing upon themselves the wrath of the powerful Haider Ali. Luckily for the Portuguese, at this critical moment

Madhavrao, who was ill at Poona was under the treatment of a Portuguese physician, Fr. Frei Leion de Madre de Deus. Through him the Portuguese ultimately succeeded in getting dropped the demand of the passage to the Peshwa's army via Phonda. The vast army under Visaji Pant Lele was ordered to march against Haider Ali by another route, and the Portuguese were spared a tricky situation. Khem Sawant who was helping the Peshwa, was also in touch with the Portuguese, informing them of the danger from Haider Ali, if they granted passage to the Peshwa via Phonda.

Dom Pedro de Camara succeeded De Mello as the new Governor of Goa on 24 September, 1774, and remained in power till 3 November, 1779. The new Governor was aware of the Portuguese problems well and wanted particularly to maintain peace with the Marathas and Haider Ali Khan. He was also particular in keeping Sawantwadi friendly with the above two powers, because he was aware that any threat to the Wadi territory meant a threat to Goa. In the month of October 1775 he requested Jivaji Vishram to maintain friendly relations with Nawab Haider Ali Khan. The idea behind this move was to keep Goa safe from any troubles from the side of Haider.

In the beginning of 1776, Khem Sawant informed the Portuguese Governor about the heavy attack of Kitturkar Desai (Desai of Kittur) with the help of Haider Ali on the Jamboti territory. Jaitoji Rane of Sakhali, his brother Krishnaji and the Bhimgadkaris also offered help to the Desai of Kittur. Further, Khem informed the Portuguese of the capture of the small kingdoms of Sriramgapatam, Bidnur and Sunda by Haider Ali, who was now planning an attack on Phonda. Khem made it clear that Haider had captured Dharwar and if Supa next fell into his hands it would be dangerous to the Portuguese. He now sought the help of Mahadaji Shinde, who despatched a force of 10,000 soldiers. Khem also sought Portuguese help and requested them to join and arrest Jaitoji's brother, Krishnaji Rane, who had offered help to the Desai of Kittur. This request was made in order to check the nefarious activities of Krishnaji Rane. Actually it is not known what action was taken by the forces of Mahadaji and the Portuguese.

The Tulaji episode

The new Governor Dom Frederico Guilherme de Souza came to Goa in 1779. He concluded a treaty with the Peshwa on 11 January, 1780, by which the latter requested the Portuguese to hand over Tulaji Pawar, one of the culprits responsible for the murder of Peshwa Narayanrao. Narayan was murdered on 30 August, 1773, after which Tulaji who was separated from Raghunathrao Peshwa by the treaty of Purandar, took service with Haider Ali Khan. It is significant to note that the Wadi Darbar was helping this murderer and was trying its level best to send him to Raghobadada. Tulaji's arrival at Dicholi was announced by Jivaji Vishram to the Portuguese Governor. According to the treaty of Purandar, Tulaji Pawar left Raghobadada and thereafter he took service with Haider Ali Khan. Meanwhile Nana Phadnis who had entered into a treaty with Haider Ali Khan, asked him to dismiss Tulaji Pawar from his service. Tulaji was then given shelter by Khem Sawant who requested the Portuguese to send Tulaji aboard their ship to Surat to his master Raghunathrao Peshwa who had then taken protection with the English. Tulaji was to proceed from Surat to Bombay. The Portuguese, however, without paying heed to the request of Khem, handed over Tulaji to the Poona Darbar. It is not known what was the intention of Khem Sawant in requesting the Portuguese to hand over Tulaji to Raghunathrao Peshwa instead of the Poona Darbar with whom he was in good terms. This act of Khem Sawant would have actually brought about a conflict with Poona Darbar, but it seems that the latter over looked Khem's actions as they were in need of his help. In 1786, the Marathas were waging a war with Tipu Sultan. The envoy of the Peshwa, Gopalrao Ramchandra, was at Goa to secure help from the Portuguese. He proposed that the joint forces of Khem Sawant and the Portuguese should attack Tipu. The Portuguese did not offer help as conditions were not favourable to them. Khem, however, allowed the Poona Darbar to pitch their camp at Banda in his territory. The Marathas stationed 10,000 troops at Banda under one Jivaji Gopal. It is not known whether Khem Sawant sent his own forces against Tipu with the Poona army. Khem at this time was at war with the Kolhapur Darbar on the question of Morchal.

Khem-Jivaji differences and the Portuguese

As already noted, when Khem Sawant was a minor, the administration of Sawantwadi was looked after by his mother Janakibai with the help of his secretary Jivaji Vishram Sabnis. When Khem assumed power in 1763, he began to make several changes in administration. He removed his secretary Jivaji Vishram from service and in his place appointed Raghunath Dalvi Bhosale, Sadashiv Narayana Chitnis and Anant Rambhat Aaroskar. Jivaji Vishram was working as the administrator for nearly eight years before Khem came to the gadi. During this period, Jivaji Vishram had established his hold over the Sawantwadi administration which was troublesome to Khem Sawant. To put an end to this situation, Khem removed him and appointed new persons in his place. Jivaji Vishram resented his removal, and leaving Wadi went to Varghat. Later he also sought shelter in Portuguese territory, but they refused to help him. They knew that any help to Jivaji Vishram would naturally bring about a conflict with his master Khem Sawant.

The newly appointed administrators were no match for Jivaji Vishram. Now, disgruntled Jivaji planned an attack on Sawantwadi with the cooperation of his son and the Hewalker Desais. It seems that Jivaji could not execute his plan and the idea of attack had to be given up.

In the beginning of 1764, Jivaji again approached the Portuguese for help and requested them to hand over the fort of Dicholi. He informed them that by doing so, the Bhosales would come to an understanding with them which would be advantageous to them in many ways. But the Portuguese rejected his request. He tried to convince them to take his side in the present conflict with his master. The result of these pressure tactics of Jivaji was that he was taken back into service for nearly one year and half after which he was again removed.

Jivaji Vishram after his second removal from service remained apparently silent for nearly two years. During this period Jijabai of Kolhapur was seeking Portuguese help against the English who had attacked her territory. This was an opportune moment for a seasoned administrator like Jivaji Vishram to regain his position. Finding Jijabai in difficulty he at once attacked the fort of Rangna and took it. Next, he attacked Bhudargad, another important fort belonging to the Kolhapur ruler and requested the Portuguese to help him. The Portuguese, of course, remained neutral. Jivaji Vishram now attacked Mahadevgad and Narayangad belonging to his former master, Khem, and occupied them. He was helped in this venture by his kinsman Krishna Sawant. From these rebellious activities of Jivaji Vishram it seems that it was his intention to create a separate position for himself by occupying important forts both from the territories of Kolhapur and Sawantwadi.

With the loss of the forts of Mahadevgad and Narayangad Khem at once took action. He requested the Portuguese for help and at the same time asked them to assist Jijabai. Jijabai was also to join Khem in restoring the forts from Jivaji Vishram. In 1767, the joint forces of Khem and Jijabai launched an attack on Mahadevgad and Narayangad and reduced them without much difficulty.

The fort of Rangna where Jivaji had now taken shelter, was the target of attack of the joint forces. As this fort was of strategic importance on the border area of Kolhapur and Sawantwadi, Jivaji Vishram tried to play a game by offering the fort to the Peshwa if he could take advantage of this situation. The Peshwa sent his own Karkun to Jivaji but nothing seems to have come of these talks between the Karkun and Jivaji Vishram. At the same time, Jivaji Vishram approached the Portuguese pointing out that if the fort of Rangna fell into the hands of the powerful Peshwa it would be dangerous to all the neighbouring powers including the Portuguese. The Portuguese, however, do not seem to have paid heed to this pressure diplomacy of Jivaji Vishram.

At last, Jijabai of Kolhapur sent her army under the command of Yeshwantrao Shinde, her administrator, on the fort of Rangna. The forces of Khem also joined Yeshwantrao Shinde. The siege of the joint forces continued for two months and a half, after which Jivaji Vishram surrendered Rangna and took shelter at Wadi. In the seige of Rangna, Jivaji lost twenty of his men and about fifty of them were beheaded. Khem took pity on Jivaji Vishram, pardoned him for all his offences and took him back in service. Jivaji Vishram in 1771, decided to leave his master's service as he was not in a position to solve some difficult problems which Sawantwadi was facing. On this occasion, Madhavrao Peshwa offered Jivaji Vishram service at Poona which Jivaji declined. The next year, Jivaji retired to Kerim Pedne but was again persuaded to take up service with Khem by Mahadaji Shinde. Owing to some differences, once again Jivaji Vishram was removed from service by Khem and thereafter he never came back on the political scene of Sawantwadi. However, Khem accepted Jivaji's successors into his administration.

The episode of Jivaji Vishram indicates how difficult it was for his master to remove him from service, though unwanted, because of his high rank and administrative experience. The rival powers around and the strong central power like that of the Peshwa were always eager to welcome in their service disgruntled persons like Jivaji Vishram by granting them political asylum, whom they could always use as a pawn on the political chessboard of the period. As a result, in such internal quarrels as the one just discussed, some kind of compromise between the master and his dissatisfied able servant was often preferred to the latter's removal.

Khem-English conflict and the Portuguese

By 1764, the English had firmly laid the foundation of their dominion in India by their success in the battle of Buxar. They had thrown off their garb as traders and had been actively interfering in the internal affairs of the Indian states for political power. Their expansionist design was very clear and they scarcely allowed any opportunity to slip out of their hands for its fulfilment. Their three important centres of power were Calcutta, Madras and Bombay. The imperial Mughals were a spent force, and the real contest for the hegemony of India was now between the Marathas and the East India Company. The Marathas had considerably restored their power and position in the North under Peshwa Madhavrao I. But when he was engaged in a war with Hyder Ali of Mysore, the

English found an opportunity to expand their power further on the west coast, south of Bombay. Amongst the strategically situated places, the fort of Malwan in the mouth of Bombay under the Chhatrapatis of Kolhapur was important. The English occupied it in 1765, when Madhavrao Peshwa was busy fighting with Hyder Ali. Its occupation by them created alarm all over the Maratha country bringing to light their expansionist objective in India. Madhavrao Peshwa was fully aware of this and had noted the British as enemy number one of the Marathas. But he was not in a position to take immediate action against them because of his pre-occupation elsewhere. Flushed with their success at Malwan, the British squadron under Major Gordon and Captain Watson attacked the fort of Yeshwantgad or Reddi along the coast, on the pretext that the pirates of this region had been endangering their coastal trade. They had easy success at both the places over the naval and land forces of Khem Sawant. The powerful English could easily call the Sawants pirates, though they had been there prior to the advent of the English on the west coast. During this event, Khem's administrator Jivaji Vishram, who was looking after the coastal region found it impossible to take a stand against the English. In order to save the situation he informed the English that the fort belonged to the Portuguese, and at the same time requested the Portuguese to hoi their flag on the fort by sending a handful of soldiers at night. st Meanwhile fearing the English attack, the people of the district of Reddi begged for Portuguese protection and pledged loyalty to Goa. Immediately, Viceroy Ega ordered Terekhol fort to stand firm, and prepared to go to its aid if necessary. However, the English did not meddle with the Portuguese possessions. At last Khem had to settle the matter by a treaty. According to it, Khem agreed to cede the land between the Karli and Salshi rivers, bound on the west by the sea, and on the east by the Sahyadri mountains, on receiving for himself the fort of Reddi. He further agreed to pay Rs. 1,00,000 as war expenses, to allow the British merchants pass freely, to keep no navy, and to help the British in the event of a war with the Marathas.

No sooner was the ink of the treaty dry than Khem Sawant again started his naval attack on the British ships, virtually breaking the treaty. The English, therefore, sent their envoy Mr. Thomas Martin for a talk, a new treaty was signed between the two parties on 24 October, 1766.

Some of the interesting terms of this treaty are that the war expenses, settled at Rs. 2,00,000 would be payable over a period of 13 years (Rs. 80,000 within 3 months) during which the fort of Vengurla was ceded to the British, extendable till the full payment was made. Hostages were to be kept at Bombay at Khem's expense, and the British flag would be hoisted over Vengurla.

Jivaji Vishram now joining hands with the English, planned to invade and conquer the Portuguese territory of Phonda. When the Goa Government was apprised of this secret plan, it planned a counter strategy. The Portuguese encouraged the Desais to rise in revolt against the Bhosáles. When the Pedne Desais revolted the Bhosales out of fear handed over Dicholi and Sakhali to Goa for protection. The Portuguese were able to secure a good income from the provinces of Pedne, Dicholi and Sakhali, without firing a single shot, or using a single soldier in combat.

Four years after signing the treaty, the hostages escaped from Bombay as Khem did not pay the war expenses regularly. (During the six years from the date of the treaty Khem had paid only Rs. 45,000). When the period of 13 years was over Khem requested the Portuguese to send their citizen Vithoji Kamat, the mediator of the former treaty to help him (Khem) get back the fort of Vengurla. Khem also wrote to Vithoji Kamat to work once more as a mediator. But the Portuguese do not seem to have sent Kamat to help Khem Sawant. Khem then requested the British to handover the fort of Vengurla to him as the period of 13 years expired as mentioned in the treaty. The British, however, turned down Khem Sawant's request as he had not fully paid the war expenses agreed to in the treaty. Upon this, Khem attacked Vengurla in 1780, and occupied it. This was a singularly notable victory to the credit of Khem Sawant against an European power. Khem informed the Portuguese about the capture of Vengurla fort. The English officials gave a detailed account of the loss of Vengurla to the English Company. The account shows the state of affairs of the English who were guarding the said territory, and the treatment which they received at the hands of the Bhosales.

Khem was expecting the Portuguese to bring about an understanding between him and the English regarding the handing over of the fort of Vengurla. But the Portuguese remained silent in the fight between the British and Khem.

In 1974, Khem Sawant captured some English ships upon which the latter asked the Portuguese to help them against their common enemy. At this time relations between Khem and the Portuguese were strained as Khem had taken Pedne from them. The Portuguese were preparing to attack Yeshwantgad by sea, but were deterred from doing so when they came to know that Khem was trying to secure help from the Poona Darbar through Jivbadada Kerkar. Thus, the plan of Anglo-Portuguese attack on Khem's territory came to a naught.

Sawant-Kolhapur conflict and the Portuguese

For several years since Khem Sawant ascended the gadi of Sawantwadi, he followed a non-belligerent attitude towards Kolhapur. In 1776, at the height of his power he started fomenting disturbance in Kolhapur. Thus Khem drew upon himself the wrath of the Kolhapur state which attacked the fort of Gandharvagad, forcing Khem to cede one-third of the revenue of Maland and Varad, and pay yearly a fixed sum from Pat and Haveli that is Sawantwadi proper.

The court of Kolhapur was never on friendly terms with Sawant. Kolhapur was a scene of serious domestic uprising due to a new revenue survey carried out by the authorities in 1781. Taking note of these disturbances Khem Sawant laid siege to the fort of Rangna. Khem called upon the Portuguese to join him in view of their close friendship and requested to send four experts in launching Garnaly. He constantly appealed to the Portuguese to consider the siege of Rangna as their own stressing that he had initiated this action not with the hope of getting help from other powers but from the Portuguese alone. He further emphasized that if this help was rendered by the Portuguese it would prove to the world their friendship with the Sawants.

The Kolhapur ruler was also in touch with the Portuguese to secure their help against the besieging force of Khem. There exists considerable correspondence between Kolhapur and the Goa Viceroy in connection with the Rangna siege. The repeated appeals of Khem to the Portuguese for help fell on flat ears. The Portuguese never wanted Khem to be stronger and were determined to see that the fort of Rangna did not fall into his hands. In this affair, they at the beginning made a show of friendship with Khem but in due course joined hands with Kolhapur. The Kolhapur ruler on receiving help from the Portuguese despatched contingents of the Amatya and the Pratinidhi (of Kolhapur). The Viceroy of Goa requested Kolhapur to destroy the navy of Sawantwadi. Khem was helpless to resist them single-handed. His position was critical as he had to face now two powers, Kolhapur and the Portuguese. The net result was that Kolhapur forces defeated Khem's army under the walls of Rangna. The conflict lasted for eight months and at last, Khem having been defeated promised Kolhapur to desist from causing further incursions into their territory.

The Portuguese, who pretended to be friendly at the beginning with Khem Sawant, actually occupied Dicholi and Sakhali belonging to him. The details of this occupation are discussed later.

Khem Sawant who had undertaken to desist from making incursions into Kolhapur territory kept his word. For nearly two years from the Rangna incident, Khem was at war with the Portuguese, but thereafter, he entered into a treaty with them as late as 1788, when he was involved in a conflict with Kolhapur known as 'Morchel War'. At the beginning of 1785, Sultanrao Malap of fort Sindhudurg, wrote to the Governor of Goa requesting friendship of the Portuguese and conveyed his happiness over the Sawant-Portuguese friendship. It is not clear why Sultanrao expressed his happiness over Portuguese-Sawant friendship.

THE MORCHEL WAR

For sometime after the agreement of 1781, Sawantwadi and Kolhapur were at peace with each other. But their relations were completely disturbed in 1785, on account of the grant of Morchel and the dignified title of Raje Bahadur to Khem Sawant by a firman, from the then Mughal Emperor. Technically by the Varna treaty of 1731, the Chhatrapati of Kolhapur was the sovereign lord of Sawantwadi and as such it was his prerogative to have the Morchel. But it came to be conferred on Khem due to his brother-in-law Mahadaji Shinde who was practically the Badshah-maker in Delhi politics. The Imperial firman containing these orders was ceremoniously taken all the way from Delhi to Sawantwadi where, on 11 May, 1785, Khem Sawant duly accepted the firman and the honours. The announcement of this grant was sent to the Peshwas, the Kolhapur Chhatrapati, the Nizam, the Portuguese Governor of Goa, Tipu Sultan and others by the Emperor of Delhi. The Portuguese Governor felicitated Khem Sawant for these honours. Unhappy with this situation, the Kolhapur Darbar lodged a complaint with the Poona Court against Khem for the receipt of Morchels. This affair involved Khem Sawant, the Kolhapur and the Poona Darbars, and the Portuguese, in wars fought intermittently from 1785—1792, known as the Morchel War.

By 1785, the Kolhapur State was hostile to Khem Sawant. A village in the Malwan sub-division had been the bone of contention between the two parties. The grant of firman which Kolhapur viewed seriously added fuel to the fire.

The stand taken by Kolhapur was accepted by Nana Phadnis. He was helpless to take any action on account of the pressures brought on him by Mahadaji Shinde, the protector of Khem Sawant, and he kept putting off matters till the end. Kolhapur was also negotiating with the Portuguese to prevent Khem from using the Morchels. Kolhapur ruler deputed two persons to Goa to secure Portuguese help. They suggested to the Governor of Goa that he should either provide help to Kolhapur or at least remain neutral in the hostilities between Sawantwadi and Kolhapur. The Governor directed them to hold talks with the secretary of State. The Portuguese Secretary asked them as to what their master desired, what were the causes of the war and what help they expected from the Portuguese. The two deputies replied that their master was intending to destroy Khem Sawant, who was insolent and treacherous, that the war had arisen because of the scandalous behaviour of Khem towards their master, and, despite being a vassal of the Raja, he had attacked one of the main forts. Finally they stated that the Portuguese should not favour the Bhosales against Kolhapur and that, if the booty of the conquest was to be shared, the Kolhapur Government would help the Portuguese in sending it to them either by sea or by land. The Portuguese Secretary asked them to produce letters of authority do deal with the negotiations. But the deputies informed him that they had come at the order of their master just to know the stand of the Portuguese. However, they agreed to bring necessary authority from their master to carry negotiations with the Portuguese.

When the news of Kolhapur negotiations with the Portuguese reached Wadi Darbar, Khem asked the Portuguese Governor to fix a day for the talks. Portuguese complied with his request and accordingly Khem deputed his emissaries to hold talks with the Portuguese. They informed the Portuguese about the injustice done to their master by the Kolhapur Raja by waging a war against him. They also explained how he needed the help of the Portuguese and reminded them of the help Khem had offered to the Portuguese when Tipu Sultan's presence on the Ghat threatened Goa territory.

In reply to the emissaries the Portuguese secretary stated that the Raja of Kolhapur wanted to destroy Khem totally and had sought Portuguese neutrality in the matter. However, the Portuguese who had unhappy experience, with Khem in the past, suggested to Khem that the Bhosales should enter into an agreement with the Portuguese before seeking any help. The emissaries urgently agreed.

Meanwhile, Nana Phadnis who had kept putting off matters because of Mahadaji Shinde's pressure, now decided to offer military help to the Kolhapur ruler.

The forces of Kolhapur under Pritirao Chavan and Ratnaker Pant Appa and those of Nana Phadnis led by Hari Pant Phadke, attacked and captured the forts of Here and Gandharvagad, which were previously captured by Venkatrao Gaod Sardesai of Khanapur. Khem Sawant reported to the Portuguese about the capture of Here and Gandharvagad. The joint forces then attacked Prasiddhagad. The Kolhapur Maharaja himself led the expedition on the fort of Prasiddhagad and after his victory there had been to a nearby river for a bath with his *zanana*. After securing success on the fort, the forces descended down the western ghats into Konkan to attack new posts belonging to Khem. Khem Sawant was in a pitious condition because no help came from the Portuguese on whom he was depending. Mahadaji Shinde who was all the time watching the developments in the Sawantwadi region anxiously, seeing the plight of Khem Sawant, despatched his forces under Rajashree Manaji Shindi. Sakubai Shinde mother-in-law of Khem Sawant also appealed to the Portuguese to save Wadi State from further disaster. However, military help from the Shinde's proved of no use to them. Kolhapur forces meanwhile captured the forts of Narsinhgad and Nivty. The Kolhapur ruler was in constant touch with the Portuguese to secure their help and alliance even though he was victorious on all the fronts. Khem Sawant while awaiting Portuguese succour, was also preparing to free some of the forts occupied by the Kolhapur army. He informed the Portuguese that their help would prove highly useful to him at this critical juncture as he had lost all hopes of succour from any other quarters. He requested them to supply 25 barrels of gun-powder, cannon balls, 1500 triggers and also a cash of Rs. 2500. But his appeal for help proved of no use, as the Portuguese wanted Khem first to enter into an agreement with them.

Khem Sawant now sent his forces and some warships to free Bharatgad, but could not succeed. Meanwhile, the Kolhapur forces proceeded to take the fortified post of Vengurla where they established their base. This newly acquired territory, which yielded an annual revenue of Rs. 1,50,000 was hereafter called the *Daruni Mahal* and remained for many years a source of dispute between Kolhapur and Sawantwadi. Kolhapur then laid a siege to the fort of Reddi. Khem Sawant, now in a very critical state, fearing that any aid to Kolhapur from the Portuguese would mean his total destruction, finally appealed to the Portuguese for help and promised to surrender to them the remaining part of the Pedne territory, and wrote to the Portuguese accordingly. This was exactly what the Portuguese wished. They asked him not only to surrender the remaining part of Padne but also to give away his right over Dicholi and Sakhali already in Portuguese possession. Finding the calamitous situation in which Khem was, the Portuguese considered an alliance with him natural and more beneficial than with the Kolhapur State. It was also inconvenient for the Portuguese to invite any of the powers existing on the Ghats to attack Sawantwadi and remove the natural barrier Goa had owing to Khem's existence. The Portuguese always preferred a small ruler like Khem as their neighbour rather than the one like the Raja of Kolhapur, who in the absorption of the Sawantwadi State, was bound to be a more powerful ruler and, therefore, more dangerous to them. The authorities in Goa knew that if they failed to help Khem now they would lose once for all the golden opportunity provided by the Morchel war of getting Pedne, Dicholi and Sakhali. The demands put forth by the Portuguese were promptly accepted by Khem, since his main aim was to secure help and prevent the Portuguese from providing help to the Raja of Kolhapur.

The Portuguese acceded to the request of Khem Sawant and negotiations were carried on by Vedashasrasampanna Rajasri Vasudev Bhat Bava, an envoy of Khem. (Visaji Mahadev, an envoy of the Bhosales who was already in Goa had to leave the place due to the death of his mother). At last, after a negotiated settlement, Khem entered into an agreement with the Portuguese on 29 January, 1788 according to which, Khem Sawant surrendered Pedne to the Portuguese in return for military help.

Portuguese-Sawant attack Kolhapur forces

Following this on 1 February, 1788, the Portuguese troops under Adjutant General and Colonel of the legion of Bardesh Joaquim Vicente Godinho de Mira, with a legion of 800 cavalry, assisted by 300 persons of the Phonda legion under Lieutenant Colonel Manoel Freitas and 900 soldiers commanded by Colonel Rodrigo reached Kolvale. They were accompanied by two companies of cavalry, one regiment of infantry and 8 pieces of artillery. The troops carried with them 50 barrels of gun-powder and a huge quantity of bullets.

On 5 February, 1788, Portuguese-Sawant forces arrived in the vicinity of Vengurla. They attacked the forces of Kolhapur besieging the fort of Reddi. The Portuguese called for naval bombardment against the besieging troops and forced them to give up the siege and to relinquish some of the wayside checkports they had captured and fall back to Malwan. The forces of Kolhapur carried heavy loot from Reddi.

Meanwhile, the Portuguese Governor informed Nana Phadnis through their envoy Narayan Shenvi Dhume, who was at Poona, that Nana should refrain from helping Kolhapur in the present war. He, however, made known to Nana Phadnis that the Portuguese did not wish destruction of Kolhapur. The joint forces of Kolhapur and Nana regrouped at Malwan deciding to attack Sawantwadi itself and caught up with the Sawants' army at Nandos where they inflicted a severe defeat on the Sawants. They further succeeded in making prisoners of some of the prominent chieftains of the Sawants such as, Rajasree Kussoba Sabnis. Usapker Desais, Babay Mana (servant of Khem), Som Sawant Mangaonker and his nephew, Corporal of Sidoba Rao, Paiim Sawant and Parmekar Desai, who for greater security, were despatched to the fort of Malwan. The joint forces of Kolhapur and Nana then decided to attack Akeri. Some of the Portuguese troops at this time were at Malgaon. When news reached about the plan of Kolhapur to attack Akeri, the Vakil of Sawantwadi, Visaji Mahadev, called upon Joaquim Vicente Godinho de Mira, in charge of troops, to come to rescue but he refused as he had no orders. The matter was immediately reported to Goa, and on 7 February upon the orders of Marshal, the Portuguese troops reached Akeri which was hardly a couple of miles from Sawantwadi to defend the territory from Kolhapur attack. But due to strong opposition from the Portuguese and Khem's army who were in full strength, the Kolhapur-Nana forces were compelled to fall back on Malwan. The Portuguese informed the Peshwa Madhavrao that they had kept their forces to prevent Kolhapur from capturing the capital of Sawantwadi which they had planned to attack. They assured him that they would withdraw the forces as soon as Kolhapur did so.

The Kolhapur ruler engaged at the help the Portuguese had given to Khem Sawant sent more reinforcements from their capital. The Portuguese on their part moved extra forces from Goa. They sent their naval forces and brought cannons and ammunitions with the idea of attacking Malwan. Kolhapur Raja now realised that it would be disadvantageous if his forces further attacked the territory of Sawantwadi. Several skirmishes took place between the two opposing forces without a decisive battle.

Kolhapur meanwhile made preparations for the withdrawal of their forces. Kolhapur managed to retain the area of the Daruni Mahal and appointed extra men to the garrison of these posts. The Raja of Kolhapur also requested the Portuguese to hold talks. Khem on hearing this, informed the Portuguese Governor not to trust Kolhapur and not to take back their forces till he was given back his lost territories. At this time fortunately for Kolhapur, Tipu Sultan laid a siege to Hubli, which naturally scared the Portuguese who hastily withdrew their forces. Fortunately Kolhapur also followed suit.

By now Kolhapur seems to have succeeded in exerting sufficient pressure on Khem Sawant to give an assurance at least temporarily, that he would surrender the Morchels to the Poona Council. This they could do by keeping a firm grip over the captured territories and by their readiness to pursue the war. At last an agreement was arrived at between Kolhapur and Sawant, but Khem did not surrender the Morchels to Poona Council as it was a prestigious issue.

Khem Sawant managed to win a respite even though he lost a valuable part of his territory. He made several representations to the Poona Court and also brought pressure on Nana through Mahadaji Shinde. At the instance of Mahadaji Shinde, Nana Phadnis organized peace talks between the representatives of Poona, the Shinde and Kolhapur. Khem also sought the help of the Portuguese in solving the conflict with Kolhapur and informed the Governor about the progress of the talks at Poona. The Portuguese on their part negotiated with the emissaries of Kolhapur and the Bhosales but failed to achieve any success. The only success Khem could obtain was to free his people kept in the fort of Malwan as war prisoners. Thus for the time being the Kolhapur-Sawant conflict came to an end.

In January 1789, the Vakil of Sawantwadi, Visaji Mahadev informed the Portuguese that the forces of Kolhapur numbering 5000, had carried out a heavy attack on Jamboti, destroyed the region and taken away prisoners. In this grave situation the neighbouring chieftain of Jamboti sought the help of Wadi state. Visaji requested the Portuguese to defend Ramghat and Chorlem. It is not known what the result of this attack was, though the loss suffered by the chieftain of Jamboti was heavy.

Nana Phadnis sends expedition against Kolhapur

Khem Sawant had been making repeated representations to Mahadaji Shinde to restore the territory lost to Kolhapur. Mahadaji on his part had kept up constant pressure on Nana Phadnis to acquire these territories by use of force against Kolhapur. The envoy of Khem Sawant who was at Poona, told Nana that his master was displeased with the Portuguese because their help proved of little use to him in restoring the lost territory. Actually it were the Portuguese who benefited by getting part of Pedne. Khem was instigating Nana inwardly to secure his help against Kolhapur.

Nana Phadnis who was pressurized by Mahadaji Shinde had a personal grudge against him and was, therefore, avoiding him. In 1792, Mahadaji personally went to Poona and was successful in pressurizing Nana, who called upon the ruler of Kolhapur to give back the captured territory to Khem Sawant. When Kolhapur failed to accept the request of Nana, he ordered his army to attack Kolhapur and thus forced the Kolhapur ruler to give up the captured territory to Khem Sawant.

The Kolhapur ruler at last came to an agreement for the return of captured territories and accepted Khem's right for the use of Morchels. The Portuguese on their part had deputed Krishnarao Dhume to meet Nana, and even Jivbadada was negotiating with the Poona Council for the settlement of the dispute between Kolhapur and Sawantwadi. All these were successful in their mission. The Peshwa even though unhappy over the title of Rajabahadur given to Khem, allowed him to make use of it and this decision was conveyed to him accordingly. In November 1793, Kolhapur handed over all the forts to Khem Sawant. The amount which Khem had to pay to Kolhapur in lieu was paid by Jivaji Ballal. Khem now decided to offer all the forts to Jivbadada to pay off the debts, but Jivbadada refused to accept them. The Portuguese Governor felicitated Khem when he was informed about the return of forts to him by Kolhapur.

It may be recalled as discussed at the beginning of this Chapter under the heading "Naro Trimbak attack Bhosales Territory Bharatgad, Masura, Vengurla, Kudal, Chedvan, Nivty and Karli", that when Naro Pant had attacked Khem's territory in 1757, the fort of Siddhagad captured by him was still in the hands of the Peshwas. In December 1793, Bhosales attacked the fort which was under the command of Gangadharpant, Subhedar of Vijaydurga. But when Khem was informed that Jivbadada was mediating with Nana Phadnis, he called back his forces attacking the fort. Jivbadada was successful and Nana agreed to return the fort to Khem, on the condition that the amount of Rs. 22,000 spent on the fort should be paid. Khem agreed to pay the amount and the fort was handed over to him by the Peshwas.

Khem Sawant was very happy with Jivaji Ballal due to high favours shown to him, and in recognition of his services he was given the inam in Talegao taraf of Varad village on 2 April, 1794. Khem also bestowed upon Narahar Ganesh Kerkar the inam of village Harambal in Pedne, in recognition of his loyal and faithful services. Narahar Kerkar had helped Khem Sawant by offering him a loan of Rs. 18,000.

The various wars Khem had to fight with his neighbours drained his treasury and he had to borrow money from various sources to run the administration. He even followed irregular methods to secure finance. In about 1795, Khem ordered the arrest of Lakhbadada Lad, a Pagnis in the service of the Shindes demanding Rs. 25,000 for his release. When news reached Jivbadada Kerkar he felt sorry over the steps adopted by Khem Sawant for obtaining money for his treasury. Jivbadada who was highly influential in the Wadi court, pressurized Khem for the release of Lakhbadada and accordingly he was released.

Kolhapur again attack Sawantwadi

The ruler of Kolhapur was keen on the developments taking place in Sawantwadi. Taking note of the situation in which Khem was involved, the Raja of Kolhapur once again attacked the territory of Sawantwadi in the beginning of 1795. The forces of Kolhapur joined by the Portuguese navy and army carried the invasion right upto the residence of Wadi. The joint forces successfully captured the forts of Reddi, Vengurla, Nivty and Banda. Khem Sawant was helpless both in man-power and money, his main protector Mahadaji Shinde being at this time dead. The Portuguese who in the past had prevented other powers coming closer to Goa, were themselves involved in this attack. They described Khem as ungrateful, ambitious and the treacherous and were out to punish him. Calling Khem a 'Small Sardesai' the Portuguese Governor was now of the opinion that he did not need even a company to punish him. The words expressed by the Portuguese Governor in his various letters indicate the anger of the Portuguese towards Khem Sawant. Nana Phadnis who was friendly to the Portuguese was not prepared to disturb it by helping the Sawantwadi ruler. Jivbadada had even lost faith in Nana Phadnis due to the policy he had adopted towards Khem Sawant. He now approached Baloji Pinge, a friend of the Portuguese to bring about a peace treaty between Khem Sawant and the Portuguese, but he was unsuccessful. Kolhapur at this time being engaged in a war at home was required to call back its forces thus saving Sawantwadi from further disaster. For the next two years Kolhapur-Sawantwadi relations remained more or less the same.

Kolhapur-Sawantwadi prepare for an attack on Goa

The rulers of Kolhapur who had more often than not remained unfriendly with the Sawants, now forgetting old enmities decided to join hands with Khem Sawant against the Portuguese. In the early spring of 1797, Shivaje Raje of Kolhapur turned his attention towards Goa with whom he had been allied against Khem Sawant just two years before. Sawantwadi was also planning an offensive against the Portuguese. The Portuguese had, for a long time, failed to pay the annual tribute, that Kolhapur considered its due and had also gone on occupying such posts that had fallen into their hands as a result of their skirmishes with Khem Sawant, the Raja of Sunda and others. These posts, the Kolhapur ruler considered belonged to their vassals because all the territory to the south of Salshi had come under their sovereignty by the treaty of Varna. Soon the troops of Khem and Shivaji numbering 5000 to 7000, pitched their camp at Naseri and Mangaon.

The Raja of Kolhapur selected Pant Amatya and Pritirao Chavan as the two commandants to help Khem in the Goa expedition. Portuguese on their part acting on information from one Bhikaji Dhume took strong measures against any intrusion by the Kolhapur and Sawantwadi forces. Meanwhile Shivaji Raje on getting information about the Patwardhan Ichalkaranji plan to attack Kolhapur, cancelled the expedition on Goa. Six months later, Shivaji despatched his forces to aid the Bhosales, against their offensive of Goa. The Bhosale-Kolhapur force attacked Ghandarvagad and Kalanidhigad. It seems that the Portuguese at this time through Nana persuaded Shivaji to keep away from helping Khem Sawants militarily. Nana Phadnis deputed Moro Baburao and Vasudev Govind to persuade the Kolhapur ruler to bring back his forces, and he acted accordingly. The invasion of Goa never gained momentum except at the border places. The Portuguese then carried on negotiations with Kolhapur for a treaty, but the terms put forth by Kolhapur were never implemented by the Portuguese.

It is worth noting that the three powers, the Portuguese, Sawants and the Kolhapur, whose borders touched each others territory waged wars against each other in which all possible combinations have taken place. This often happens in disputes over borders where three or four powers are involved.

Jivbadada's death and the Portuguese-Kolhapur attack on Sawantwadi

Jivbadada Kerkar died on 6 January, 1796. With his death whatever support Khem had after Mahadaji Shinde totally disappeared. Shivaji of Kolhapur who had joined hands with Khem just a year back against the Portuguese had now become their ally. In October 1798, the joint forces of Kolhapur and the Portuguese attacked Sawantwadi. They created havoc in Khem's territory. Khem deputed his army under Chandra Farzad who encountered Kolhapur's forces at Avalegaon and inflicted a heavy defeat on them on 25 October, 1798. Chandra fought valiantly and was appointed a permanent Sardar of Khem.

Relations with the Portuguese

Khem Sawant did not remain friendly with the Portuguese as expected by them in the beginning. In 1763, the Marathas having captured a Portuguese vessel coming from Macau, the Viceroy requested the King of Sunda and Khem Sawant to assist him in punishing the Marathas. The King of Sunda promised to send 10,000 men but sought the neutrality of the Bhosales. However, the Portuguese failed to punish the Marathas and the ship remained in Maratha custody.

The Bhosales permitted the Portuguese in 1765, to construct a church in their dominion agreed to by the treaty of 1761. His Majesty, the King of Portugal, though pleased with this, cautioned the Viceroy of Goa, to take care that the church allowed by the Bhosales to be constructed in their dominion was not subjected to any insults nor dishonoured in any way.

In 1767, Khem Sawant requested Jaitoji Rane of Sakhali for help in an attack on Portuguese territory. But Jaitoji was not willing to help Khem and informed the Portuguese commander accordingly, requesting them to protect the interest of the Ranes in the event of signing any agreement with the Bhosales. As Khem failed to secure any help from Jaitoji Rane, the attack was given up.

In 1773, one important incident took place in Sawantwadi. Khem Sawant who had been without a son for the last 10 years that is since his marriage in 1763, was now blessed with a son in April 1773. The news of the birth of a boy to Queen Laxmibai was communicated to the Portuguese Governor. The Portuguese conveyed Khem Sawant their happiness over the news and wished his son long life.

As already noted, a treaty was concluded by the Portuguese with the Bhosales on 14 October, 1768. By this treaty, the three provinces of Pedne, Dicholi and Sakhali, were ceded to the Bhosales, on the condition that all past dues to Goa were paid up and that their rents were collected for the Bhosales by Goan rent-receivers. This was done with a view to control the provinces and keep a watchful eye on their political activities. From 1768 to 1773, there were no open hostilities between the two states.

The humiliating clauses of the 1768 treaty, kept the Bhosales restive. In 1773, the Bhosales requested the Portuguese to hand over Terekhol fort, Mahem village, and also for full control of Pedne and Dicholi. In view of this demand, the Portuguese Governor cautioned the king of Portugal that Terekhol guarded the Kolvalle river from the Bhosales piratical attacks, while Pedne and Dicholi were good buffers in the event of an attack. He further stated that the twice-ceded Mahem was no more than a just compensation for the defence expenditure imposed on Goa by the Bhosales. It is to be noted that the Portuguese had entrusted the work of collecting rent from the above provinces to the Desais. In 1773, the two Desais who were rent-receivers for the province of Pedne, revolted against Khem Sawant, because they were tortured by him. The Portuguese added fuel to fire by supporting the revolters. Open hostilities took place at Gorgao and Vaidongar Heights in Pedne. In the beginning the Bhosales were successful, but later when Portuguese troops openly appeared on the scene Khem's forces retired.

On 10 January, 1774, Dom Joao Jose de Mello died, and Filippe de Valadares Souto Maior succeeded him by Patent of succession. He looked after the administration of Goa till the arrival of a new Viceroy. In September 1774, Dom Jose

Pedro de Camara came to Goa as Governor and Captain-General. The title of Viceroy had now become absolute, and henceforth Camara and his successors were appointed with the title of Captain-General of India.

The new Governor-General acting on the advice of the King of Portugal tried to abstain from the conflicts either with the Marathas or the Sawants. The Portuguese tried to secure by way of friendship and not by war whatever they wanted. This being the proper time for Khem Sawant, a negotiated settlement between the two Powers was worked out in 1774.

The earlier treaties of 1712, 1754, 1759 and 1771, were ratified by this treaty of 1774. The Bhosales agreed to build a church at the site where Christian population existed and also permitted the missionaries to practice their religion. They also undertook to return run-away Negroes, soldiers and captives. The Bhosales also agreed to discontinue piracy, the main cause of all troubles, and not to construct big ships without obtaining permission in advance. They exempted the ships of the Portuguese and their vassals from paying duties whenever their ships touched their ports. The Desais were permitted to enjoy their 'Desaites'. The village Ussagaon was given to the Portuguese to garrison its troops. Both the states promised aid in times of need.

The terms of the treaty were of some advantage to Khem and in view of this treaty of friendship, the Portuguese remitted to the Bhosales the contribution of four thousand xerafins annually which he owed to the Portuguese. Khem had agreed to pay 1000 xerafins if he failed to provide 2 Arab horses as decided before. This payment was not cancelled. The treaty was more beneficial to Khem economically.

Khem's campaign against the Ranes of Sakhali

Khem Sawant at the end of 1778, started armed action against the Ranes of Sakhali. It is probable that the Wadi ruler intended to install fear in the Ranes who were growing strong and harassing the Bhosales by raids into their territory. But the Bhosales were strong enough to repell their attacks. Fearing Khem's armed action the Ranes took shelter in the Province of Hemadbarshen belonging to the Portuguese. They appealed to the Portuguese to come to their rescue. But the Portuguese did not do so openly as they were not willing to disturb existing relation with Khem. However, they secretly favoured the guerilla movements of the Ranes. Khem on receipt of the news that Jaitoji Rane had sought Portuguese help, ordered temporary suspension of operations against them. Khem Sawant had planned total destruction of the Ranes. He was also joined by the petty Desais near Sawantwadi. Some members of the Rane family had raised their banner against their own brothers. Among them Umaji Rane, was actively helping Khem against his own kinsmen. Jaitoji Rane faced with this calamitous situation again appealed to the Portuguese to provide him with ammunition and forces without which he was not in a position to defend himself. Jaitoji reminded the Portuguese of the help he had received in the past from them when the Ranes were attacked by the Bhosales. Meanwhile the Bhosales destroyed the *vatans* of the Ranes impoverishing them. The appeal of Jaitoji had no effect on the Portuguese. Lack of help from the Portuguese prevented the Ranes from retaliating against Khem. At this time Jaitoji with his family was at Satardem. Though the Portuguese did not provide any help openly to Jaitoji against Khem, they helped Jivba Rane and Suryaji Rane who were friends of the Bhosales. Jaitoji knew that the feud in the Rane family would be beneficial to the Bhosales. Jaitoji requested the Portuguese for the protection of his family. They at last intervened and mediated, bringing to an end Khem's action against Jaitoji and others who supported him. Khem Sawant succeeded in installing fear in the minds of the Ranes and also kept the Portuguese from providing succour to them.

Portuguese attack Khem's territory

Dom Federico Guilhermo de Souza succeeded Camara as the new Governor-General of Goa. The arrival of the new Governor was welcomed by the Wadi ruler. Khem requested the new Governor that he should maintain friendship with him and submitted a proposal to him. The proposal is in the form of a letter, a summary of which follows :

Khem Sawant informed the new Governor that due to the injustice done to him in the treaty he has signed at the time of Dom Joao Jose De Mello in 1768, lapses occurred from him in complying with the terms of the treaty. The Sawantwadi state could not cope with the expenses, as the villages, paddyfields and the fortresses remained with the Portuguese and as the Portuguese continued to get the income, he further asked the Portuguese to return back whatever had been taken by them and keep them as neighbours under the orders of the Portuguese State. Khem Sawant also made it clear to them that if everything was returned to him he would be ready to sign a new treaty, which would be a permanent one. He further stressed that he would allow the Desais to continue with their ancient grants, and would also pay annual sum of money to the Portuguese, and that the merchants would be compensated for the property that was stolen from them.

Khem Sawant had to incur the hostility of the English because he was under the protection of the Portuguese. The Portuguese, however, alleged that he was an ally of the English. Khem pointed out that this was not correct and that his position should be clarified. He would be at a loss if the Portuguese let him down by calling him an ally of the English. Actually no document is available, wherein the Portuguese called Khem Sawant an ally of the English.

The Portuguese after considering the proposal of Khem Sawant replied that the former Governor and Captain-General Dom. Joao Jose de Mello, had acted with justice in connection with the peace treaty of 14 October, 1768. It was duly signed by Khem Sawant's representatives duly empowered, so the question of injustice did not arise at all. To justify the action of Joao Jose de Mello, the Portuguese cited various conventions, agreements, etc., according to which once the party agreed to abide by them it could not state afterwards that injustice was done to it. Khem's complaint that injustice was done to him by the treaty of 1768, was actually an after thought and an excuse by which he intended to break the treaty.

In the Khem-English conflict of 1780, the Portuguese remained neutral. They brought to the notice of Khem Sawant that they could not help him against the English as they were at peace with Great Britain. The English did not attack Khem when he took Vengurla from them.

In December 1780, the Desai of Pedne informed the Portuguese that the Bhosales were mobilizing their forces, and Vithal Vishram with about ten to twelve cavalry men and nearly hundred infantry men had arrived at Wadi from Varghat. He was received by Raje Khem Sawant and other high dignitaries of Wadi. The Bhosales were probably planning an attack on Kolhapur. In June 1781 Khem laid siege to the fort of Rangna. The details of this attack are discussed under the heading "Sawant-Kolhapur conflict and the Portuguese". Seeing that the Sawantwadi ruler was involved in a conflict with Kolhapur on Rangna fort, the Portuguese began concentrating their forces for an attack on Khem's territory. The Portuguese Governor was actually waiting for the opportunity to strike Khem who had for several years failed to pay to the Portuguese Crown his annual tribute of 4000 xerafins. The Bholsales had also made continual piratical attacks on the Portuguese merchant vessels and had usurped the rent of the Desais, vassals of the king of Portugal.

Actually in leading an attack on the fort of Rangna, Khem had relied more on Portuguese support and had asked from them gun-powder and ammunition. But the Governor was cunning. He knew that if he had provided succour to Khem he would have lost the opportunity of striking on Khem's territory. The Governor General immediately sent forces under Yerik Carlos, Yerik and the Portuguese troops attacked the fort of Dicholi. After several skirmishes the Portuguese successfully captured the fort from Khem's forces. The conflict between the two states brought much loss and misery to the people, and they requested the Portuguese to end the war. But the Governor who had determined to carry on the war ordered his troops to march to Sakhali. The Portuguese troops laid siege to the fort of Sakhali which was near the temple of Vithoba. The siege continued for nearly 14 days as the soldiers in the fort defended the fort very bravely. But further defence was not possible as the Portuguese began to attack vigorously, and the fort was ultimately surrendered to them.

In this action, the Ranes Kustoba and Jaitoba helped the Portuguese and provided them with all facilities against Khem. The Ranes were waiting for an opportunity for revenge on Khem who had taken armed action against them previously. The Ranes once again demonstrated their superior skill in guerilla warfare and earned Portuguese friendship. Once the territories of Dicholi and Sakhali came to be occupied by the Portuguese, the Governor General issued an ordinance granting freedom to the population to carry on their life according to their old customs.

Bhosales attack Dicholi and Sakhali

The Portuguese inflicted a crushing defeat on Khem. Khem Sawant now decided to secure the lost territories by way of negotiation and deputed his envoy to Goa to hold talks with the Governor General. But the Portuguese were not willing to surrender Dicholi and Sakhali to the Bhosales pointing out to them their failure to pay tribute from 1774, and their piratical attacks on the merchantships of the Portuguese. They further communicated that the matter of surrendering Dicholi and Sakhali to the Bhosales had been referred to the King of Portugal and a reply was awaited. This was just a time-killing device of the Portuguese. The envoy of the Sawants had to leave Goa without any hope of getting back the lost provinces.

Khem Sawant now saw the necessity of capturing the lost provinces by force. He realized that the Portuguese had deceived him and captured Dicholi and Sakhali. Actually the Governor General had promised Khem when his forces had attacked Rangna, that the Portuguese would come to help him, but instead of providing succour, the Portuguese troops attacked and captured the two provinces. Once the motive of the Portuguese was clear, Khem ordered concentration of troops at Wadi and Maneri. The movements of Khem's forces were made known to the Portuguese commandants of Dicholi and Sakhali by one Suryarao Desai of Pedne. The Ranes of Sakhali were also in constant touch with the

Portuguese to secure their help as they feared that Khem would retaliate against them because of the help they had rendered to the Portuguese in the Dicholi and Sakhali campaigns.

Thus, after making necessary preparations the troops of the Bhosales numbering one thousand attacked Gululem on 1 October, 1782. The attack was successful. It was the beginning of the Portuguese-Sawant conflict for Dicholi and Sakhali. The troops of the Bhosales then attacked Maneri, Mencurem, Sal and Dumacem. There were several skirmishes resulting in the victory of the Bhosales. The Bhosales then attacked a batch of the Portuguese troops at Mulgaon and also a detachment of their cavalry, in which the Portuguese lost seven soldiers and five horses. The Bhosales dislodged the boundary garrison of the Portuguese, conquering the entire company off the walls of Bardesh, and the border of the river (Mandavi) that separated the Island of Goa. The Bhosales caused considerable loss to the settlements in the cultivation of kharif and rabi crops. The Portuguese had to grant exemption in the payment of *foros* for the Gaonkars. They appointed Justice Feliciano Ram Nobre Mourao, Intendant General of the new conquests of Dicholi who drew up a plan showing the losses suffered by the Portuguese.

The campaign of Dicholi was a great success to the credit of Khem Sawant. He then turned his attention on Sakhali. The troops of the Bhosales attacks on the fort of Sakhali on 16 November. The Portuguese opposed the Bhosales and attacked the trench of Morgim, with the idea of diverting the attention of the Bhosales. A body of select and well disciplined Portuguese troops passing through the river Chapora dislodged the Bhosales. The Marshal of the troops then ordered to keep ready 40 longish and straight African boats for the passage of troops. The boats were protected by artillery. In order to forestall Bhosales advance and to secure back the lost places, the Portuguese took defensive measures. Lieutenant Colonel Joao Baptista Viera Godinho was entrusted with the work of planting artillery pieces on the enemy border. The launching boats were under the command of Lieutenant of artillery Euginio Rodrigues, assisted by Manoel Lopez. The longish and African boats carried 400 soldiers in which there were some corporals whose names are recorded as Joao Ignacio, Joao Marcell, Jose Vaz and Vishvambar Shenvi. There were also 150 grenadiers of the 1st and 3rd regiment commanded by Major Manoel Antonio Diniz de Ayalla, with the captain of grenadiers Jose Nunes de Silva and the Lieutenant Manoel Joaquim Sarmento, Agostinho Jose de Mota and Joaquim Paes Raboxo. The Marshal under orders of Jose Tristao Vaz da Viega Cabral was assisted by his brother.

With hue and cry the Portuguese troops attacked the Bhosales who had camped in the fort. The attack was resisted by the Bhosales in the beginning but later they retreated. The troops of the Bhosales plundered and burnt several villages. In the face of the Portuguese artillery the Bhosale's action proved ineffective and their troops began to flee for life. Portuguese lost three soldiers and two naval persons in the ambush, and one grenadier was hit by a bullet in the neck, and two others were seriously wounded. On the side of the Bhosales, thirty soldiers died and their commander succumbed to the injuries.

To restore the Provinces lost to the Bhosales, the Portuguese troops were sent under General Henrique Carlos. The strength of the Bhosales' forces was 5000 infantry and 300 cavalry. On 6 December 1782, the Portuguese troops numbering 2400, attacked Dicholi fort which was garrisoned by eighty infantry men and 220 grenadiers. There was not much resistance from the Bhosales as the attack was very heavy, and the Portuguese troops occupied the fort without much difficulty. Next, the Portuguese troops under Adjutant General Joaquim Vicente Godinho de Mira with Sergeant Major Manoel Antonio Diniz de Ayalla were sent, for an attack. The light infantry was commanded by Colonel Antinio de Assa Castel Branco with Lieutenant Colonel Manoel Godinho de Mira. Two companies from Bardesh and Salsete were also despatched. They were commanded by second Lieutenant Venture Manoel de Carvalho and Sergeant Major Rodrigo respectively. They carried a large quantity of ammunitions with them.

Khem Sawant who had lost Dicholi but still held Sakhali, in order to retain it, thought it necessary to end the conflict. Meanwhile, at 10 o'clock in the night, the Portuguese Brigadier received from the camp of the Bhosales a letter from Vithal Vishram (brother of celebrated Jivba) informing them of the death of his wife and further stated that a Maratha General Manaji Phadke had joined them with 1000 infantry and 150 cavalry. By informing this, Vithal Vishram tried to create panic among the Portuguese soldiers who were certainly afraid of Marathas joining Khem's forces. But the Portuguese paid little heed to the letter of Vithal Vishram and continued the war. The Portuguese troops then laid siege to the fort of Sakhali. The siege continued for nearly 25 days and at last Portuguese troops entered the fort. It is significant to note that the *killedar* of the fort was a Portuguese Lieutenant by name Antonio Barbosa. Bhosales suffered heavily in the said attack, and according to the Portuguese sources the evaluation of the dead soldiers was difficult. The Portuguese captured from the Bhosales 62 arms, 25 digo, and 8 swords of the corporals, much provisions and ammunitions. The loss on the side of the Portuguese was very light ; the Portuguese lost one grenadier of the 2nd regiment who was hit by a bullet on the head. Two corporals also died in the siege. Besides, Lieutenant of the light infantry Joao Caetano Gerlego lost his left hand, and nearly 22 soldiers were wounded.

On 8 December, 1782, the Marshall of the troops proceeded from Dicholi to St. Stephen and reached Panjim on 9th where the Governor received him with the demonstration and civility.

Khem Sawant though failed to achieve victory over the Portuguese, was yet determined to continue the war. He made use of his good offices to secure money and persons and was certain that his mother-in-law, brother-in-law and the Desais of Hevale would come to help him. But his hopes were dashed to the ground, and he failed to secure any help against the Portuguese.

Next, the Portuguese preparations for an attack on the Bhosales territory of Pedne where they had stationed a force of 2000 strong. In old Alorna the Bhosale forces were under the command of Ram Shet Sirsat and Raghu Shet Sirsat who were in the esteem of the Bhosales. In a mountain fort, immediately named as New Alorna, Bhosales forces were under the command of Hanumant Sawant with 150 Pednekars and some Portuguese soldiers who had deserted to Khem. Shivaji Londe was in charge of the fort Avaro with eighty soldiers, while Apaji Rane garrisoned the fort of Maneri. By these arrangements Khem Sawant had kept his forces well defended. The Portuguese army consisted of 1700 soldiers. The artillery consisted of six calibres, two howitzers of the same calibre, four excellent carriages with a competent equipment and firearms respectively of 200 shots for each gun. The Portuguese also carried cannons of high quality.

On 21 March 1783, nearly 1000 soldiers who were in the service of the Desai of Kittur joined Portuguese troops. They were under the command of a artillery man Estique, an Italian. Thus having made the plan for an attack, the Portuguese troops dashed on Pedne. There was heavy fighting and the Portuguese succeeded in making much advance in the Pedne territory.

On 2 April, day of St. Francisco of Paul, the Portuguese troops attacked the old fort of Alorna. The attack was led by Lieutenant Colonel Manoel Godinho de Mira, assisted by Adjutant General Joaquim Vicente Godinho de Mira and Colonel Antonio de Assa. The Portuguese troops carried heavy bombardment and successfully captured the fort. Their next target was the fort of New Alorna. The Marshal ordered the old fort of Alorna to be garrisoned with 200 soldiers of light infantry, and the new fort was demolished. In the Pedne attack the Portuguese burnt several villages like Orddem, Contuale, Talorna, Usuri, Tuem, etc. Some of the temples were also hit by the Portuguese attack. Khem Sawant now feared that the Portuguese who had almost occupied half of Pedne would capture the entire province. Portuguese too were afraid of the Peshwa joining hands with Khem. Meanwhile Khem sued for peace which was accepted by the Portuguese Governor, and accordingly he ordered a ceasefire, but did not surrender the captured places.

The gaonkars from the places of Alorna, Ibrahimpur and some other villages who were victims of the Portuguese attack rendered oath of vassalage to His Majesty the King of the Portugal. The Portuguese Governor-General took various measures for strengthening the provinces captured by his forces.

Khem Sawant who had lost militarily with the Portuguese, now started diplomatic moves to get back the lost provinces. He also sought the help of the Peshwa in this matter through Mahadaji Shinde. Accordingly, in May 1783, Khem deputed his envoy to meet the Governor. The Peshwa also sent his envoy Govind Laxman to bring about peace between the Portuguese and the Sawant. But the envoys of both the sides failed to reach any settlement, however the Governor informed them that he would act on the advice of the Home Government, and the envoy of Khem left Goa. Khem wrote to the King of Portugal requesting for the return of the territories of Dicholi, Sakhali and a portion of Pedne.

Meanwhile, the envoy of the Peshwa, Govind Laxman, who was in the Portuguese jurisdiction suddenly died in August 1784. His death brought about a severe setback to Khem who was hopeful of Peshwa's mediation. But the Portuguese were happy over his death and the Governor of Goa informed the Home Government accordingly. The death of Govind brought to an end the negotiations Peshwa had with the Portuguese. Immediately the King of Portugal issued order whereby the captured provinces were joined to the Goa territory. The cherished desire of the Portuguese authorities was then fulfilled.

Khem Sawant though discouraged with the above developments did not lose hope entirely, as he was still confident of the Peshwa's help. In March 1785, the Governor of Goa wrote to the King that the Peshwa was still backing Khem Sawant, and that Tipu Sultan's attack on Goa was not completely ruled out. Considering this, the plan of capturing the remaining part of Pedne was kept in abeyance for some time. Further steps to get back the part of Pedne was to be taken at the appropriate time. The Governor at last got a proper opportunity to secure the part of Pedne without the use of force. On 12 May, 1785, the emperor of Delhi bestowed on Khem the title of Raja Bahadur and the privilege of using the morchels. This distinction gave rise to so much jealousy between Khem Sawant and Kolhapur, that the Raja of Kolhapur threatened Sawantwadi with destruction. The details leading to this war have already been discussed under 'Morchel War.' The Portuguese Governor was pleased with the honours Khem had received from the Delhi Emperor. But he did not fail to exploit the conflict to his own advantage. By lending support to Khem Sawant, the Governor forced him to surrender to him the remaining part of Pedne. Thus by 1788, the Portuguese became masters of the provinces of Dicholi, Sakhali and Pedne.

Once the conflict with the king of Kolhapur came to an end, Khem Sawant made repeated representations to get back the lost provinces which were viable both from an economic and defence point of view, Khem also sought the intervention of Nana Phadnis to free his provinces from the Portuguese control, and the latter sent his envoys to Goa to negotiate matters with the Portuguese. In 1795, Jivbadada Kerkar who was friendly with Khem, offered two lakhs to the Portuguese for the return of the said provinces to Khem. But all the efforts from Nana, Khem and even Jivbadada could make no effect on the Portuguese, and the Governor firmly refused to return the provinces to Khem.

Khem attacks Pedne

In 1792, due to scanty rainfall there was scarcity of grains and prices began to soar. Under this state of affairs the army of the Bhosales established posts on the borders of Pedne and began to govern the area. It is probable that their aim was to get loot from Pedne. The Portuguese were afraid that the Peshwa might join Khem, and to avoid the danger they deputed Bahugun Kamat Wagh to meet the Peshwa. Deoba Sinai also assisted the Portuguese, but Jivbadada strongly objected to his move and sent succour to Khem through the Peshwa. The Portuguese desired that Khem should accept payment from them and once for all give away his right over the Pedne territory. Mahadaji Shinde who had been a great supporter of Khem Sawant, died on 12 February, 1794. This was naturally an irreparable loss to Khem Sawant.

Khem now decided on his own to secure the territory of Pedne and negotiated with the Portuguese to restore it. As no settlement could be reached the troops of the Bhosales under the command of Som Sawant and Santo Ram Akerkar attacked Pedne fomenting a rebellion. The rebellion was successful and Pedne was occupied by the Bhosales. Portuguese now in order to distract the attention of Khem's forces, brought some ships for an attack on Reddi. Khem too alerted his navy, but the idea of attack was given up by the Portuguese. However, the Portuguese ordered that the ships of the Bhosales anchored under the protection of the fortress of Reddi be blockaded. The troops of the Bhosales then assaulted Bardesh but they were repelled by the Portuguese. Khem inflicted much damage to the Ranes who had allied with the Portuguese and also killed many of the Portuguese soldiers and imprisoned some. Som Sawant succeeded in arresting Satroji Rane and took him to Wadi.

Attack on Phonda

In September 1794, Khem attacked Phonda. There was heavy fighting between the Bhosales and the Portuguese, and the Bhosales compelled the Portuguese to retreat. Ultimately Phonda fell into the hands of Khem Sawant. Now the Portuguese infantry numbering 2000, and a naval force under Candido Jose de Mourao assisted by sergeant of artillery Mor Antonio Rodrigo Ferreiro, attacked Phonda in the beginning of 1795. The naval force of the Bhosales attacked them from the river Durbhat. But the Portuguese resistance being too strong could not be met adequately by the Sawants. Bhosale forces scattered in different directions. The Portuguese made it difficult for the Bhosale's army to gather together. Many soldiers including some officers died in the action and once again the Portuguese conquered Phonda.

Francisco Antonio da Viega Cabral succeeded Menezes as the new Governor-General of Goa. Khem sought his help in establishing friendship. But the new Governor was displeased over Khem's relation with the previous Governor. At last after some years of respite the Governor attacked the territory of the Bhosales. The neighbouring chieftain of Khanapur also suffered due to the hostility Portuguese had with Khem. He appealed to the Portuguese for peace. The attack of the Portuguese was concentrated on Maneri and Ibrahimpur from the fort of Alorna. Shivaji Raje of Kolhapur also promised help to the Portuguese but his help was not necessary as the

Portuguese considered Sawantwadi as a small kingdom. However, they informed Shivaji Raje that Kolhapur should secure back whatever Khem had taken from Kolhapur. The Portuguese attack was heavy and the defeat of Khem was inevitable. The Bhosales began to retreat. One of the principal *commandant* of the Bhosales cavalry was seriously hurt while some cavalrymen were wounded later succumbing to injuries. Under this critical situation, the Bhosale's troops began to flee and the Portuguese inflicted punishment on the Bhosales. The Portuguese though they could not benefit much territorially, caused much loss to the Bhosales.

Portuguese attack Pedne

Pedne remained a bone of contention between the Portuguese and Khem. With the death of Nana Phadnis on 13 February, 1800, the Portuguese decided to attack Pedne. The Portuguese Governor, desirous of regaining the lost province which was kept in a constant state of disturbance by the Bhosales, ordered Colonel Joaquim Vicente Godinho de Mira to send his Sergeant-Major, Jose Callado to attack Pedne. There were several skirmishes between the two forces. The Bhosale's forces at this time gathered near the temple of Rawalnath. The Portuguese in their action captured some of the persons of esteem of Khem. They were three corporals, Ram Sawant Bhosale, Dhondo Govind Farzand and Bhagwant Sawant. The Portuguese transported them to Fort Aguada and treated them with all courtesy. The troops of the Bhosales then surrendered Pedne to the Portuguese, and Pedne was once again added to the Portuguese dominion. All the Desais of Pedne then took oath of allegiance to the Portuguese.

The Bhosales made several representations to the Portuguese for the repatriation of their prisoners. Khem was also interested in signing peace agreement with the Portuguese. The Portuguese on their part requested Khem to send an able envoy to adjust peace settlement, and also asked him to send the proposals. The Governor also sought from Khem the payment for the losses the Portuguese had suffered when he had attacked Portuguese territory in 1794, and also asked him to restore cannon balls taken by his forces. Actually, the Portuguese wanted a 'solid and permanent' peace with the Bhosales. Khem was also eager to sign it and deputed his envoy Zaitoji Mohite, who was received at Goa with all courtesy. He was accommodated in Panjim. The Bhosales forgetting the past, began negotiations with the Portuguese but they could not come to a lasting settlement as the Portuguese failed to accept Khem's line of argument. Khem again renewed his desire for friendship with the Portuguese. But all his attempts were turned down. The Portuguese neither entered into agreement with him nor released prisoners who were actually kept as hostages, so that Khem should bow down and enter into a treaty with them. Shortly, thereafter, Khem Sawant died on 6 October, 1803, at the age of 54. He had no male heir. As recorded before, a son was born to him in 1773. But it seems that he did not survive as he is not referred to in the published or unpublished records. The Desai of Pedne, Govindaji Jaswantrao wrote to the Portuguese Secretary of State informing him about the death of Khem Sawant Bhosale. He requested therein that if he be pleased, he should order the Colonel of Pedne for sending clothes of mourning to the relatives of the bereaved as it was the custom. On getting the same, Govindaji would despatch the said mourning clothes.

Khem Sawant had deep interest in education and made magnificent grants of land to temples and learned persons. Khem gave inam lands to the temples of Raeerakhumaee and those at Parule and Malgaon, which are continued to this day. Amongst the inams which were enjoyed till 1911, and a few years thereafter, half were given by Khem. In 1799, Khem laid the foundation stone of the temple of Shri Atmeshwar. It is said that once a saintly person by name Atmaramhava Ramdas while returning from his pilgrimage to Kashi brought him a Shiva Linga for installation in Sawantwadi. When he was at Valavali God Shanker appeared in his dream telling him that "I am in the house of a person where my body is burning due to chilly powder. Please rescue me and install me properly". The next day the saint approached the concerned person and to his surprise found that he was using the (Shiva Linga) stone for crushing chillies. He brought it from him (Bana Linga) and informed Khem Sawant about the whole story. Khem then built a temple today known as Atmeshwar. The Linga rescued by the saint was also installed in a temple built nearby, named as Praneshwar. All religious ceremonies of the temples are performed out of the income received from the land granted by Khem.

Khem was a person of learning. Poets and Pandits used to come from far off places to Khem's court because of his love of learning and the liberal grants which he offered. In 1780, one Gopal Kundavozul, a poet from Andhra Pradesh came to Sawantwadi. He wrote a work called *Samanta Vijaya* in Sanskrit at the instance of Khem Sawant. It has six cantos and 347 stanzas. It states that the ancestor of Khem came from the north. The founder of his dynasty in Sawantwadi was *Mangalik* or *Mang* who is a historically known person. The whole work is a panegyric describing the exploits of Mang and his successors up to Khem and therefore has little historical value. It was later rendered into Prakrita by Narsinha Sankhwalkar, running into 907 verses.

The famous saint Sohirobanath Ambe lived during the reign of Khem. He was born in 1714, at Palaye in Pedne. He wrote Akshayabodha, Mahadanubhaveshvari, Purnakhsari, Advasananda and Siddhantasanhita and a number of songs. Mahadaji Shinde built a *Math* at Ujjain in honour of Saint Ambe. In 1792, the saint left the Math secretly and was never seen thereafter.

Around this time, another saint belonging to the Kudaldeshastha Gaud Sarasawat Brahmin community came into prominence; he was born at Parule. He was a famous Kirtankar. It is said that he used to perform many miracles, and due to his blessings a 90 years old woman gave birth to a son at the village Baon. He died in 1840.

Khem Sawant was one of the most successful rulers of the Sawants of Wadi. The year of his death 1803, is very critical in the Modern History of India because, around this time a number of important powerful Maratha states like the Peshwas, the Shindes and the Bhosales of Nagpur, had entered into subsidiary alliances with the expanding British power. Khem's kingdom escaped the calamity because it was situated too far to the south, away from the scene of political activity. However, after his death the internal quarrels of his family gave an opportunity to the British to grab his kingdom finally in 1818. To the credit of Khem it may be said that he took Vengurla from the British by defeating them in 1780.

PORTUGUESE DOCUMENTS

No. 1

HAG :* MONCOES dO REINO, No. 69-70, 1671-1707, Fls. 42-42 v.

Your Majesty,

The excesses, thefts and tyranical acts committed by the rebel Khem Sawant have rendered him powerful and most feared by the Indian Princes, his neighbours. He tried similar excesses, thefts and tyranical acts in this State and was quite successful. He entered Bardesh through various places, using for this purpose his galleys, and made landings on the shores of the same part of territory. Nonetheless, at the time of his last attempt of attack, forewarned as we were, he had to withdraw with a loss and we managed to capture two of his galleys, some ammunitions and arms. Later, he entered one night the small island of Calvy, where he killed with blows of cutlass five men and women, who could not run away. On the sea, all of our ships had to surrender and the white men aboard were arrested and taken to his forts in fetters and they were not freed until he was paid some money as ransom. All this compelled me to declare war on him and make hostilities to the fullest possible extent, this resolution having been unanimously taken in the meeting of State Councillors, as Your Majesty will see from the copies attached herewith.

I was crowned with such a tremendous success in this task that the resolution I took was considered to be timely one and I availed myself of this opportunity to encourage the Mughal, who had also declared war on the said Khem Sawant and asked me for the help to fight against the said rebel, who was becoming a second Shivaji and had captured many

*HAG=Historical Archives of Goa.

territories in Konkan and all the territories in Phonda. I am not going to give more details about what was done since it has been reported separately.

As regards the loss Your Majesty says to have been caused by destroying totally the rebel Khem Sawant, I feel that his total destruction has proved to be greatly creditable and useful, because the territories of his dominion are not going to be annexed to Mughal or any other powerful Prince, as they are situated far away. They will be divided among the neighbouring Desais and friendly dependants of this State, for their conservation. They have witnessed with much dependance and respect the punishment given to that petty King, from whom we could not expect any loyalty, but rather we had to fear him. He used to resort to any means to take revenge even by seeking the help from Arabs, with whom he had close friendly relations. Also I feel it convenient to inform Your Majesty that there are some people in Goa in favour of Khem Sawant, supplying him with information, forgetting totally the duties of loyal vassals, as I am informed. Your Majesty will accordingly order me to act conveniently.

May God protect the most Catholic and Royal Personality of Your Majesty, as it is desired by your loyal vassals.

Goa, 13 December, 1706.

No. 2

Dated : 2-6-1738

HAG : LOOSE PORTUGUESE DOCUMENT No. 2032

I am in receipt of Your Excellency's letter of this date, reporting therein about the entry of Bounsulo within the jurisdiction of Ponda town as also about the flight of women from that town to our towns, and I am inclined to say that you did well in not preventing the coming of the said women, but it should be noted that it results in the increase of our people for the consumption of provisions and that no men, lascarins and dancing-girls, should ever be allowed to come.

As regards five men that Your Excellency is asking me for the purpose of patrolling, I am writing to General of River to send them to Your P. and no artillery-fire should be opened against Bounsulos, in cases when they are sighted while carrying women who might be withdrawing.

May God protect Your Excellency.

(Count of Sandomil)

No. 3

HAG : MS No. 652, AUTO dE JURAMENTO dOS RANES, 1746-1797, Fls. 2-3

Instrument of the oath of allegiance, obedience and fealty being pledged to the King, Our Lord, by the Desais Satroji Rane, Desai of Sakhali, Zalba Rane, Fssoba Rane, Vantoba Rane, Ganesh Rane, Rodraji Rane, all Desais also of Sakhali, cousins and relations of the same family and house of the said Satroji Rane ; Hari Gaunsa Desai of Maneri Province, Kustam Gaunsa, also Desai of Maneri, Ranganath Parab, Desai of Dicholi and Male Parab his relative ; Ramaji Desai of Rivem, Rama Sawant Desai of Sanvardem, Fatoba Desai of Carambali, also of Sakhali Province ; Kustamaba Desai of Haddavai, also of Sakhali Province, Tuka Sinai, Ambu Sinai and Ramachandra Sinai Nadkarni, Chief clerks of the said Sakhali Province, who are also military officers ; Dattu Sinai, clerk, proprietor of the Sakhali custom's post, and also a military officer. At your feet we pledge the sincere obedience and total submission of perpetual fidelity to the State of India of the very High and Powerful King of Portugal, our Lord and this on our behalf and on behalf of all our dependant and descendants. And, as vassals of the High and August Majesty, benevolently allowed by Your Excellency to live under his Royal protection, we promise and pledge, of our free and good will, to comply with and inviolably keep all the obligations of loyal vassals. This pledge we make and ratify with the greatest oath in our rites, which is to solemnly place our hands on our swords, as we do now . . . under penalty of those same swords turning against us should we fail to keep our word at any time.

HAG : MONCOES dO REINO, MS No. 128 B, Fls 95-96

Your Majesty,

I submitted to Your Majesty last year the text of the Treaty of capitulations signed with Sardesai Ramachandra Sawant Bhosale, who has so far observed the same faithfully, the State having enjoyed the income from the Provinces conquered by the Viceroy Marques de Alorna.

The said Sardesai expired a few days ago and it is said that he was poisoned. Some vested interests got excited and wanted to hand over the Government to one uncle, brother of his father, which I prevented by sending two hundred soldiers and a regiment of cavalry, who enthroned the minor son of the said Sardesai, under the tutelage of his mother, Secretary and his first Dalvi, as they have shown themselves to be faithful to our friendship.

I have also acquainted Your Majesty with the prorogation of the peace granted to the King of Sunda for a period of six months and the monsoon having followed this period, I came to know before a fresh renewal, that your Majesty had resolved on the report submitted in connection with this issue by my predecessor. I was given two more letters; one by the State Secretary, Diogo de Mendonca Corte Real and the other by the Council of Overseas Provinces. Your Majesty has ordered me in the first letter that I should sign the treaty of peace with Sunda, by retaining the possession of the forts of Piro and Ximpim. In the second letter I have been ordered to make a peace agreement with Sunda and Bhosale taking care of the strongholds that we are still having in the North and restoring those we have lost. I would have really liked to comply with these orders had I not been embarrassed for want of necessary reinforcements, which I hope the Royal Clemency of Your Majesty would fulfil, the present needs of the State having been placed before Your Majesty. The shortage of the same is the main reason of its decadence.

No peace agreement can be made with Sunda, by ignoring the cession of the said forts of Piro and Ximpim, whereby the State will have nothing to lose, as they are causing unnecessary expenditure towards the maintenance of their garrisons, absorbing at least four companies of infantry and five companies of sepoys besides other expenses for the maintenance and repairs of the fortifications. There is no safe port for big ships, except the creek of gales, which is situated nearby, where even eight big ships can be accommodated during the monsoon. Sunda can afford to pay to the State four hundred thousand xerafins and to give four villages nearer to the Province of Salsete with a consignation of twelve thousand xerafins in the Province of Zambauli. A fortress can be built at his cost in the said creek, where an anchor-ground can be maintained under the protection of a garrison. The execution of this agreement was embarrassed with partialities caused by the drunkenness of the said King and wide powers enjoyed by his Secretary in the Administrative affairs, and even though he has not brought forth any doubts worth being considered, I am always trying to devise means to force from him the said demands.

Most of the petty kings and rulers in this continent, including the very kingdom of Mughal have formed a league in order to destroy Nana, Prime Minister of Shahu Raja, with a view to avoiding the repeated extortions and thefts with which he is oppressing all of them, without exempting even his own King, on account of powers he has usurped from him. Almost all of them have sent their envoys to this city asking for help, but, as I am deprived of troops, I have entertained them politically by giving them good hopes and stirring up trouble. If they continue to preserve their alliance, and if the Nabab of Arcate favours them with as many as sixty thousand men, they will no doubt achieve their task. If I can keep them sufficiently distraded, I could attend to the recovery of our positions in the North, for which I have made all the necessary arrangements, with utmost care, to bring success to our side. It is true that very often such a machinery among the Asiatic people fizzles out owing to their interests, which constitute their intimate goal and, as such, I cannot execute my plans, without carefully studying their mind.

May God bestow upon the highest and most powerful Royal Personality of Your Majesty, the Most Faithful, a happy long life.

Goa, 6 January, 1756.

No. 5

HAG : MONCOES dO REINO, MS No. 138B, Fl. 518

Most Illustrious and Most Excellent Sir,

The letter of Conde de Ega, dated the 28th January of last year, regarding the churches, which have been founded in the Province of Phonda and Zambaulim, and regarding the permission that Bhosale had given to found another one in his dominion, was submitted to His Majesty, and royal approval has come to everything worked out in the same connection. His Majesty has, however, ordered to advise you to be careful and wise in the matter of the construction of the said churches, so as to enable them to subsist with decorum, without being exposed to the insults of the natives.

May God protect you.

Palace of our Lady of Ajuda, 9 April, 1765.

Francisco Xavier de Mendonca Furtado.

No. 6

NAI* : BHENDE COLLECTION, DOC. No. 14— NAI (NEW DELHI)

Representation of the Great and Honourable Sardesai Khem Sawant Bhosale to the Most Illustrious and Most Excellent Dom Frederico Guilhermo D'Souza, Governor and Captain General of India and of Portuguese Asia.

The most fortunate and honourable Sardesai sends his representation to His Excellency who is known to be a lover of justice. On hearing of his arrival, Jivaji Vishram was sent to pay respects and to present this representation orally and in writing. Since no reply was forthcoming it has become necessary to state that injustice was done by John by the treaty signed during his time. It was not possible for us to fulfil the terms because the loss of villages, fields and defences reduced the revenues of the state and made it difficult for it to pay its dues. We represent that what is due to us be returned and we will be good neighbours.

If the complaints are attended to and justice is done we are ready for a new treaty which could be lasting; otherwise, there is no need of a new treaty. We have not asked anything new. The Desais will retain their old rights, the state will receive its annual contribution as before, and the merchants will receive compensation for the thefts. We believe that after having given so much generously the state will not grudge little. If permission is required from Portugal we would like to know from where come the orders to take Gauntalem and Canealem and recently Ussagao. Let it be decided whether it is useful or not to have good neighbour and if we are protected by the State we should not seek our good. The English are our enemies because we sought the protection of the State and if now the State is allied with the English and fails to come to our service or rescue we are lost. It is urgent to know the exact situation to enable us to take necessary measures.

*NAI =National Archives of India, New Delhi.

Reply of the Governor and Captain General of India and Portuguese Asia to the above representation.

Clear and just answers have been given to every representation made by Jivaji Vishram.

The most illustrious and the Most Excellent Dom Joao Jose de Mello, former Governor and Captain General of this State acted with justice in connection with the Peace Treaty of 14 October, 1768, entered into with the Great Sardesai with solemnity and signed by the Honourable Antaji Ramchandra Sabnis, Sido Pandit, Datagi Parab, member of the chamber of Satarda and Narayan Mulgy under the respective powers granted by the Great Sardesai.

It is an unheard thing, rare and strange that, after a treaty is agreed and signed, it is not complied with under the pretext that it includes an injustice. If such a proposition was admitted, no treaty could be firm and all of them would be ridiculous with the specious pretext of injustice.

The Great Sardesai should think over the point that a desire to infringe the treaties to which one did bind himself voluntarily is not a way conducive to and coherent with the firmness of friendship.

All the nations have always religiously complied with the treaties and with the promises made therein because all of them respect the Divine Law, the natural law and the law of people which prescribe the compliance. The Great Sardesai signed the said treaty through his envoys giving them legitimate powers and concluded an agreement with the Majesty's State because what anybody does through other persons or through his lawful attorneys is, according to the customs followed by the nations, adjudged as done by himself.

According to the first principles and elements, rules have been established which were deducted from the Law of the People. The agreements at the beginning are voluntary and afterwards they become of necessity. The Great Sardesai at the beginning and before that could not have promised or bound himself, could have not signed the said treaty by his attorneys ; but as he did promise, bind himself and did sign it through them, his obligation becomes now a necessary one and it is not becoming to his person to offer resistance and to be evasive.

Also, it is a certain rule and principle deducted from the said law of the Peoples ; that the agreements acquire the legal force by convention of the parties ; because they can bind one another, to fix rules among themselves as for the manner, time, place and conditions which would bind them.

The Great Sardesai who agreed and promised in the said Treaty should comply with his promises because it is a law which he imposed upon himself.

Also under principles and rules, the justice of the Majesty's State is established : Nobody is entitled to change his resolution harming other man's interest after the acquisition of a right. The Majesty's State has acquired the right to what was promised to it in the treaties and the Great Sardesai is not entitled to change his decision and opinion.

What pleases at one time cannot ever displease and the reason is : that there is nothing in keeping and more coherent with the human faith and beneficial for trade than to keep word and to implement promises. And also there is nothing more contrary and opposite to the equity and the natural law than not to comply with the given word, promise and trust, thus harming the interests of the third party.

Against all these principles and rules deducted from the natural law and from the law of the peoples embraced and accepted by all the nations, the Great Sardesai is willing to infringe the treaties and, what is more to be noted, is that he even denies the tribute and does not wish to pay the feudal dues as acknowledgement of the vassalage due to the Majesty's State forgetting the great benefits he received from the Royal greatness and magnanimity of the Most Faithful Majesty. Because, when the Majesty's State had the domain and possession of the three provinces of Dicholi, Pedne and Sakhali acquired under the legitimate title of conquest and war by the Most Excellent Viceroy, the Marquis of Alorna, having maintained their possession and domain during many years and, in its capacity as the legitimate owner, having given them on rent to the Great Sardesai in consequence of his requests and representations for the annual sum of fifty thousand Ashrafis as it is found recorded in Chapter 4 of the peace treaty entered into with the most Excellent Viceroy Count of Ega on 26 July,

1759 lately it was ceded to him (the Great Sardesai) the domain and possession of the said three provinces under the treaty of the said Count of Ega dated 24 December 1761, following orders of His Majesty when the Great Sardesai bound himself in chapter 9 of the same Treaty to pay the tributes of four thousand ashrafis and that, in case it was not paid, the Majesty's State could take possession of the paddy-fields Donossil Indalem and Digui and Vanganim of the village Naroa. This was confirmed by the treaty of the Most Excellent Dom Joao Jose de Mello, former Governor and Captain General of this State in Chapter 6 with declaration, in Chapter 24, that in case it was not paid within one month to be counted from the last day of the year in respect of which it is to be paid, the State could take their immediate possession.

Not only one month had elapsed but all the years of the Government of the Most Illustrious and Excellent Dom Jose Pedro da Camara and the same commissioner continued during the times of the most happy Government of the Most Illustrious and Excellent Dom Federico Guilherme de Souza and, notwithstanding the lack of payment of the said tribute, the Majesty's State has behaved with utmost restraint and loving regard towards the Great Sardesai by not taking possession of the said paddy fields as it could have done ; thus showing the high esteem and value in which the friendship with the Great Sardesai is seen, hoping that he will be convinced smoothly and amicably to pay the said tribute and to fully observe the treaties, because the Majesty's State is not willing to have new treaty, but it wishes only that which were made be observed and in case they are not complied with by the Great Sardesai the Majesty's State is entitled to make use of its rights and to preserve its decorum.

The most Illustrious and Excellent Governor and Captain General of the State gave and swore homage in the Royal Hands of the Most Faithful Majesty binding himself to preserve and to defend the State with all its fortresses, lands jurisdictions and possessions in the same form as he found them and were handed over to him, he came to build, defend, restore and to augment the Majesty's State and he did not come to destroy or to diminish ; and, therefore, without explicit order of His Majesty he shall not hand over any lands from those which he took under his care, vigilance, custody and protection.

The two localities Gauntolem and Cancalem were taken when the Great Sardesai had lost them ; as they belonged formerly to the jurisdiction of Reddi the English had already conquered this fortress from him and there was dispute between the Majesty's State and the said English about the possession of the said territory ; it was submitted to His Majesty and the Great Sardesai bound himself in Chapter 19 of treaty dated 14 October, 1768, and that the said territory with its rental be kept as a deposit in the hands of the Majesty's State until when the Royal resolution is received and one has to avail of this resolution.

In spite of this, the Most Illustrious and Excellent Governor and Captain General, desirous of making firm the friendship with the Great Sardesai, promises to write to His Majesty and to perform the role of an obsequious attorney on behalf of the Great Sardesai so that he may direct that the said villages or localities be handed over to him (Sardesai) and the Great Sardesai also should address his petitions to the Royal presence of His Majesty and he should hope from his unblemished justice and Royal greatness that he will order to hand over to him.

If the English are enemies of the Great Sardesai the Majesty's State shall not and should not give him aid against them because the Court of Portugal has an alliance signed with the King of Great Britain under many solemn treaties and the Majesty's State cannot infringe the said treaties nor it can violate the friendship it has got with the British Nation and, thus, the State shall not, directly or indirectly, give aid to the Great Sardesai against the said English. If they invade and attack the domains of the Great Sardesai, the Majesty's State shall remain neutral, and this is permitted by all the laws and also it shall not give aid to the said English against the Great Sardesai, keeping at the same time friendship with the said English and with the Great Sardesai.

Also, to what further might be represented verbally, reply will be given.

Goa, 25 August, 1780.

No. 7

HAG : MONCOES dO REINO, No. 176A, Fl. 12-12v

Most Illustrious and Most Excellent Sir,

The news that spread of my death produced in the ungrateful heart of Bhosale the same effect as it happened when Aidar Ali Khan feigned to be dead in order to know the frame of mind of his sons and Chief corporals. Believing that I was dead, Bhosale, considered himself freed from the enemy most feared by him and freed from obligations to his great benefactor. He committed without any delay such ungrateful acts as a meanminded and traitor is capable of, thus showing that his expression of thanks was false. The Province of Pande revolted and welcomed his forces. The companies of Sepoys we had formed there also revolted. And in the course of so sudden an incident, the small detachments of his Legion, which were at Pedne, came to the Province of Bardesh, without any losses through the same places where the selected forces from Goa perished in the month of February 1759.

I ordered reinforcements and warned the forts of Alorna and Terekhol. I ordered assault on ships of Bhosale anchored under the protection of the fortress of Reddi. But this operation did not cause the loss I expected to cause. And much cold-bloodedly, I am using the forces in sufficient number to punish the ungrateful Bhosale in such a manner, May God bless my plans to serve as a lesson to the neighbours.

May God give you a long life.

Goa, 6 November, 1794.

No. 58

HAG: REIS VISINHOS No. 19, Fl. 7

Illustrious and most generous Babu Rao Subhedar (of Kolhapur) May your friendship be perpetual :

Jose Caetano Pacheco Tavares, Chief Judge of the House of Supplication, Councillor and State Secretary of India, etc.

Your letter brought by Honourable Venkatrao was submitted to the Most Illustrious and Most Excellent Sir Francisco Antonio da Veiga Cabral, Commander of the order of Christ in the Council of His Majesty, the Most Faithful, Lt. General of his armies of Portugal and Governor of India. He was happy with the good news and knowledge of the admirable qualities of Your Illustrious Personality. He has ordered me to reply to the points raised in the said letter.

His Majesty's State is acquainted with the qualities of Royal Nobleness that concur in the person of the Magnificent King of Kolhapur and holds him in a high esteem, in preference to the representatives of neighbouring powers and on account of these fundamental reasons your alliance is highly praised. The State is ready to receive with full attention your ambassador in order to conclude the convenient and perpetual agreement between His Majesty's State and the Magnificent Raja.

It seems that God Almighty chose the most opportune occasion to punish the Sardesai of Kudal Khem Sawant for his ungratefulness, ambition and treachery, by restoring to the Magnificent Raja his forts and the respective territories. At the same time, His Majesty's State has overcome the insurrection at Pedne by considerable hostilities, by capturing the forts of Reddi, Vengurla, Nivty and Banda and by invading the region right up to the residence of Wadi. With God's blessings and the forces of the State and the Magnificent Raja, both on the land and the sea, the task was made easy, while the resources of Khem Sawant in people and money were so limited and he is at present deprived of any help on account of the death of Valorous Shinde, his protector.

I am not writing any more. I recommend myself to be ever graced by the Illustrious friend. May our Lord protect you.

Written in Goa, on 2 January, 1785.

Jose Caetano Pacheco Tavares.

No. 9

HAG : REIS VIZINHOS No.19, Fls. 133-134

To the Illustrious and Great Laximibai Bhosale, Sardesai of Kudal Pargana and other provinces.

May you live in perpetual happiness!

I, Francisco Antonio Veiga Cabral da Camara Pimentel, etc.

Being in good health, I received with much pleasure the letter of Illustrious and Great Sardesai and was happy to know about your welfare.

The repeated acts of ungratefulness which your Illustrious and Great husband has committed against me, after I had saved him from an eminent danger to which his dominion and he himself were exposed to in the year 1788, as it is known to all, had led me to be determined not to have any letter from him and to order all kinds of hostilities against him, as permissible in the present juncture, as a punishment for the insults made to his Majesty's State and to myself.

The Province of Pedne, offered by your Illustrious and Great Husband as a token of just gratitude of that beneficial act, was made to rise in insurrection by himself in the first year of my rule, and this being a scandalous act to be committed against any other Governor and Captain General of Portuguese India, only because it was an ungrateful act, how could it be conceived to have been committed against the very Governor, who had personally gone to verify the said benefit.

I could have ordered the destruction and burning of the Province, but, as I always hate cruelty, I hoped that time would persuade those people about the advantage of living in peace under the benign Portuguese dominion, and I promised to help them when their disillusionment convinced them of their error.

The circumstances changed and a time came when the Desais of the place and other prominent personalities of Pedne made declaration of their loyalty and asked to provide them with the help immediately. On the entry of the Portuguese forces in that Province, the rebels fortified themselves in the Temple of Pedne. The corporals and others your Illustrious and Great Husband had sent on account of mistrust, had already caused a revolution in the Province. The Portuguese forces attacked the Temple. The said corporals surrendered and the men ran away, without any agreement, and no agreement could take place under similar circumstances. The said corporals were sent to Goa as prisoners.

When I came to learn that the three corporals Ram Sawant Bhosale, Dhond Govinda Farjad and Bhagvant Sawant enjoyed certain status under your Illustrious and Great Husband, I ordered to keep them in the fortress of Aguada and to treat them in the same way they would be treated if they were at Wadi.

For just reasons mentioned in the beginning of this letter, I refused to consider any attempts at reconciliation made by your Illustrious and Great Husband and it did not occur to me that the Illustrious and Great Sardesais, whose esteemed qualities and honourable conduct I have always appreciated could intervene.

Consequently and paying much attention to this mediation, I permit your Illustrious and Great Husband to send to this Palace in Goa a plenipotentiary to adjust Peace, by making good the damages that his act of ungratefulness in the year 1795, has caused to His Majesty's State and by returning the pieces of artillery that remained at that place and also were taken from Phonda. This treaty of Peace will be followed by the release of three corporals mentioned above and the ratification of a stable peace.

Your Illustrious and Great Husband shall have to let me know about the plenipotentiary's departure, so as to enable me to issue the necessary orders for his safe passage to His Majesty's State and to this Palace.

May God illumine the Illustrious and Great Sardesai with His Divine grace.

Goa, 9 February, 1801.

Francisco Antonio da Veiga Cabral.

No. 10

HAG : REIS VISINHOS, No. 19, Fls. 157

Illustrious and Great Raja Khem Sawant Bhosale, Bahadur Sardesai of Kudal Pargana and other provinces :

May your friendship be perpetual !

I, Jose Caetano Pacheco Tavares, of the Council of His Royal Highness, Councillor for the Overseas Provinces, Chancellor of the High Court of Goa, and Secretary of His Majesty's State of India.

Your letter, in which you have expressed your desire of restoration of old friendship between the two, admitting the justice of the treatment extended to you by His Excellency, was submitted to the Most Illustrious and Most Excellent Sir Governor and Captain General of His Majesty's State of India. He has ordered me to let you know that all acts of ungratefulness committed by you will be forgotten to restore peace and old friendship granted that your proposals are sincere and consistent with decency and greatness of His Majesty's State which has welcomed you so often under its powerful protection, giving proofs of its sincere and permanent friendship.

May God grace you with His Divine Grace.

Goa, 22 April, 1803.
Jose Caetano Pacheco Tavares.

MARATHI DOCUMENTS

तारीख १३-४-१७३९

नं० २७४९

हू

अजम अकरम अंतोन फिरेर दे आंन
द्राद सफतायें दे इस्ताद जंजिरे
गोवा दाम मोहबत हू

मोहिबानपन्हा व मुखलिशान दस्तमाहाः अजी जयराम सावत भोसले व रामचंद्र सावत भोसले सरदेसाई प्रा कुडाळ व माहालानिहाये सलाम बादज सलाम येथिल नेकी जाणोन मोहिबी आपली कारनेकी कलम करणे दिगर कितबत पाटविली पोहचोन दिल आराम जाहला व राजश्री पांडुरंग विश्राम यांसी लिहीले प्रमाणे व सांगोन पाटविले प्रमाणे व मुदेहि लिहून पाटविले प्रा सविस्तर विदित केले व राजश्री जगनाथ विश्राम याकडहि जबानी सागितले कि इस्तादाचा व इजानेबांचा श्नेह बहुकाल सुरळीत चालावा यावास्ते कितेक सागोंन पाटविले प्रमाणे त्यांणि विदीत केले मुख्य गोष्ट इस्तादांचा व इज्यानेबांचा पुरातन स्नेह चालला त्यास बारदेस घेऊस कारण म्हणावे तर मराठ्यांची सबलता पाहिली आण सवदेकर यांची ठांणी अवघी घेतली फुडां बारदेस घ्यावा या कार्यावर ते आले तेव्हा इजानेबास येसे दिसोन आले कि बारदेस मराठयाचे हाती पडलेने इस्तादासहि बरे नव्हे येसे समजोन बारदेस घ्यावा लागला तेव्हा आपलेच फौजेनसीं मराठयांची फौज न आणिता घेउन आजबेर राखला मराठयां फौज काय निमित्य न आणिली म्हणाल तर इस्तादाचा व इजानेबाची कदिम दोस्ती तेव्हा ते राज्य आमचे व हे राज्य इस्तादांचे येसें समजोन आपल्या फौजेनसीं घेऊन राहिलो फुडा तरी बारदेस मराठयांस सहसा देणार नाही हा मोहिबांचा खातरनिशा असो घ्यावा परतु खाजगत फौज टेऊन बारदेस राखावा लागला तेव्हा फौजेस खर्च लागला तो याविसीचा भावार्थ पुर्वपश्री मोहिबांस लिहून गेलेच आहे तेणे प्रमाणें मोहिबी कार्य केलेने मोहिबांचा व ण व्यंकटराऊ यांचा तह होउन व्यंकटराव यांची फौज वरघाटी जाई पावेतों बारदेस आम्हाकड असावा तदनतर तुमचे स्वाधिन करु येविसीचा भावार्थ राजश्री जगनाथ विश्राम यांकड सांगितला आहे मोहिबास सांगतील त्यावरुन मालूम होईल वरकड लिहीणे ते राजश्री पांडुरंग विश्राम यांणि लिहीले आहे व

मुदहि अलाइदा लिहून पाटविले आहेत मालूम होतील प्यार मोहबत असा दिजे रा ४ मोहरम हे किताबत.

करार मुदे करुन यावे

खोरजुवा व पनाले दोन गांव आमचे आम्हास पोटसहित घ्यावे कलम ?

दारु व गोळी भांडेचे गोळे सिवभट यांचे मुंदतीमध्यें दर आहे तेणे प्रा ध्यावे कलम ?

सिवभटाचे विघ्यमानेचा तह जाहला आहे तो कागद येन जिनस आमचा घ्यावा कलम ?

हिंदुधर्माचा मुदा बारदेसामध्ये व्यंकटराऊ यांकडून कबुल केला असेल तर जहालो न कबुल केला तर आम्हास करुन घ्यावा कलम ? नकद पैके आम्हास खर्चास घ्यावे कलम

तुमचे भांडते आरमार आहे त्याचे आम्हास वाटेस तुम्ही जाऊ नये कलम दूर .

येणे प्रमाणे मुदे करुन घ्यावे करार करुन लिहीले आहेत.

तारीख : २०-४-१७३८

.नं० २८१४

श्री

याद मुदे होऊन यावयाचा तपसील खोर्जुवां पनाले दोनहो गाव हि चोली महालचे आमचे आम्हास घ्यावे कलम ?

म्हापसे व कोळवाली तपे बारदेस यां दोन हो गावांत हिंदुधर्म चालावा तुळसी ब्राह्मण भट अतीत वृतबंध लग्ने गणेश सिमगा इतर देवकार्य व कलावते व याच्ये हे त्या बिना सर्व चालावी गोहत्या करु नयेत कलम ?

आम्हास खर्चास पेके पाहिजेत कलम ?

सिवभट याचे विद्यमाने तहनामा पुर्वी कस्न घेतला होता तो आमचा आम्हास फिराऊन घ्याया कलम ?

आम्हास दारु व गोळी व माडिचे गोले पाहिजे होतील तेव्हा सिवभट याचे मुज तिस दर आहे तेणे प्रमाणे आम्हास घ्यावे कलम ?

आम्ही इस्तादास व वासालांस इस्ता-दाच्या देणे असेल व इस्तादानहीं

आम्हास देणे असेल तें आज तागावेत
उभये पक्षी सांगणे कलम ?
इस्तादाची तारवा खासा दिवाणची
खेरीज करुन ऊदेमी याची तराडेस
आमची काडता घ्यावी कलम ?

इतुका निवाड़ा जाहले नंतर आम्ही मागा पुढा तुम्हावर चुकू नये तुम्हीं मागां पुढां आम्हावर चुकू नये येणे प्रमाणे तहनामे करावे यानंतर तुमची आमची बोली येणे प्रमाणे व्हावी त्यास तुम्ही व्यंकटराऊ याची बोली करुन फौज वरघाटी चालवावी म्हणजे बारदेस आम्ही तुमचे स्वाधीन करावा आण तुमचा व व्यंकटराऊ यांची बोली न जाहाली आण व्यंकटराऊ फौजेनसी सास्टिस राहिला तर बारदेस आम्हाचकड असावा आम्ही राखावा मराठे यास देणार नाही परतु बारदेस आम्हाचकड राहिला तेव्हा व्यंकटराऊ प्रसंगी बारदेस आपणास घ्यावा आपण राखतो म्हणेल तर तुमचा आमचा गावपणा असतां देतां कार्यास नये तेव्हा जो उपाई टांकेल तो करुन बारदेस राखावा लागेल तर त्यास जो खर्च लागेल तो तुम्ही घ्यावा आम्ही येत्न करुन बारदेस राखतों।

तारीख : १६-११-१७३९

नं० २९४

हू

अजम सकटतार दे इस्ताव वाम
मोहबत हू

मोहिबानपन्हाही मखलिशान दस्तगाहा अजी नाग सावंत भो सरदेसाई पा/ कुडाल व माहालनहाये सलाम बादज सलाम मोहबल मकसूद आकी ता/छ २८ शाबान सोमवार मु जाबोटी ये × न नेकी जाणून मोहिबी आपणाकडील कार-नेकी कलमी कराव × फर्माविले पाहिजे दिगर इज्यानेबाकडील वर्तमान तर सर्व तयारी जाणजा (गो) करुन येका दिवसात येक होऊ × ते आणि खाली उतरोन मोहिबांनजीक यावें असा करार केला इतके दि × × फौजेनसी येऊन मुलाजमत होती त्यास आज पनरा रोज पावेतव प्रज्यन चोर सर्व सामान स्वाराचे······येक घटका अवकास प्र × × न × × नाही याकरितां दिवस

लागले त्यास आदि (त्य) वारी वर्तमान अहकिले जे (वाडि) करानी बारदेसांत प्रवेश केला तेव्हा मोहिबांकडील लोकास व त्यास जुजही जाहले असे अँडकून परम संकोच पावलो मोहिबी अगोदरघ त्वरा करुन मुरास आपला जमाऊ आणून बसविला त्यामुळे मनिमास शरे होहून जवळ येऊन बसावयास पा (ट) वलें इज्यानेब इस्तादाचाच म्हणविला असतां हेगिस येऊन पावतील न पावतील हा कांही भास मोहिबास होहून हेगी केली असेल तर उताविली न करावी होती कदानचीत मूर मजबूत केला उत्तम केले त्यासकल गनिम जात गेलेवर घोड़ा जमाऊ त्यांवर पाटऊन × ×हले त्यांस येश घ्यावे हे काये (व) तंमान बरें जाहली गोस्त येत नाही ते गोस्तिचा काये हि (सा) व आहे इज्याने (बा) कडील जमाऊ व मोहिबांकडील जमाऊ ये (क) जाहलेवर × × × × × ×आहे आण कोण तो × ×आहे याऊपर इज्यानेबाचा बेत इस्तादा खेरीज असेल (तर) खुदा साव आहे इस्तादाचा कामावरची व ज्याहपनसी हाजीर आहू हे येकबाल-पन्हा विजरे यांस व मोहिबास मागांच कलमी केले आहे ते बराबरी करणें इज्या-नेबास जरूर असेल तर सामना फौजेनसी येऊन यां दिवसांत पोहचतों हा खतिरनिशा मोहिबावा असों घ्यावा मोहिबास दिसेल कि वाडिकर व इजानव बंधु आहेत हे प्रसंगी येकत्र होतील येसे कदांनचीत दिसेल तर ते बंधू न्हवत केवळ दुशमन आहेत वा मर्यादा करुन वर्तणूक केल्याचे हर प्रकारें पारपत्यच करावें तेव्हाच कोणही प्रसंग आहे असे असतां इस्तादाकडे दुसरा अर्थ धरुन मागां पुढां पाहून वर्तणूक करुं तर इज्यानेच येका बापाचा नसेल जाती भोसले आहू जो शब्द बोलावा तो······आहे तो बरा करावा हा आमचा स्वधर्म आहे बरें येवडा तपसील लिहावा असा अर्थ नाही परतु काल विपरीत आहे दुष्ट संधि साधतात या करितां सुचनाई लिहीला असे आतां सहश्र गोष्टिची ×स्ट इज्यानेब आपले बळकटीने येऊन पोहचतच आहे त्यास मोहिबाकडील जमाऊ सिध असावा आतां येकाकी ऊतावीळ न करावी आपले सिधतेन तयार असावें इज्यानेब फौजेनसी त्वरच साखलीस मुकाम करुन मोहिबास खबर देतो ते क्षणि जमाऊ मोहिबास चितास येईल तेथ पवावा ते जागां आमचा व मोहिबाचे फौजेची मुलाजमत होईल गनिमाचा तरी कोण तो × ×आहे त्यांनी तो आपला पुढार केलाच आहे याउपर इज्यानेब आपले जमावानसी मोहिबांकडिल जमाव-नसी कर्तुत्व करुन दाखवीन तो आमचा मजरा येकबालपन्हा विजरेपासी होईल आणखी कितेक विचार याच मनसबेवास्ते इज्यानेबांस पाहिले आहेत ते प्रसंगी दृष्टिस पडतील इज्यानेबासा काडिचा अवकास या मनसबे विरहीत नाही दिवस गत लागली म्हणतील तर येकाकी फौज जांबोटीस आणिली म्हणजे गोस्ट (१) होऊन गनिम शेर होतों याकरिता जागजाग तयारी करविली आहे त्यास मध्ये

प्रज्यन दोन याकरितां इतके दिवस लागले प्रज्यन तो दूर होत याऊपर जलदी करावी ते करतो मोहिबा काडिमात्र दुसरा विचार न समजावा इज्यानेबाचा बेत म्हणावा तर इस्तादाचें बरें जाहलें म्हणजे त्यामुळे इज्यानेबाचे बरें हाच निश्चये असाच करार आहे याऊपर इस्तादाच्या कामावर जिव ज्याबनानसी मारुन खरे होतो हा निशा चिनाचा असों घ्यावा हे खरे प्रज्यनाने केवल (साव ग) लोक नाही तर येवडा प्रसंग याचा मोहिबाकड त्याचा न होता बरें याऊपर त्वरा आहे याच उतर बहूत जलदिने येकवेळ पाटवावें तुम्हावर झूंझ आम्हाआधीं पडेल तेव्हां आम्ही तुमच्या साहित्यास न पावलों तेव्हा जिवंत असोन नाहिसें झालों आतां जे दिवसा तुमची आमची भेट होईल ते दिवसी आहों असाच प्रसग घडला बरें याऊपर अधिक काये लिहावे आपणा बहूत ऊताविली केली हे माणूस पावतांच प्रत्योंतर देऊन रवाना करावा पण दिलगीर न व्हावे आमचा येंता माहराज संभाजी राजे याचा लखोटा व × रा हिंदुराव घोरपडे याचा लखोटा व × नारो राम मंत्री याचा लखोटा पाटविला असे व मोहिबांस येक लखोटा येकून च्यार लखोटे पाटविले आहेत पाऊन ऊतर पाटवणे ·····पाटवावा ऊतराचा मार्ग पाहतो येकवेळ ज्याब जलदिने पाटवावा हे ज्यादा लिहीणे न लगे हे किता (बत).

तारीख : २०-१-१७४०

नं० ७०

हू

सुज्याहतः सामत दस्तगाह अजम
अकरम सियोर लुविस अफोंस दात
सकटतार जंजिरे गोवा बा मबत हू इनाशा
खुशबक्त बाशद

अजि दिलयेकलास सवोजी राणें देसाई ता/ साखली सला बजत सलाम येथिल नेको बजनर जाणून न कारनेकी कलमे रजा फर्मावली पाहिजे दिगर केरिचे वर्तमान तर सेनवारी प्रातकाली केरिवर स्वारी आली देखील फोणेची फौज केरिच्या लोंकांनी व रा विठोजी राणे व सिवबा राणे याणीं मारामार बरि केली गनिमांचे दाह पनराजण ठार जाहले व दाह तिस जखमी जाहले यांमध्यें·····याच धोगे पडिले आहेत कळले नाहीं आम्हाकडील दोगे ठार

जाहले व दोगे जखमी जाहले दारूगोलेचे सामान सरोन फजित जाहली जर दारूगोळे संग्रयास असते तर गनिमास मारुन काडुन मोड करु येता सामान न होहून राहिले खासगत व लोकांचे घरामधे होते ते बराबर घेहून लोकानिसी काडोन घरावरील डोंगरावर सवरी मध्यरात्रिनंतर कडोन आले सेनवरी आम्ही नारवेस होतो केरिचे येव येकोन दाह च्यालिस माणसानसीं केरिच्या ऊपराळे करणे रात्रीन डिचोलीवरुन केरिस आलो आम्ही यावयाचे पुर्विच केर गनिमाने घेतली मग आम्ही आमच्या समुदायास मिळोन घेहून सर्व लोकांसहीत आपल्या समुदायाच्या व आपल्या कविलेनसीं कागज येहून नाणस आंहू येथिल कबिले ठेहून भिमगडच्या लोकास तुम्ही ठिकाणी ठेहून वरवड लोकानसी व रा विटोजी राणे व सिवबा राणे देसाई लोकानसी वा घेऊन आम्ही नारवेस यावयास येतो नारवेहून विठोजी राणे व सिवबा राणे लोकानसी आपणाकडे सेवेसी रवाना करुन देहू हे वर्तमान आपणास कळावेया बदल लिहीले आहे बहूत काय लिहीणे प्यार असो दिजे हे किताबत हे वर्तमान सावरेचे मुकामी लिहीलें होते त्यावरी गनिमाने येऊन चोंहोकडून वाटा धरुन मागास स्वारी आली त्यानंतर आम्ही जांबोटीस वर्तमान लिहीलेवरुन राजश्री कृष्ण गावडे सरदेसाई ता/ खानापूर हे जमावांनसी घांटमाथा येऊन गनिमाने भेट मारले गनिमाचे पांच जण मारले व पांच दाहा जणास जिवे धरलें आम्हास जांबोटिस येणे येसें सांगोन पाटविले वरून आम्ही कबिलेनसी जांबोटीस आलो येथं आटच्यार रोजाची लोकाच्या कबिलेची खार्चाची अनुकुलता करुन देहून आम्हीं सत्वरच जमावानसी गोवे यास येतो जुवेकर राणेहीजमावानसी वा आणतों कळवेयाबदल लिहीलें आहे नारवेस यावयास हे वाटेने वाट न चुकली तर आम्ही जमावानसी बारदेसाहून मलियेस तारिवरी पणजेस यावेयास येतो भितर घेणे म्हणोन पासास वोडत लाविली पाहिजे हे किताबत हू हे किताबत ।

तारीख : १७४७

नं० ७२०

हू

रफाअलपन्हः हिसमत व शोकत दस्तगाहा
दोतोर अजम लुविस आफोस दांते सकडतार दों
इस्ताद दां मशफकत हू

अजी दिलयेखलास कृष्णरा (ऊ) (गुरकार) दिंमत संवस्थान सोधे सलाम मकसुद आंके येथिल खेरखुसी आणुन बां रफाअलपन्हाः सेहत सलामती खुद

निविस्तन केले (पाहि) जे दिगर भोसले येऊन सुपेच्या कोटाश्र व मेढयास मोर्चे देऊन भांडत आहेत कोटकरी व मेटेकारी बरी मारामार करित आहेत आरंक्चि भोसल्याकडिल दाहा पांच ठार जाहले दाहा पांच जखमी जाहले परंतु ऊपराला जाहलंयाविना भोसला निघोन जात नाही सुपेस पावल्याची खबर दाखल होतांच इजानेब फोंडयाहून निघोन सांग्यास येऊ (त) धारोजी पोंवार सुभेदार व नागबा देसाई वरकड पतकांचा जमावस होत च्यारसे मनुष्य डिगावरुन रवाना केले आणि जांबोलीस येऊन कुंडल घाटच्या मार्गे जाऊन इकडून मारामार करात्री येसे करुन अजम वासुदेव पंत व दुलबा नाइक व बुर्वे या समागमे जमाव देऊन खाना केला आहे परंत इस्तादाकडिल जमावाची मदत जाहल्यावितरीक्त भोसला निघोन जात नाही यैसी यासी ह्या समई ऊपराला करुन सुपेचा कोट रक्षून द्यावा आरेभी इस्तादांनींच सुपा संपादुन दिले आहे ह्या समई ऊपराला करुन रक्षुन घ्यावे हरयेकविसी रफाअतपन्हा, सांगतील त्या गोष्टिवितरीक्त इजानेव आहेत पैंसे नाही हे सर्वही मुलाजमती-चेत्रक्ष जाहिर केलेंच आहे भोसल्याची योजणा सुपे हातास आलिया मार्गाचे नास धरिले होते त्यावर मग पुढे जे कर्तव्य ते करावे·········आहे भोसले दुष्ट त्याणी योजिले सिद्य गोलिया इजानेबांस·········णच पडणार व इस्तादां सही उत्तम आहे येथे नाही भोसल्या ········साथ आहे मार्ग हातास लाग-लिया येक प्रकार हे सर्वही रफा······पन्हास दखलच आहे पैस पाठावयाचे पुर्वीच ऊपाये व्हावा याकरिता मनावर घेऊन येकबालपन्हास जाहीर करुन ऊपराला करावा याविसी······सोल इजत असार लक्षुमण शेणवी जाहीर करतील ते खातिरेस आणुन लवकर ऊपराला करावया आकिल आहेती खुदायेताला वा रफाअलपन्हा: स आपले पन्हा: मधें हिसीयार बरस खुषाल रंखों तारीख १५ माहे मोहरम हे सलामे.

तारीख : ५-४-१७४८

नं० २६०

हू

अजम अकरम दों पेद्र मिगेल दालमेद
कोंदी दे आसुमार मार्केज दे कस्तेल नोव
बिजुरई जंजिरे गोवा हरमसनव हुकू
मत मुतमकी बाशव

अमारत व अयालतपन्हा हिशमत व शेकत दस्तगाहा अंजी जयराम

सावंत भोसले व रामचंद्र सावंत भोसले सरदेसाई पा कुडाळ व माहाला-निहाय सलाम बाजद सलाम येथिल नेको जाणन मोहिबी आपणाकडिल कारनेकी कलमे करीत असिलें पाहिजे दिगर मोहिबांकडून बहूत दिवस खत येऊन दिल आराम होत नाहीं हे बात दोस्तीचे जागां वाजीव आहे अैसे नाही तरी हरबक्त किताबत पाटऊन दिल खुश होई तें करित असीलें पाहिजे ऊंकी इजानेबांकडिल वर्तमान आंगरे याच्या मुलूकांत मुलूकगिरीस गोवलकोट अंजन-वेलच्या सरदो पावेंत जाऊन तेथोन माघारें येऊन मुडागढ आगरा यार्णे नुतन बांधिला होता त्यास मोर्चे बंदि करुन हस्तगत केला आण तेथोन आपल्या टिकाणास आलों स्वस्थलास आले नंतर माहराज राजश्री छत्रपती यांकडून बहुमान व वस्त्रे व रोक खर्चांची बेजमी होऊन आली आण लेहून आलें जें आणिखी त्याच्या प्रांतांत मनसबा करणे साहित्य लामेल तें पुरवीलें जाइल म्हणोंन त्यावरुन सांगुतिही जाणेचे तरतुदी होत आहे मोहिबांस मालूम व्हावे यास्तव कलमे केलें असे यानंतर इजानेबातर्फेने भले माणूस ऊभय पक्षींच्या खुलासेवास्ते गेले होते त्यास जाऊन बहूत दिवस जाहाले अैसे यास अभयपक्षीचे खुलासेचा धंदा ऊरकोन जलदीने येऊन पोंहचे तें करावेया मोंहिब आकील आहा ज्यादा काय लि छ ९ रविलाकर हे किताबत.

तारीख : १७४९

नं० ५७

हू

श्री रामो जयती

राजश्रि या विराजित राजमान्ये राजश्री

विट सेणवी घुमे स्वामी गो ।

सेवक येसवंतराव माहादेव (खा) सनिवीस विनंती ऊपरी येथिल कुशल जाणून स्वकिये कुशल लेखन करित असिलें पाहिजे विशेष राजश्री तुलाजी आगरे सरखेल गर्वारुष होऊन मनमाने सारिखी वर्तणुक करुं लागले यास्तव राजश्री स्वामीचें अंतराव विशम येऊन त्याचे पारपत्य करावें यैसा मनसबा योजिलाराजश्री भगवंत राव रामचंद्र पंडित आमात्य व राजश्री सरदेसाई कुडाळ-कर यास आज्ञा करुन त्याचे मुलुकांत धामधून आरंभिली जलमार्गे आरमार आणाऊन त्याचे स्थंलास तंदी पोहचवावी म्हणून अजम अंतोन फिरगी याज

बा वस्त्रें पत्रें देऊन गोत्रयास तुमचे यजमानाकडे रवाना केले यासी त्याजकडोन सांगितल्या प्रमाणे देऊन आले नाही सांप्रत दोंतोर याज बराबर लेहून पाटविलें कि आम्ही मनसब्यास तयार आहो यैसी यास माहराज राजश्री स्वामीस मनसब करणें अगत्यच आहे तुम्हाकडिल निश्चये जाला पाहिजे यास्तव सांप्रत राजश्री अंताजी भास्कर यां सभागमें पत्रे देऊन पाटविले असेल येथिल विचार सविस्तर सांगतील तो अर्थ ध्यानात आणून आपले येजमानास विचारे करुन सांगोन दो महिन्यानी या मनसब्यास ऊपित होत ते करणें राजश्री पंतप्रधान व इंग्रज याजकडून राजकारण आले होते परंतु ते आम्ही घडों दिल्हे नाही आणि तुम्हाकडे पत्रे वस्त्रे पाटऊन राजकारण केले त्यासी साल ग्गुा तुम्हाकडोन मनसबा घडोन आला नाही याउपरी ये गोस्टिचा विचार दृढोतर मनास आणून ऊतर सत्वर पाटवणे म्हणजे दुसरी योजना केली जाइल बहूत काये लिहीणे हे (विनंती ?)

तारीख : १७४६

नं० ७

हू

अजम अकरम दों लुविस केतान

दे आलमेद गोबेर्नदोर इंदी

बार मसनद हुकूमत मुलमकी बाशद

अमारत व अयालतपन्हा हिसमत व शौकत दस्तगाहा—अंर्जी दिलयेखलास पांडुरंग विश्राम सलाम बादज सलाम बनजर जाणेन अमारतपन्हाही खैर खुसी कलमे करावया रजा फर्माविली पाहिजे महबल मकसुद उंकी सध्या मालवणकरी याचें आरमार तुलाजी आंगरे याच्या आरमाराने धरुन न्हेले याकरितां सिवाजी पंत यांही राजश्रीस लिहीलें जे माहराज राजश्री छत्रपती यांचे आरमार तुलाजी आंगरही चाकरच असोन त्याणे बेइमानी केली याक-रितां तुम्हां व आम्हां सर्व साहित्यानंसी मिलोन आंगरे यास सामना नतिजा घ्यावा म्हणोन आग्रहें करोन सांगोन पाटविलेंवजरुन राश्रीनी श्वांर व जमाऊ कुलीं मालवणास रवाना केला आहे मालवणचेही साहित्य होतच आहे पुढां आंगरे यांच्या मुलूक व टाणी घेऊन नतिजा पोंहचवावा तर हा मनसबा मागां-पासून इस्तादासही आवशक होने त्यास हाली त्याचा प्रसंग आला आहे मागां-पासून राजश्री चे चितीं हा मनसबा करावा होता परंत निमित्य न्हवतें त्यास

ह्याली माहराजाचें साहित्य होऊनं आपलेही कार्य होते याकरितां अविलंबावें लागलें तर राजश्री तर्फेन या मनसोबत अगाध आहे यैसे नाही आण इस्तादातर्फेन आंगरे यांस नतिजा घ्यावा राजश्री कडेस आपले साहित्य करावें यैसे इस्तादा-कडून होऊन येतें किंवा नाही हे समजोन हुजरु येणेविसीं आज्ञा आली आहे याकरितां राजश्री नारायेण भट पेटकर यांस रवाना केले आहेत याचे उत्तर येइल त्या सारीखा विचार करावा लागेल इजानेबही हे समजोन सत्पर याहिस जाणार आहेत ज्यादा काये लिहावें मेहरबानी असावी हेकिताबत.

तारीख : १७५०

नं० १३

येकबाल व इजलालपनाहा : हशमत व शोकत दस्तमाहा : खुलत व येकजहत इतिवाहा: दो पेंद्र दे आलमेद कोंद असुमार माकेंज दे हलोर्ण दे कस्तेल नोव विजरे कपिताव जनराल दा इंदी जंजिरा गोवां परही फजखुद

अर्जी सवाइ इंमडी सदासिव राजेंद्ररु सोधा सलाम महबल मकसुद आंकी येथिल खुषी बनजर जाणोन वां येकबालपनाहांनी आपली खेरखुषी कलमी मरकुम करुन दिल ताजा करित गेलें पाहिजे दरिवाला सांप्रत मसलत करुन मनिम भोसुल्याकडिल सेंवटाचे ठाणे निवती दर्या किनारेस होते तें काबिज करुन पैंले केलें कलेंची वाड आपले कबजात आणुन तेथें अमल चाल-विला व ते जागां गनिमाने नंवि तराडी बांधवित होता ती जालून टाकिली व त्यामधिल तिन तराडी मालवणच्या आश्रयास गेली होती तिही जबरदस्ती दाखवोन मालवणकरांकडून आणुन घेतली आणि तेच समई डिचोली प्रांती जंरोन कोस्त सरदार याणे संस्थानची फौज सभागमे घेऊन गनिमास खुब्रवजा तंबी पोहचविली आज इस्तादाच्या खुबित्रदल व संस्थानच्या किफायतेलीवास्ते केले म्हणोन सर्व हकिकत जाहीर होणेवास्ते मुबारक किताबत निवीष्टन केली ती पोहचोन खानदाने यांस खुमहाली ते कलमी करितां येत नाही आंयेकबाल-पनाहाः यशस्वी आहेत जे इदिस विजेरे होऊन दाखल जाहल्यापासुन संस्था-नाटाई बहुतसा प्रितीचा आदर चालविला व गनिम भोसुलेस खुबवजा तंबी पोहचविली जें यामागा बहुतजण इंदिस विजुरे होऊन आले परत येकबाल-पनाहा प्रमाणें संस्थानाटाई प्रितीचा घरोंबा विशेष चालविला या प्रकारें अवलही चालिले नाही आगेही होणार नाही या प्रमाणें ऊभयेपक्षीं अश्राई व येगानगी चालोन आली व गनिम भोसुलेस हि तंबी पोहचविली ती अवलही

जाह्ली नाही व आगेही होणार नाही या प्रमाणें सजा देऊन दाहाशत लाविली आणि ठाणीं कांबिज केली हेजर दुसरेचे वांटेस येते यसं नाही रेहित आहेत तेथे दिनबदीन प्रिती विशेष चालवावी आणि गनिमास तंबी पोहचवावी हे शास्त्र प्रमाण निती आहे याप्रमाणें आंयेकबालपनाह यांचा प्रवर्तक आहे यावरुन खुदायेतालाची मेहरबानगी पुरी होऊन नेसवंत होत आहेत आंयेकबाल-पनाहास गनिमाचे शेवटचें ठाणे काबिज जाहले तें खानदाने यांसच जाहलें इज्यानेबांमध्यें व येकबालपनाहाः मयें कांही जुदाई नाही गनिमाची सर्व ठाणी काबिज जाहलीं तेव्हा पेशजी पाही हमराह येकबालपनाहाः याणी सजून दिल्हे प्रमाणे डिचोलीचा अमल संस्थान निसबताने चालऊन देतील हे खानदाने यांचा विशाच आहे आणी पेशजी सभासद कृष्णजी पंडित गोवेस आमदन जाहले समई इज्यानेव मुजबानी मफसल केले होते कि इसमाल खांस मुषहाल करुन राखावे हे आज इस्तादास व आं राजेच्या संस्थानास बहुत वाजिब असेल म्हणून कांजे मामुलें रजिस जाहलेवर केव्हांच आगरे याकडे जाऊन राहिलेवर दरियामधें जेर्बाद होऊन फिरेल याबदल इंज्यानेबो मानिलेस वश्य व्हावे यास कितेक वजा आपलेर्फेतने अनुमोदन केलें परत कोणिही गोष्टीने ऊगाश हात नाही कि अजम कलपैया मअरफतिने उंशनेनी मानिलेस जें घ्यावेयाचे कबुल केले होते त्यावर दृढ घ्या सरा दिला तेव्हां त्याची रजाबंदी संस्थानतर्फेच व्हावी हे बदल येकबालपनाह याणी निवोस्तन केलेस अवल येकबालपनाह इंदिस आले पासुन खानदाने यांची पुरी ममता धरुन संस्थानचे राज्यास गनिम भोसुला सर होऊन बहुत वजे तसदी देत असता खानदाने यांचा मुलुक तो इस्तादाचा मुलुक यैसें असोन भोसुला बहुतवजेने संस्थान-तर्फेस तसदी देऊ लागला तेव्हा इस्तादास मुख्य गनिम यैसे समजोन खामखा तंबी पोहचवाऊन गनिमाची ठाणी तबल रेडि पावेतों काबिज करुन गनिमास हालखुद ठेऊन संस्थानचा मुलुक निरुपद्रव करुन हेजेस सहज पुर्तुकाल पावेतों मशहुर करुन घेतले हरवजे खानदाने यांस येकबालपनाहाः होऊन दुसरा मित्र आहे येसें नाही तेव्हां मानिलेस इस्तादाचे व संस्थानचे खुबिवा-स्ते रजाबंद करुन ठेऊन घेतलें यैसे म्हणोन तर येकबाल पनाहली केले ते खानदाने यांनी केले ब खानदाने यानी केले ते येकबालपनाहनीच केले हेत्रजे ज्यानोबंन दोस्ति चालत असे मागेहो हेचवजे तरकी होऊन चालावे हे खान-दाने यांचे स्वाहित आहे तर आंमा मएरनिलेचे विवेखावास्ते जे फर्मावणे ते मरला सभासदार कृष्णाजी पंडित यास फर्मावििलें असे वकंड हकिकत सभासद अधिकारी विरेया कलमी करितील व सभासद कृष्णाजी पंत जाहीर करितां सर्व हकिकत जाहीर होईल तेथ जियादा काये त्याद्वावे खुदायेताला येकबाल-पनाहा : यास''''''बरस खुषहाल रखो।

तारीख: १७५०

नं० ४१२

हूं

भजम अकरम फ्रांसिस्क आफोस
दे ताव्र कोंद दे सांजुवाऊ ये मार्के
ज दे ताव्र विजुरे ये कपिताऊ जेरा
ल दा इंद हमेश खुशवक्त बाश
द

अगारत व अयालतपना: हिसमत व शोकत दस्तगा: अजी जयराम सावंत व रामचंद्र सावंत भोसले सरदेसाई पां कुडाळ व माहालानीहाय सलाम बादज सलाम येथिल नेको बानजर जाणून मोहिबां आपणाकडिल खैरखुसी कलमे करुन दिल ताजा करित गेले पाहिजे मकसूद उकी इस्तादातर्फेने व इजानेबातर्फेने पहिलेपासून बहुतसी येकलासी चालत होती अलिकड कांही अंतर आले यास्तव इस्तादातर्फेचा जोरा होहून कितेक नाशाड जाहली ते संधी पाहून तुलाजी आंगरा याणे भरधगड सिधगड हे टाणेस अपाये केला इस्तादाचा व इजानेबाचा खुलासा चालत असतां त्याचा हात न लागता त्याऊपर इकडून जबरदस्तीने भरतगड धेतला ते इरेस्तवं आंगरेने आपल्या जमावानसी कुडालास येवत नाही याकरितां येक वरीस पावेतों सामान गुस्तेंद केले आण कितेक द्रव्य खर्च करुन भारी जमाऊ करुन कुडालास दगेनेच आला आण आरमाराने येहून कारलिचा नागा धरलाउ त्याऊपर इकडून फौजेनसी बिदवणेंस मुक्काम केले आण त्याची फौज जागा सोडून बाहिर आली होतो तेथ गांट घालून त्याची फौज मोडली त्याऊपर दुसरे रोजी त्याणे अवघा जमाऊ येकवट करुन गोटवर चालून आले हे इज्यानेबांकडिल फौजेस दखल जाहले काही येकाकी फौज निघोन आली तें वर्तमान परस्पर मोहिबांस ज्याहिर जाहलेच असेल इस्तांदाचा व इजानेबांचा पुरातन खुलासाच आहे त्यामध्ये अंतरावे आली तेव्हां इस्तांदाकडून कितेक इजानेबातर्फेची करावी जाहली तर इस्तादाचा भरवसां इजानेबांस आहेच इस्तादाचा व इज्यानेबाचा पुरातन सेजार त्यामध्यें आंगरेने उत्पात योजीला याचा अभिमान इस्तादातर्फेस आहे कि नाही हे इज्यानेबांस मालुम व्हावे यास्तव किताबत पाटविली आहे जवाब पाटवावेया मोहिब आकिल आहेत ज्यादा काय लिहावे हे किताबत.

तारीख : १६-१२-१७५०

नं० १०४१

रफाअलपन्ह : हिसमत व शौकत बस्तगा:
बोतोर अजम लुबीस आफोंस दांत सकडतार
बो इस्ताद बामाफकत हू

अजी दिलयेखालास कृष्णराऊ फाऊगुरकार दि 1 संवस्थान सोधा सलाम मकसुद ऊफी येथिल खुशी बानजर इलाही जाणऊन आरफाअलपन्ह: सैयत सलामती खुद निविस्तन केले पाहिजे दिगर भोसुले यावरी आंगरे चालोंन येऊन दोनी भांडणे होऊन दोघांकडिल भलें भलें लोक नाया जाहले व पावरखलक हिसार व जखमी जाहलें व वाडीकराचा भाऊ निबालकराचा मुल आगरोनी दस्त केला व आंगरेकडिलही भोसुले यास सापडेले ते भोसुले यांनी ठार मारीले करीतां उभयेताल ईरे पडोन आगरेनी तल धरुन कुडाळाचा कोट पाडीला होता तो बांधोन दुरुस्त केला म्हणे व ऊपरालेंवास्तें इस्तादाकडे किताबती लिहून तेजीबहि पाटविला आहे म्हणे व भोसुलेकडीलहि किताबती लिहून पाटविलेले पोहचलें म्हणों यैसे वर्तमान यैकिले जाते व आगरे यास इस्तादाकडील काही उपराला करितील यैसेही बाद अवाई आहे तर इस्ताद व रफाअलपना: आकील आहेत कीं भोसुला गनीम होती खरें परंतु इस्तादाच्या आजमासांत असोन होता आता जेव्हा आगरेंनी भोसले यास मोहाबा म्हणून केले आणि इस्तादानी ऊपरात्क आंगरे केला तरी आंगरेची रितीरवेस अवधी रफाअलपना: स जाहीर आहे परंतु भोसलेहून आंगरा हशमजादा आहें तेथे उपराला पोहचोन त्याची पलकही जाहली यापुढे हरयेकबाये दुर व दिसोन येते यैसै नाही हे इज्यानेत्रांस जाहीर जाहलें यास्तवें रफाअलपन्हा:स निवीस्तन केले आहे यावरी रफाअलपन्हा: आकील फमीदे आहेत सिवसेंजार म्हणायाचा पहीले भोसुले याचा बरा नहुन आंगरेचा बरा नव्हे या गोस्टीची पेरोदेशी व पेरवी रफाअलपन: स न कळे यैसे नाही परंतु इजानेबास सुचला प्रसंग निवीस्तन केले आहे आणि वरघाटीच खबर कोर काही अधीकोतर नाही. आणि हुजरोन किताबती व दिलायेत लवकरीच येऊन पावणार आहे तेथे पावतांच इजानेब मुलाखातीच्या अभिप्रयास रफाअलपन्ह:स विदीत करीत आहों मालूम जाहले पाहीजे जियादा लिहीणे येत्तीयाज नाही प्यार अर्जानी राखणे खुदायेताला आपलेपना: मधे: हिसीयार बरस रफाअलपन्ह स खुशाल रखो निवीस्तन भा. मामलें फोंडा ब तारीख २७ माहे मोहरम प्रमोद सवछर मार्गसीर या १४ दसी हे सलाम .

तारीख : १३-१-१७५१

नं० १०३९

रफअलपन्हः हिसमत व शोकत दस्तगाः
दोतोर अजम लुवीस आफोंस बांत सकडतार
दो इस्ताव वामशफकतहू

अजी दिलयेखलास कृष्णराऊ गुरकार दि सवस्थान सोधे सलाम मकसूद आंकी येथिल खुशी वानजर इलाही जाणाऊन आरफाअलपन्हः सँबत सलामती खुद निवीस्तन केले पाहिजे दिगर भोसुले याच्या मदतीस मराटेची फौवज आली आहे त्याची तहकीफ बातमी आणवावीया करीता तेथेच आदमी पाटवीलें होतें ते पारगड पावतों जाऊन बातमी घेऊन आलें पारगडास वाडिहून व मसुरेंस आमदरत्फी माणसें येत आहेत तेथें सर्व वर्तमान मनास आणिलीयां बेकटरायाचा पुत्र नारायेणराव येक व मानाजी पायेगांडा व अवडीला वडीयाचा पुत्र व हरीपंत ? येसे ४ सरदार चौघे व फोवज च्यार हजार पांच हजार आहे वरचेवर रामघाटाने शेगर दोबीसे स्वार येतच आहेत मराठेकडिल येक नगारेचे ऊट व नगारासहीत आगरेने नेला त्यावर मराठेची फौवज सारी मसुरेस जाऊन बसली यार बोली होऊन आगरेने मसुरेचे गडास मोर्चे लावीले होते ते काढीलेच त्यावर मराठेची व आगरेची बोली होत आहे तिनी लक्ष रुपये व सात ठाणी आगरेकडे आहेत ती द्यात्री म्हणोन त्या तिन लक्ष रुपये घ्यावयास आगरा मान्ये जाहला व सात टाणी म्हणायाची देवत नाहीं म्हणतों सात टाणी दिल्याखेरीज सोडणार नाही म्हणउने मराटे म्हणतात यामुळे अध्याप सला जाहला नाहीं परंतु आट चौदा दिवसात सला होईल सला होताच मराठे व भोसुलेसहीत इस्तादाच्या व संवस्थानाच्या मुलकांता यावे यैसी सिधांत केला आहे म्हणोन तहकीक बातमी खबर या प्रमाणे घेऊन आलें व दुसरे बातमी वर्तमान नजुरेने पाहून आले जे संभाजी राणे याणी सदोबास पेशवाई दिली हक दक्षण प्रातीच्य जिल्हेच्या सनदा दिल्या पारगड मनोहरगड व भिमगड व कळानिधीगड समानगड यैसे पांच गड सदोबास दिल्हे सदोबाकडिल किलेदार व सबनीस व लोक यैसे आलें सनदे प्रमाणे पारगडावर सदोबाचे निशाण चढविलें किलेदार सबनीस लोकासहीत गडावर जाऊन पहिली व किलेदार व सबनीस गडाखाले ऊतरोन हुकूमेप्रमाणें हुजूर जावयास गेले हे नजरेने पाहून गेले माणूस आलें मनोहरगडास व भिमगडास सदोबाकडील निशाण व किलेदार सबनीस लोक येस येणार होते आट चोहू दिवसामधें पावतील हे हकीक घाटमाथाचे गड सदोबांची टाणी बसली व फौवजाद सदोबाच्या तर्फेची आली आहे भोसल्यानी तो बोलीचाली करुन चौथाई वसूल करुन इस्तादानी घेतली टाणी सोडवून घ्यावी

म्हणाऊन बोली करुन घेऊन आले आहेत हे वर्तमान तों पहीलें तागायेत आहेच या प्रमाणे जाहलीया इस्तादास व सर्वस्थानास बाधक होणार यास सदेह नाही याची तरतुदी करीतां राहिलीया मग कटीण पडणार या करिता इज्यानेबास पासोन आलें ते जाहीर होणेवास्ते निवीस्तन केले आहे व इजानेबी हुजूर सोपेस सलतनन्हः साहेबाचे खिजमतेस ही बातमी वर्तमान निवीस्तन करुन पाटवीलें आहे रफाअलपन्हानी दिली आणून येकबालपन्हः मार्केज दे तावर यास जाहीर करावयास आकील आहेत इज्यानेब हि बतिमी येत आहे ती रफाअलपन्हास दखल करीत आहे रफाअलपन्हानी बातिमी येत असेल ती इज्यानेबास दखल होयेसें करावे वाजीब आहे जियादा लिहीणे येतीयाज नाही प्यार मोहबत असो देणे खुदायेताला आपले पन्हामध्ये हिसीयार बरस खुशीवत रखो निवीस्तन गो मामले फोंडा व तारीख २५ माहे सफर प्रमोद सवंछर पुस्प बहूलं १२ दसी हे सलाम.

तारीख : १७५२-५३

नं० १६११

हू

अजम अकरम फ्रासिस्क असेस दे ता
व कोंद दे सा जुवांव मारकेज दे ताव्र वि
जुरे कवितांव जराला दा इद हमेशा खुशबक्त बाशद

अमारत व अयालतपन्हा हिशामत व सौकत दस्तगांहा अजीं रामचंद्र सावंत भोसले सरदेसाई प्रां कुडाळ व माहालानिहाये सलाम बाजद सलाम महबल मखसुद येथिल नेको जाणऊन मोहिबीं कारनेंकी कलमे किताबत केली पाहिजे उंकी संवदेकरी यावर मोहिबां मोहिम करुन जमात्रांनसी खोलगड प्रांती स्वारीस गेले म्हणून परभारें श्रत जाहले मोहिब मसलतीस गेलें तेंव्हा शेत्रुस नतीजा देऊन फते करुन येतील परन्तु जाते समई इजानेबांस दखल करविले नाही यावरुन चितास येक प्रकार वाटलें जे इस्तादाचें श्नेह केला तेंव्हा इस्तादाचें काये ते इजानेबांस अगत्ये मोहिबांचें शेत्रु पराभवातें पावावें हेच अवशेक असतां किताबती वरुन विदीत न जाहले मोहिब व इजानेबासहू वर्तमान स्वारीस जावें यैसे चिती होते परंतु येथिल कलहावा मजकूर यास्तंव टिकाण सोडून जाणे घडत नाही जलमार्गे गलबते खाना करावीं तेंही स्वारीस अगोदरच गेली मोहिब मसलतीस गेले आण इज्यानेबातर्फेने साहित्ये घडोन आले त्यामुळे

इजानेब बहुतसें बेदिल जाहले तें कलमें करवितां नय हाली पास वाटेने पायांचा जमाव मोहिबांकडेच रवाना करावा हा हेतु धरोन हे किताबत निवीस्तन केली असे जमाव सांखळीस गेले नंतर कोणते मार्गे मोहिबांकडेस पावावें पायवाटेने किंवा तरांडी पाटऊन न्हेवाल ते दयावार लिहावेंया मोहिब अकिल आहेत व गलबतेंही स्त्रारीहून येताच आपलेकडेस रवाना करुन देववितो किताबत येताच जमाव रवाना करुन दिला जाइल मोहिबांच्या ज्यावरी निकर्ष त्यास नतिजा फले व्हावे हेंच च्याहत आहों. त्याज प्रमाणे सिधीस पावले ज्यादा काये लिहीणे प्यार मोहबत असो दिजे हे किताबत छ × माहे जिल्हेज.

तारीख : १७५३

लालिक वाडिची

नं० १९३०

श्री

सियोर मार्केज विजरह यांस अताजी कृष्ण हेजिबनिया राजश्री जये राम सावंत भोसले सरदेसाई प्रा कुडाल व माहालानिहावे यांचा अनवा यैसा जे इस्तादांचा पुर्व श्नेह चालता आला त्यास मध्ये मार्केज हलर्ण याचे मुजतित विकल्प वाढोंन मुलूक व ठाणि घेतली त्यामुळे रयेत कुल परंगदा होऊन वोशाड पडला रयेत गरिब दुखउन काये याजकरितां सियोर मार्केजांचा पुर्वापार श्नेह उभयेपक्षिचा व्हावा आणि तहरह पुर्वापार आमच्या वडिलांही केला त्या प्रमाणे करोन कितेक गोडि राखावी या विचारावरी आम्हांस खाना केले. गोस्टीनंतर सांगितले प्रमाणे सियोर मार्केजास अर्ज करुन तहमुलें आणि ठाणी मागा घेतली ती आमची आमचे स्वाधिन करुन मुलूक रयेत नादऊन पुढें पाहावे कामकाज करुन सिफार-सिमध्यें मार्केजांची मेहरबानी संपादुन घ्यावी त्यास भेटी होतां सांगितलें कि घर कलह वाडऊन तिसरा आगरा सामिल करुन आपले घर नासावें प्रयोजन नाही उभयेपक्षी समाधान होऊन रयेत नादवावी आगरेस सामिल करु नये त्या वचनावरुन त्याकडिल मनसबाही स्तंगित केला परंतु मुलूकामध्यें उपद्रव त्यां-कडून अनिवार जाहला आमचा उभयेपक्षिचा विवेक करुन रयेत नादवावी म्हणून सियोर मार्केजाही सांगितले वरुन आम्ही कबूल जाहली तुमचा मुदा लिहून देणेविसी सांगितले वरुन उभयेतांचा वेव्हार जे तपसील.

१

राजश्री फोंड सावत भोसले सरदेसाई यांचे पुत्र नव जण त्यामध्यें वडिल राजश्री नार सावंत यांणी आपला बाप देसकत करित असतां दुष्टवासना करुन बापास बंदिस टेऊन आपणा सिका नवा करुन बरिस दिडबरिस पावेतों देसकत केली पुढें बंदिमध्यें बापाने राजकर्ण लाऊन त्यास मारिला त्याऊपरी तिसवर्षे पावेतों आमचा बाप देसकत करित होता दुसरा राजश्री नाग सावंत बापासी बदलून वरघाटी मेला तेथेच मृत्यू पावला त्याचा पुत्र व बाइको आम्हाकडे आहे आम्ही सात भाव व येक पुतण्या येकत्र आहों कलम ।

२

आमचा बाप निवर्तलेनंतर मजकूर जे राजश्री रामचंद्र सावंत येकत्रच होता आम्ही आट जण व हा येक येणे प्रा नव जण येकत्रच होतों ममताही सर्व समानधपणें होती सिका आम्हाकडे होता तो आमचे चिती त्यां आम्हाटाइ दुसरा विचार नाही याकरितां त्याकडेस आम्हीहून दिला कितेक दिवस चलत आलेंपरित नावे दोन कामदी पत्रां आधी आमचे मग त्याचे या प्रा कांही दिवस गेले पुढे त्या आम्हाटाय्र ऊगाच विशाद वाढला मग सिका आमचा आम्ही घेतला वरिस परित होता माग तो आमचे त्याचे निखालसपणे चालले कृत्रिम भाव हा काहिच समजला नव्हतां ममता होती तेव्हां पुन्हा त्यांकडेस आम्ही दिला त्याजवरी आज दोन वर्से परियेंत त्याकडे आहे तों दिवसही थोडके समाधानपणित्र गेले मग तो कामकाजामध्यें विकल्प वाढत आला पाहतां कृत्रिमच तेव्हा सिका मागतां देत नाही म्हणून लागला आम्ही आट जण उभे राहून यासच सिका कैसा देतां येतो याचवरी अतिशये वाढला तो आजवरी वाढत आला याजऊपरी सियोर मार्केजांही क्षिरिनीर परिक्षा करुन उभयेपक्षिचा इत्यर्थ करावा कलम ।

३

आम्ही सात बंधु व येक पुतण्या राजश्री नाग सावताचा पुत्र असे आट जण ऊगे असून हाच सिका करिन म्हणतो आम्ही आट जण त्या प्रा हा नवा वरकंडा प्रा असावे पैका घ्यायाचा तो येवज देऊ मुलूकांत उपसर्ग करुं नयं सात आहेत त्या प्रा त्याणें असावे कलम ।

४

तो वडिलाचा पुत्र म्हणून मागतो तरी वडिलांची कर्तव्यतात कलोन गेली आम्ही आट जण असून यासच करु देवत नाही त्याणे बारा वरसें पावेतों केला त्या प्रा बारा वरसे आम्ही करु व वरकडही त्या प्रा करितील पुढें श्री सागेल त्या प्रा करवावे कलम ।

५

येणे प्रा करिना उभयेतांचा पडला यावरी सियोर मार्केजांही निश्चयात्मक उभयेतास सांगावे ते सांगोन सुक्षित करावेया प्रा घर कलहाचा मजकूर जाहला त्याची जाप तो काये कागदावरी लावया प्रमाणें घ्यावी.

येणे प्रा घर कलह मुदा जाहला पुढें निरोतर काये ते करार जाप लिहिली पाहिजे दिवस गतिवर पडलेने मुलूक भयान जाहला पुढिल कामाविसी राहिली तो चलूस पाहिजे कमल.

तारीख : १७५३

नं० २०७०

हु

अजम अकरम फ्रासिस्क आफोंस ताव्र

कोंद दे सांजुवांव मार्केज दे ताव्र

विजुरे कपितांव जेराल दा इद दर मसन

द मुलमको बाशद

अमारत......जिवाजी विश्राम......प्रस्तुत राजश्री जयराम सावंत साहेब याणी आंगरेसी राजकर्ण करुन आरमार त्यांचे आणून वेगुर्लेस भांडताहेत हे वर्तमान येकबालपन्हास ज्याहिर झालेंच आहे व राजश्री सरदेसाई साहेबी किताबत पाटविली आहे की खमखा एकबालपन्हाही आपले वचन दिले ते गोस्टिचे स्मरण करुन आरमार तातडिन फौज रवाना करुन गनिमास मारुन काडून कोट राखनील यैसा पुर्ण भरवसा धरुन किताबत पाटविली आहे इज्यानेब इतुके दिवस उभयता राजश्री सरदेसाई साहेब यांचे मध्येस्तीस होतो आंता राजश्री जयराम सावंत साहेब याणि आंगरेसी राजकर्ण करुन त्यांचे आरमार आणून वेगुर्लेस भांडताहेत याजकरितां इज्यानेब राजश्री. रामचंद्र सावंत साहेब याकडेस मिळोन गनिमास स्तंबी पोहचवावी या कतृत्वांत राहून येकबालपन्हास ज्याहिर होणेंवास्ते कलमे केले आहे आणखी कित्येक मातबर सरदार राजश्री दलवी आदि करुन बाहिर गेलो होते त्यांसही हाली आणविले आहेत सर्वांही राजश्री रामचंद्र सावंत साहेब याकडेस मिळून इस्तादाचा जमाव येईन त्यांकडेस अनकुल होऊन आंगरा यास नतीजा देऊ त्यास येकबालपन्हाही दुसरा अर्थ चितांत न आणिता फौज व आरमार रवाना

करावे गनिमास मारुन येश घ्यावे ज्यादा कय लिहीणे मेहरबानी असो घ्यावी किताबत.

तारीख : ७-१०-१७५७

नं० १३८८

हू

अजम अकरम गोबेनंदोर दो इ
स्ताद दा ईदि हमेशा खुशवक्त बाशद

अमारत व अयालतपन्हा शौकत व हिशमत दस्तगाहा अजी खेंम सावंत भोसले सरदेसाई पां। कुडाल व माहालानिहाय सलाम बाजद सलाम येथिल नेको आणून कारनेकी कलमे केले पाहिजे ऊंकी चंद रोज गुदरले मोहिबांकडून किताबत येऊन खुशवक्त हासील होत नाही हे दो (स्ताचे) जागां मुनसीब नाही हरवक्त किताबत पाटवून दोस्ती दिनवदिन ज्यादा होई ते बात करावेया मोहिब आकिल आहेत दिगर रा। नारोपत सुभेदार जंजिरे विजयदुर्ग···रा पेशवे याकडिल फौज सामानसुधा तोफा देखील घेऊन किले पारगडास वेडा घालोन बसले होते हें वर्तमान इज्यानेबांस दखल होतांच राजश्री दलवी जिवाजी विश्राम यांजबरोबर फौज देऊन रवाना केले, याणी जाऊन त्यांसी लडाई केली, मोटे जुज जाहले. त्यांकडिल फौज पराभव होऊन पलिकडेस जायास गेली। पुन्हा मागु ती भारी फौजेनसीं इकडे लडाइस यावेया तरतुदीत आहेत. मोहिबांस मालूम व्हावें यावास्ते कलमे केले असे इस्तादाचा व इज्यानेबाचा येखलासीचा विचार चालत आहे. तेव्हा, दारुगोळा व जमावानसी इज्यानेबांचे साहित्य करावेया मोहिबास योग्य आहे. व मोहिब करितील हा इज्यानेबाचा खातरनिशा आहेच. व हाली इस्तादाकडिल लोक पेडणे माहलां येउन नदिबागचे नदिकिनारेस वाजपुसी करितात. व येत जातात त्या रहदारीस अटक करितात व तरांडीं खाडितून आंत आली आहेत. अशा दुतर्फा श्नेह अ (ऋ) श्रीमपणीं चालत असतां आदमी लोकांस कजया व्हावा हे गोष्टि मोहिबास विदीत नाही, दुतर्फा आदमी लोक आहेत ते उगेच मदिच वेव्हार करुन मोहिबांस मनस्वी सांगतील. आण मोहिबांचे चिवास विषाद येईल या करिता मोहिबीं पहिलेपासुन चालत आले आहे त्या रितीने उभयपक्षी स्नेह ज्यादा व्हावा हेच इज्यानेब च्याहात आहेत. मोहिबांचे पैलेहून इज्यानेबांस अधिकोतर आहे यैसे नाही. आदमी लोक मोहिबांचे

तर्फेचे पेडणे महाली आहेत त्यासही ताकिद मोहिबी करावेया मोहिबी आकिल आहेत . ज्यादा काय लिहीणे प्यार मोहबत असो दिली पाहिजें . हे किताबत छ २२ मोहरम सुभा समान खमसेन मया अलफ .

तारीख : १७६३

नं० १२८६

हू
अजम बेल च्योर जुजे वास दे करवाल
सक्रतायें वो इस्ताव वा इंवो
दाम मोहबत हु

मोहिबानपन्हां मुखलिसान दस्तमाहा अजीं खेम सावंत भोसले सरदेसाई पां कुडाल व माहालानिहाय सलाम येथिल नेकी जाणुन कारनेकी कलमे केले पाहीले दिगर अलिकड मोहिबाकडन किताबत येऊन दिल खुशवस्ती पोहचत नाही हे दोस्तिचे जागा मुनासिफ नव्हे हरवक्त किताबत पाटऊन दोस्ति दिनव्रदिन जियादा होइ ते बात केली पाहीजे ऊकी इज्यानेब लग्नाकारणे वरघांटी जात्रेयाचा निश्चय करुन मागील बंदोबस्ती करुन वरघाटी जावयास सुमुहूर्त करुन निघालो आहो मोहिबांस मालुम व्हावे यावास्ते लिहीले आहें जियादा काय लिहीणें मोहबत असो दिली पाहिजे हे किताबत छ १६ रजेबु .

तारीख : १७६३

नं० १२८८

हू
अजम बेल च्योर जुजे वास दे करवाल
सक्रतायें वो इस्ताव वा इंवो
दाम मोहबत हू

मोहिबानपन्हा मुखलिसान दस्तगाहा अजी खेम सावंत भोसले सरदेसाई पां कुडाल व माहालनिहास सलाम येथिल नेकी जाणुन कारनेकी कलमे केल पाहीजे दिगर चंद रोज मोहिबाकडुन किताबत येऊन दिल खुशवक्त पोहचत नाही हे दोस्तिचे जागा मुनासीब नव्हे हरबक्त किताबत पाटऊन दोस्ती दिन-

बदीन ज्यादा होइ ते बात केली पाहिजे इज्यानेब लग्नकार्या करितां श्री गोदेस वरघाटीं सहपरीवारे जाऊन ऊत्तम प्रकारे कार्य मोहत्साह सपादीन फौजसह वर्तमान छ ५ रमजानी स्वस्थलास यावेयास जालो दोस्तिचे जागा मोहिबास मालुम व्हावे यावास्ते निवीस्तन केले असे हरबक्त किताबत पाटऊन दोस्ती ज्यादा होइ ते करावे ज्यादा काय लिहीणे मोहबत असो दिजे हे किताबत छ २० रमजान.

तारीख : ८-९-१७६४

नं० १४०९

॥

अजम बेल चि·········दे करवल सक्र

तार्य दा इस्ताव महफुंज बाशद

मोहिब येखलास असार शफकत हिसार अजी खेम सावंत भोसले सरदेसाई पां कुडाल व माहालानिहाये सलाम बादज सलाम येथिल नेकी जाणून मोहिबी कारनेकी कलमे करित असिले पाहिजे दिगर मोहिबाकडून किताबत येऊन दिल आराम होत नाही हे दोस्तिचें जागा मुनासीब न्हवे हरबस्त किताबत पाटवित असोन दोस्ती दिनवदीन ज्यादा चाले ते यात करित असिले पाहिजे तर श्रीमंता कडून धुलप याचे विद्यमाने (मर्दनगड) तालुके या करिता जमाव सांखलिस येऊन बैसला आहे त्याच्या (साहित्यास) जमाऊ देणेविसी श्रीमत राजश्री प्रधान· पंत यांची पत्रें आलीं आहेत प्रस्तुत येविसीं. कारकुनही येऊन बसले आहेत जमाऊ तयार करुन रवाना करावे न होय तरी जाबसाल श्रीमंतास लेहून घ्या यैसे म्हणतात या पधरा रोजांन खासा धुलप जमाऊ सुधा याच मार्गे येणार यैसे ही आहे हे तपसिलवार मजकूर मोहिबास मालूम व्हावा पुढां येविसींची पेरवी इस्ताद कोणे रितीने करिता इजानेबी जाबसाल कैसा कराव याविसींचा बुधिवाद कार्य तो लेहावा त्या सारिखा विचार केला जाइल जलदिने जाब पाटऊन घ्यावा येविसीचा भवार्थ सांगोन पेशजी राव दताजी प्रभू मतकरी सातर्डे यांस खाना केले होते परंतु निखालस जाबसाल नाहीं मोहिबास दिसेल जें प्रधानपंताकडील ऊधार लिहीतात तर तैसे न समजावें आहे तो मजकूर मोहिबांस लिहीला आहे इंजानेबांचे मानस इस्तादातफेंसी अकृतिम जावें असावे त्यांत (तिसरा) (अर्थ) नाहीं परंतु सध्या मनसबा प्राप्त जाहला

मोहिबांस (कल्हवे) यास्तव कलमे केले असे इजानेबास साहित्य जमावाने न देता सुधें नाही यैसेव प्राप्त जाहले आहे दिलांत आणून निश्चयात्मक उतर जलदिनें रवाना करावें त्या सारिखा विचार कर्तव्य लागतो आले कारकून यांसी आम्ही कितेक इस्तादातफेँच जाबसाल केले परतु त्यावर त्यांचा करार किमपी नाही मालूम व्हावें याकरिता कलमे केले असे ज्यादा काय लिहीणे महबत असों दिजे छ १२ रविलाचर हे किताबत ।

तारीख :१७६४

नं० २०२१ अ

हू

अजम अकरम बेल चियोर जुजे
वास दे करवल सक्रतार्य दो द
स्ताद वाम मोहबत हू

मोहिबानपन्हा मुखलिसांन दस्तगाहा: अजी जिवाजी विश्राम सलाम बादज सलाम येथिल नेकी जाणून ......दिगर इंग्रज रेडिस जुजायास गेला आहे या करितां तेरेखोलास इजानेबी लिहीलें कि इस्तादाचें निशाण व पाच जण फिरंगी रातोरात किलेवर चडऊन इंग्रजासही सागुन पाटवावे कि किला इस्तादाचा आहे तुम्ही न जुजावे यैसे सागुन पाटवावे म्हणून कलमे केले आहे तर मोहिबी सिताबीने या प्रमाणे हुकूम तेरेखोलास करावयाऊपर आमची इरे—त नाही इस्तादाबाह इरे आहे आम्ही इस्तादाचें नांव सारिले आहे त्या सारिखें इस्तादा-कडुन साहित्य जलदिने पुरवावे दारु गोला व गोलंदाजही किलेस पाटवावे आम्ही हुबळीस असता याचविसीं मोहिबांस सांगून पाटविले होतें कि हा समई पोटवला यास मोहिबीं चिता घातले बिना परिणाम लागत नाही यास्तव मोहिबीं कामे टेऊन हा तर्तुद करावा हे किताबत .

तारीख : ५-४-१७७३

नं० ३२४६

दिगर सौभाग्यवती लक्ष्मिबाइ सरदेसाई प्रसंगुल सुपुत्र जाहलेचे खुश वर्तमान

निर्वास्तन केलेवरुन बहुत दिल आराम पोहांचलो श्री ने मोहिबांच्या मुलास आयुश व यैस्वर्य ऊदंड घ्यावें मोहिबा पाहून सुखा पावावें हेच च्याहात आहों ज्यादा काये लिहीणे प्यांर मोहबत असों देणे जाणिजे रा ता ५ माहे आब्रिल सन १७७३.

तारीख : १३-८-१७७७

नं० २९९९

हू

अजम अकरम दो जुजे पेद्र दा कामरा गोवर्ण
दोर ये कपिताव जनराल दा इस्ताद दे इ
दो बर मसनद हुकूमत मुलमकीं बाशद

अमारत व अयालतपन्हां शौकत व हिंशेमज दस्तगाहा अजी खेंम सावंत भोसलें सरदेसाई पा कुडाल व महालानिहाये दिगर इंग्रज किलें येशवतगडास आला तेवक्ती राजश्री विटोजी कामत सावकार गोवें पणज यांचे गुजरातीचे बोलिचाली होऊन बंदर वेंगुर्लें टाणेसुथा कामत मशारनिलें याचे स्वाधिन केले वन्दर मजकूर येथ इंग्रजाचा गुला नाही त्यास आज दोन वर्सें परयेत अजम मेस्त्र राबेट दिनशा बंदर मजकुरी आहे टाणे टुणेचे काम करितो व सावकारिही चालिस लाविली आहें अस्ता विशेष आहें . व तेथे खेतीस मनस्वी ऊपद्रव करितो तेव्हा इंग्रजाकडिल जो प्रकार असेल तो वाजही चौगमते ऊरकोन देऊन बंदर मजकूर टोणेसुध्दा इजानेबाही घ्यावें हा करार याजकरितां राजश्री विटोजी कामत यास येणेविसी इजानेबाही लिहीले परंतु अध्यापी येत नाही इज्यानेबास तंगा व टाणे घेणे जरुर आण कामतीचे विद्यामनाचा मजकूर कामतविणे फडशा होत नाही यैसा विचार आहे याज करितां हे किताबत मोहिबास कलमे केली असे व इस्तादाचा व इजानेबाचा स्नेह धरोबा पुर्वापार चालत आला आहे जे इज्यानेबाचे बरे ते इस्तादास पाहिजे ते मोहिबाचे दिलात तेव्हा मोहिबी कामत मानिले यास आज्ञा करोन इजानेबा जवळ रवाना करुन देवावा कामत येणेविसी चितात आशंका येईल तर मोहिबी त्याची समतर जमाकरुन देऊन इजानेबास कलमे करावे मोहिबाचे जवाबानरुप त्याचा विचार इजानेब करितील परंतु इंग्रजाचा लागला नाजिक आहे तो आपले टिकाणी गेलेने उभयेपक्षी उत्तम आण ज्या गोष्टीचे इजानेबास अगत्य तेच मोहिबास यैसे चितात आणोन माणसे पाटविली

आहेत याज बार कामतीस रवाना करावा गाव टाणे या पनरा रोजात घेणे यास्तव कलमे केले असें रा० छ ६ माहे जमादिलाखर जादा काय लिहीणे मोहबत असो दिजे हे किताबत .

तारीख : १-११-१७८६

नं० ४६८

श्री

राजमान्ये राजश्री नरहर गणेशा केरकार या प्रती राजे खेम सावंत भोसले बाहादर सरदेसाई प्रा कुडाल व माहलानिहाये सुभासीत समातेन मया व अलफं तुम्ही स्वामी कार्याटाई निस्टेने वर्तता यास्तव तुम्हावर कृपालू होऊन मौजे हरमल बागा व सरकार व बागायेत व कटुबणे व मिटं आगर वगैरे जी जमा असेल ती कुलबांद कुलकाज् सालाबाद श्री देऊ व ब्राम्हणं धर्मादोऊ व हकदार खेरीज करुन इनाम करुन दिले असें सालमजकूर पासून जलस्थंल कास्ट पाशाणं गुणादी करुन तुम्ही व तुमचे पुत्र पौत्रादी वोंशपरंपरेन भोगवटां करीत जाणे येविसी गावास आलाइदा सनद सादर केली असे जाणिजे रा छ ९ माहे मोहरम .

तालीक सनद हुजूर .

तारीख : ८-२-१७८८

नं ६६१

हू

अजम अकरम सेबास्तीयांव जुजे फ्रेरेरे बारोंक सक्र
तार्य दो इस्ताद वाम मोहबत हू

मोहिबान पन्हा मुखलिसान दस्तगाहा : अजी विसाजी माहदेव सलाम येथिल नेको जाणोन मोहिबी कारनेकी कलमे करीत गेले पाहीजे दिगर मोहिबी करारापेक्षां विशेष फौजेची व सरजामाची तरतूद करुन श्रीमंत राजश्री राजे बाहादर सरदेसाई यांचे कुमकीस रवानगी केली ते कुली लस्केर पेडणे पलिकडेस सातर्डेस व पुढा मदूरे मलगावपर्यंत वाडी नजीक गेले आज मळगावास आगाहू

पोहचतांच वाडीचा जमाव तेथ येऊन सामील होणार अजम अजुदांत जनराल हे मुकाम मंजकुरां पोहचतांच खासा राजेबाहादर फौज कुली तुर्त असेल ती वाडीचा बंदोबस्त राखून वरकड जमाव दरात हती अंबारी निशाण नगारे अवघे सलतनतसुधा येऊन सरदारास भेटणार नंतर गनिमावर जाणेची तजवीत उभयेपक्षिव्या विच्यारे करुन स्वारी करीतील माहाराजाचा मुकाम वेंगुर्लेस आहे वरकड त्याचा जमाव व स्वार रेडिकडेस गांवगना लुटीस फिरतो काल आरमार त्याचे रेडिनजीक आले तेथ इस्तांदाचे आरमारांची गाट पडून चांगला मार देऊन पळविले येकादी गुराब त्याची दस्त केली असणार बातमी आहे पळून गेली तराडी त्यांवर आरमार गेले आहे गांट पडतांच जाळून टाकतील वच्यन दिले प्रमाणे येकबाल व इजलालपन्हा गोवर्णदोर ये कपितांव जराल दो इस्ताद साहेबी निदर्शनास जेनाच्या आणिले व सरदेसाई राजे बाहदर यांची पुरी खातरजमा केली तो संतोश कोटेवेर लेंहावा सर्वत्रात कर्तुत्व करुन दाख-वीलेवी शर्त जाहली आज तगायेत बहुत प्रसंग सरदेसाई याजवर पडले परंतु या अन्वये कोणिच साहीत्य केले न्हवतें इस्तादाचा लौकिक भारी जाहला आंता अंगी मारीले तें पुर्तेपणी सेवटास न्यावें टाणि माघारे घेऊन गनीम राज्यांतून काडून घ्यावा स्वस्थानचा बच्याव करुन राजे बाहादर निर्वेघ हजरतीचे कल्याण इछुक मोहिबांकडेस विस्वास सर्व प्रकारे टेऊन वर्तत असे करणार मोहिब दाने आहेत इजानेब तंव मोहिबाचे आज्ञेसिताई नाही बरी वाइट सेवा केली ति मान्य करुन घेऊन इजानेबानेही ऊजांत यांतच करावे हे मोहिबाच दिल आहे पुर्ण भरवसा मानून स्वस्थ आहों गोवर्णदोर साहेब व राजेबाहादर ऊभयेतां येकरुप तेव्हा इज्यानेबाचे सर्व मनोरथ सिधीस जातील राजेबाहदर उभयेताच्या कर्तृत्वामुळे फारच आभारी आहेत येकवेल मुलाखत व्हावी हेच इछितात अजम अकरम मार्चाल दे कांप हे येतील आपण भेटीस जाणार तर तुम्ही यावे तसेच माघारे जावे म्हणोन धणी याणी इजानेबास आज्ञा केली आहे निकडच असली तर यां······जाऊन येतो रा छ २९ रविलाखर ज्यादा काय लिहीणे प्यार मोहबत असावी हें किताबत.

तारीख : ९-१०-१८०३

नं० २०१९

अजम जुजे काइतान पाचेक दा तावर

दाम मोहनत हु

मोहिब्रानपन्हा मुखलीशान दस्तगाह अजी गोविंदाजी जयवतराव देसाई तपे पेडणे सलाम बाजद सलाम येथिल नेको कारनेकी कलमे फर्माविली पाहीजें दिगर राजेश्री राजेबाहदर भोसुन्ले केलासवासी जाहले त्यास इजानेबाने दुखावटेची वस्त्रे पाटवावी ही रवाज पहिली पासोन आहे आता मोहिबाची आज्ञा होईल तर पाटऊ मोहिबांचे मर्जीस आल्यास अजम तेनेत कोरनेल यें कोमेदात माहल ता पेडणे यांस आज्ञापत्र मोहिबी पाटविलेवर वस्त्रे रवाना करुन देऊ यावर साहेबाचे आज्ञे प्रावर्तणुक करु ज्यादा काय लिहीणे प्यार मोहबत असो दिली पाहीजे तारीख ६ माहे वईतुब्र १८०३ वरुसे हे किताबत.

SUMMARIES OF MARATHI DOCUMENTS

No. 1—A letter of 13 April 1739, from Jairam Sawant Bhosale and Ramchandra Sawant Bhosale, to the Portuguese Secretary of State, Antonio Ferraira de Andrade informed the Portuguese that the occupation of Bardez by the Maratha forces would be harmful to the Portuguese. This position alone, they preferred to explain, prompted them to retain Bardez, which they had occupied without the help of the Marathas. Further, Bardez was to remain under the control of Sawantwadi, until Venkatrao settled the Peace Treaty and sent his army up the Ghats.

No. 2—Terms proposed by the Bhosales to the Portuguese, following their attack on Bardez in 1739.

No. 3—Letter of 19 November 1739, from Nag Sawant Bhosale to the Portuguese Secretary of State, informing that the Portuguese might think that wadikars (Jairam Sawant and Ramchandra Sawant) and himself are brothers and would unite on this occasion. In fact, he remains their worst enemy and confirms his loyalty to the Portuguese and promises his vow as a religious duty and in keeping with the best of Bhosale tradition.

No. 4—A letter of 20 January 1740, from Satroji Rane Desai to the Portuguese Secretary of State, Luis Affonso Dantas, informing the enemy attack on Keri. He further informs the fall of Keri due to ammunition shortage.

No. 5—This letter of 1747, addressed to the Portuguese Secretary of State, by Krishnarao Gurkar of Sonda, informing the attack of the Bhosale forces on Supa fort. He further requests the Portuguese to join them with their forces, as it will be not easy to defeat the Bhosales, without the Portuguese help.

No. 6—A letter of 5 April, 1748, from Jairam and Ramchandra Sawant Bhosale, to the Portuguese Viceroy, informing about the attack on Govalkot, Anjanvel and the capture of the fort of Mudagad from the Angres.

No. 7—A letter of 1749, from Yeshwantrao Mahadev to Vitha Shenvi Dhume, the envoy of the Portuguese, informing that in alliance with the Bhosales, their forces have heavily attacked Tulaji Angres territory. Requests the Portuguese to join them.

No. 8—A letter of 1749, from Pandurang Vishram, to the Portuguese Governor, informing that Tulaji Angre, a servant of the Peshwa, had captured some ships from Malwan. He further informs about the request for help made by the Chhatrapati of Kolhapur and asks the Portuguese if they would come to their help in the event of an attack on the Angres by the joint forces of Kolhapur and the Bhosales.

No. 9—Letter of 1750, from Sawai Emodi Sadashiv Rajendra of Sonda to Dom Pedro de Almeida Conde Assumar, Marquez de Alorna, informing the capture of Nivti from the Bhosales. He also informs that the ships of the Bhosales which were under construction in the Kerli river are burnt.

No. 10—A letter of 1750, from Jairam and Ramchandra Sawant, to the Portuguese Viceroy, informing about the attack of Tulaji Angre on Kudal and Karli. They request Portuguese help.

No. 11—Krishnarao Gurkar of Sonda, writes to the Portuguese Secretary of State, on 16 December, 1750, informing about the attack of Tulaji Angre on Bhosales territory. He further informs that the Sondas prefer Bhosales to the Angres as good neighbours.

No. 12—A letter of 13 January, 1751, from Krishnarao Gurkar of Sonda, to the Portuguese Secretary of State informing that the Peshwa forces have come to the help of the Bhosales. He further refers to the talks held with the Angres.

No. 13—Letter of Ramchandra Sawant Bhosale (1752-53), addressed to the Portuguese Viceroy, expressing his desire that the Portuguese should have informed him of their attack on Sonda, would be willing to join them. Promises to send his army and wants to know which way they should go.

No. 14—In his letter of 1753, Antaji Krishna hejib of Jairam Sawant, giving all the details of the family conflict to the Portuguese. He further appeals to the Portuguese Viceroy to settle the family dispute and the right to the use of seal.

No. 15—Jivaji Vishram informs the Portuguese Viceroy of Goa, dated 1753, that Jairam Sawant Bhosale joining hands with Tulaji Angre attacked the fort of Vengurla. He further requests that the Portuguese deploy their navy in repelling this attack of the enemy.

No. 16—Khem Sawant Bhosale writes to the Portuguese Governor, dated 7 October, 1757 informing the siege of Bharatagad fort by the forces of Naro Pant, Subhedar of Peshwa. He further informs about his defeat and states that he plans to renew his attack. Requests the Portuguese for the supply of arms and ammunition.

No. 17—Khem Sawant informing the Portuguese Secretary of State, dated 1763, that he is leaving for Srigonda to celebrate his marriage.

No. 18—A letter of 1763, from Khem Sawant to the Portuguese Secretary of State, informing that he has returned after marriage to Sawantwadi.

No. 19—A letter of 8 September, 1764, from Khem Sawant Bhosale, to the Portuguese Secretary of State, informing the arrival of the Peshwa's forces under Janoji Dhulap in Sakhali. He further informs the Portuguese about the help Peshwa had sought from him.

No. 20—A letter of 1765, from Jivaji Vishram to the Portuguese Secretary of State, stating that the English had been informed that the fort of Reddi belonged to the Portuguese. He further requests the Portuguese to hoist their flag on the fort by sending a handful of soldiers at night.

No. 21—This is a news letter dated 5 April, 1773, giving to the Portuguese, news of the birth of a boy to Queen Laximibai. It refers to greetings sent by the Portuguese authorities on this occasion.

No. 22—This letter of 13 August, 1777, addressed by Khem Sawant to the Portuguese Governor, requests the Portuguese to send their citizen Vithoji Kamat, who was the mediator when the treaty was signed between the British and Khem Sawant to negotiate the return of the fort of Vengurla to the Sawants.

No. 23—This is a firman dated 1 November, 1786, bestowing upon Narahar Ganesh Kerkar the inam of village Harambal in Pedne, in recognition of his loyal and faithful services to Khem Sawant.

No. 24—A letter of 8 February, 1788, from Visaji Mahadev to the Portuguese Secretary of State, informing about the loot being carried out by the forces of Kolhapur. He further informs about the capture of their Gurat by the Portuguese navy.

No. 25—Govindaji Jaswantrao Desai of Pedne writes to the Portuguese Secretary of State, dated 6 October, 1803, informing him about the death of Khem Sawant. He further requests that if he be pleased, he should order the Colonel of Pedne for sending clothes of mourning to the relatives of the bereaved as it was the custom. On getting the same he would despatch the said mourning clothes.

Glossary of Historical Marathi Words

Aarmar	:	Armada
Bandar	:	Harbour. Sometimes the word seems to have been used for an Island
Caadat	:	Letter
Cornel	:	Colonel
Comendant	:	Commandant
Cruzados	:	A silver coin of ninetenth of a rupee
Darbar	:	Court
Estado	:	Portuguese state
Gohatya	:	Cow slaughter
Governador	:	Governor
Garnals	:	A kind of cannon piece
Hons	:	The well known gold coin
Ingraj	:	English
Innam	:	Award
Jaghir	:	Land grant
Kapitan	:	Captain
Karbhari	:	Administrator
Lascarins	:	Sepoys
Mahajan	:	A devout member
Nodati	:	North
Nagara	:	War drum
Pargane	:	An Administrative Unit
Pradhan	:	Chief Minister
Pagnis	:	Officer of the cavalry
Simga	:	Shimga (The holy festival)
Sawkar	:	Money lender or a merchant
Sanad	:	Title deed
Santos	:	Saints
Tulasi	:	Celebrations concerned with the Plant Tulasi
Vratbandh	:	Sacred to the Hindus
Topkhana	:	Artillery
Taraf	:	Administrative Unit
Taluka	:	Administrative Unit
Varghati	:	Up the ghats

Bibliography

ORIGINAL UNPUBLISHED SOURCES

Goa Archives

1. Assentos de Conselho da Fazenda
2. Auto de Juramento dos Ranes
3. Catalogo dos Vice-Reis
4. Cartas e Ordens
5. Livro de Bacaim
6. Livro dos Moncoes do Reino
7. Loose Marathi (Modi) documents
8. Loose Portuguese documents
9. Portarias do Governo
10. Reis Vizinhos
11. Regimento e Instrucoes

National Archives of India—New Delhi (Govt. of India)

1. Private Collections of Dattaram Manguesh Bhende from Arabo, Pedne, preserved in the National Archives

Bombay Record Office, Govt. of Maharashtra

1. Secret and Political Department Diaries.

Mhamai Family Records

IMPORTANT PUBLISHED PRIMARY SOURCES

Aragao, A.C.T. de : *Descripcao Geral E' Historica das Moedas Cunhadas em Nome dos Reis, Regentes E Governadores de Portugal*, Tomo 3, Lisbon, 1880.

Barbuda, E.L.M. de : *Instruccoes com que El-Rei O Jose I Mandov Passar Ao Estado da India O Governador E.C. General E.O. Arcebispo Primas do Oriente No Anno de 1774*, Panaji, 1841.

Biker, J.F.J. : *Coleccao de Tratados e Concertos de Pazes que o Estado da India Portugues fez com os Reis e Senhores com quem teve relacoes nas Partes da Asia e Africa Oriental desde o Principio da Conquista ate ao fim de Seculo XVIII*, Lisbon, 1881-1887, 14 Vols.

Chaves, B.M. : *Annal Indico Historico do Governo do Illustrissimo Tavora*, Photostat editions of the original MSS (Pr. w), Printed Version (Pt. III) of 1755 and 1754, resp. Lisbon.

Costa, Dioga da : *Relacaum das Guerras da India desde anno de 1736 ate de 1740*, Lisbon, 1741.

Correia, Germano : *Historia da Colonizacao Portuguesa na India*, Lisbon, 1948, 6 Vols.

Desai, S.S. : *Marathyanchya Itihasachi Sadhane* (two parts)—Part I deals with the translation of Documents from A.P.O., and Part II with Portuguese Daftar Khand, Bombay, 1968-74.

Gracias, J.A.I. : *Catalogo dos livros Assentamentos da Gente de guerra que veio do Reino Para a India desde 1731 ate 1811*, Goa, 1893.

Gracias, J.A.I. : *Instruccoes q'o Illmo, e Exmo. Sr. Marques de Tavora deixou ao Illmo. e Exmo. Sr. Conde de Alvo que lhe veyo succeder no Governo da India*, Photostat copy of the MSS. The National Library of Lisbon, 1754, and catalogued as No. 3620 in C.P.I.R.

Kloguem, Diniz : *Bosquejo Historico de Goa*, Nova Goa, 1903.

Machado, J. de S. : *Relacao dos Successos da India e Principio do felicissimo Governo do I.E. Ex. senhor Conde de Ega*, Lisbon, 1759.

Mascarenhas, J.F.M. : *Epanaphora Indica*, Part I to V, Lisbon, 1746.

Mascarenhas, J.F.M. : *Epanaphora Indica*, Part VI, Lisbon, 1753.

Nazareth, J.D.S. : *Nova, e Curiosa Relacao das Batalhas que os Portuguese deram na India E das Grandes victorias que Alcancarao Centra o Bounsulo*, Lisbon, 1785.

Perreira, A.B. de B. : *Arquivo Portuguese Oriental*, 10 Vols., Bastora, 1937-40.

Pissurlekar, P.S.S. : *Agentes da Diploma Portuguesa na India*, Bastora, 1952.

Pissurlekar, P.S.S. : *Assentos do Conselho do Estado*, Vols. IV, V, Bastora, 1957.

Pissurlekar, P.S.S. : *Antigualhas*, Bastora, 1943.

Rivara, Cenha : *A Conjuracao dos Pintos*, Goa, 1857.

Soares, J.P.C. : *Do Cementos Compravatidos do Bosquejo Dos Possessoes Portuguese no Oriente, Tomo 3*, Lisbon, 1853.

Xavier, F.N. : *Coleccao De Bandos, E outros differentes Providencias que servem de leis Regulamentares Para o Governo Economico, e Judicial das Provincias Denominadas das Novas Conquistas*, Panjim, 1840.

Xavier, F.N : *Bosquejo Historico das Communidades das Aldeas dos Conselhos das Ilhas*, Salcete e Bardez, Goa, 1852.

Xavier, F.N : *Instrucao do Exmo., Vice Rei Marquez de Alorna ao seu Successor o Exmo. Vice Rei Marquez de Tavora 3a edicao*, Goa, 1903.

PERIODICALS

Boletim do Governo do Estado da India, Nova Goa, 1873-75.

Boletim da Filmoteca Ultramarina Portuguese, Lisbon, 1959-69.

O Oriente Portuguez, Nova Goa, 1906-7

In many cases the sources published in these Periodicals were subsequently reproduced in the books such as Archivo Portuguese Oriental, Coleccao de Tratados e Concertos de Pazes etc.

SECONDARY SOURCES

Apte, B.K. : *A History of the Maratha Navy and Marchantships*, Bombay, 1973.

Bhandarkar, R.G. : *Early History of the Deccan*—Translated by N.V. Bapat (1887).

Boxer, C.R. : *Fidalgos Portugueses e Bailadeiras Indianas, Seculos XVII e XVIII*, Sao Paulo, Brazil, 1961.

Carre, B. : *The Travels of the Abbe Carre in India and the near east, tr. lady Fawcett & Ed. Fawcett and Burn Hakluyt*, 1947, 3 Vols.

Chandorker : *Sawantwadi Saunsthancha Itihas*, Poona.

Correia, A.S. G. des : *Les Ranes de Satary*, Bastora, 1928.

Costa, A.D.D. : *Os Portugueses E os Reis da India* (Separada do B.I.V.G.) Bastora, 1933.

Danvers, F.C. : *Portuguese Records relating to the East Indians*, London, 1892.

Danvers, F.C. : *The Portuguese in India*, Vol. 2, London, 1894.

Deshaprabhu, V.A. : *Nagdevacha Tamrapat ani Pednyatil 'varade' gaom*, Bombay, 1950.

Dighe, V.G. : *Peshwa Bajirao I and Maratha Expansion*, Bombay, 1944.

Duff, G. : *History of the Marathas*, Bombay, 1873.

Fonseca, N.J. : *A Historical and Archaeological Sketch of the City of Goa*, Bombay, 1878.

Forest, George, G. : Selections from the letters, despatches and other State Papers in the Bombay Secretariat, Marathas Series, Vol. I, Bombay, 1885.

Garge, S.M. : *Karwar, Riyasatachi Kagadpatre*, Poona, 1970.

Garge, S.M. : *Karwar Riyasat*, Poona, 1968.

Gazetteer of the Bombay Presidency : *Ratnagiri and Sawantwadi*, Vol. X, Bombay, 1885.

Gazetteer of the Bombay Presidency : *Kolhapur*, Vol. XXIV, Bombay, 1885.

Gazetteer of the Bombay Presidency : *Kolhapur*, Vol. XXVII, Bombay, 1904.

Gazetteer of the Bombay Presidency : *Ratnagiri district* (Rev. edition) Bombay, 1962.

Gazetteer of the Bombay Presidency : *Ratnagiri district*, Vol. I, Part 2, Bombay, 1896.

Ghosh, Nath Loke : *The Modern History of the India Chiefs, Rajas, Zamindars*, etc,. Part I, Calcutta, 1879.

Gokhale, Kamal Mrs. : *Shivaputra Sambahi*, Poona, 1971.

Gracias, Amancio : *Portugal na India*, Goa, 1946.

Gune, V.T. : *Glimpses of Goa's History*, Goa, 1964.

Gujar, M.V. : *Karveer Chhatrapati Gharanayachya Itihasachi Sadhane*, Vols. 2, 3, 4, 8, Poona.

Imperial Gazeteer of India : *Provincial series*, Vol. 2, Calcutta, 1909.

Kakodkar, P.R. : *The Portuguese and the Marathas* (Translation of Articles of Pissurlekar "Portugueses E Maratas") Bombay, 1975.

Kelkar, Y.N. : *Vasaichi Mohim*, Poona.

Kelkar and Apte : English records on Shivaji, 2 Vols., Poona, 1931.

Khobrekar and Shinde : *Source Material for the History of Konkan*, Bombay, 1971.

Lobato, A. : *Fundamentos da Presenca de Portugal na India*, Lisbon, 1954.

Lobato, A. : *India-Relacoes Luso-Marata (1658-1737)*, Lisbon, 1965.

Maharashtra State Gazetteer : *History*, Part 3, Bombay, 1967.

Martins, J.F.F. : *Cronica dos Vice Reis E Governadores*, Goa, 1919.

Malgaonker, M. ; *Chhatrapatis of Kolhapur.*

Mendes, A.L. : *A India Portuguesa*, 2 Vols., Lisbon, 1886.

Meersman, A. : *The Ancient Franciscan Provinces in India*, Bangalore, 1971.

Menezes and Telles: *A Fortificacao de Tivim*, Bastora, 1939.

Moraes, George : *Kanhoji Angrias Relations with the Portuguese from J.U.B.*, Vol. X, Part I, July 1941.

Moraes, George : *Shivaji and the Portuguese.*

Nayeem, M.A. : *External relations of the Bijapur Kingdom*, Hyderabad, 1974.

Pawar, A. : *Tarabaikalin Kagadpatre*, Kolhapur, 1970-72.

Pissurlenkar, P.S.S. : *Subsidias Para a Historia das Relacoes Diplomaticas dos Portugueses com Haider e Tipu.*

Pissurlenkar, P.S.S. : *Rivalidade Luso-Holandesa na India durante a dominacao Filipina* (B.T.V.G., 1940).

Pissurlenkar, P.S.S. : *Marathyanchya Govyakadil Swarya*, Bombay 1938.

Pissurlenkar, P.S.S. : *Portuguese-Marathe Sambandh*, Poona, 1967.

Pissurlenkar, P.S.S. : *Shivaji no Concao*, in B.I.V.G. No. 42, 1939.

Pissurlenkar, P.S.S. : *A Presenca do Brazil no Arquivo Historico de Goa*, Lisbon, 1960.

Pissurlenkar, P.S.S. : *Colaboradones Hindus, de Afonso de Albuquerque*, separada do B.I.V.G., No. 49, Bastora, 1941.

Pissurlenkar, P.S.S. : A Proposito de Alguns Vocabulos Luso Indianos, separada do B.I.V.G., No. 49, Bastora, 1963.

Pissurlenkar, P.S.S. : *Goa Pre-Portuguesa Atraves dos Escritores Lusitanos dos seculos de XVI E XVII*, Lisbon, 1960.

Pissurlenkar, P.S.S. : *O enigma do Morte do Vice Rei Conde de Alva esclarecido A Luz de Documentos Maratas*, Lisbon, 1957.

Pissurlenkar, P.S.S. : *Portuguese E Maratas I Shivaji*, Goa, 1926.

Pissurlenkar, P.S.S. : *Portuguese E Maratas II Sambhaji.*

Pissurlenkar, P.S.S. : *Portuguese E Maratas III Rajaram*, Goa, 1929.

Pissurlenkar, P.S.S. : *Portuguese E Maratas V, A Retauracao de Bardez e Salcete*, Goa, 1933.

Pissurlenkar, P.S.S. : *Portuguese E Maratas VI* (Tentativas Para Reconquista da Provincia do Norte, Bastora, 1940).

Pissurlenkar, P.S.S. : *A liga dos Portugueses com o Bounsulo contra Sambhaji.*

Pingulkar, V. : *Sawantwadi Saunsthanchaa Itihasachi Sadhane*, Sawantwadi, 1911.

Rajadhyaksha, N.V. : *True History of the Scindhias containing the life of the Bakshi Bahadur Mujafardaul Jiwajee Ballal alias Jivbadada Kerkar*, Bombay, 1907.

Rao, R.P. : *Portuguese Rule in Goa*, Bombay, 1963.

Sardessai, G.S. : *English Records of Maratha History*, Poona affairs, 1936.

Sardessai, G.S. : *A History of Modern India*, Maratha Period, Part I, Bombay, 1925.

Sardessai, Kulkarni & Kale : *Yethihasik Patravyavahar*, Poona, 1933.

Saldanha, M.J.G. : *Historia de Goa*, Bastora, Vols. II, 1925.

Sanvardekar, B.V. : *Gomantak Parichay*, Goa, 1930.

Sarkar, J. : Shivaji, *Calcutta Review*, Calcutta, 1952.

Selections from the Peshwa Daftar : Nos. 16, 34 (1931-33).

Sen, S.S. : *Studies in Indian History*, Calcutta, 1930.

Sen, S.S. : Half a century of the Maratha Navy, Kanhoji Angria, (separated from the *Journal of Indian History*, Vol. X. Part III).

Sen, S.S. : *Indian Travels of Thevenot and Kareri*, New Delhi, 1949.

Sen, S.S. : Early Career of Kanhoji and Angria and other papers, Calcutta, 1941.

Sen, S.S. : A Preliminary Report on the Historical records at Goa, Calcutta, 1925.

Sen, S.P. : *Sources for the History of India*, Vol. I, Calcutta, 1978.

Sen, S. : History of Shivaji, *Calcutta Review*, 1928.

Sharma, S.R. : *The Founding of the Maratha Freedom*, Bombay, 1964.

Sharma, S.R. : *Maratha History Re-examined*, Poona, 1944.

Telles, R.M. : *Fortalezas de Goa e as suas Legendes* (O.P. Bastora, 1938).

Varde, Valawliker : *Goekarachi Goyabhaili Vasnuk*, Bombay, 1928.

Index